Conflict to peace

MANCHESTER
1824

Manchester University Press

Conflict to peace

Politics and society in Northern Ireland
over half a century

Bernadette C. Hayes and Ian McAllister

Manchester University Press

Published by Manchester University Press
Altrincham Street, Manchester M1 7JA, UK
www.manchesteruniversitypress.co.uk

British Library Cataloguing-in-Publication Data is available

Library of Congress Cataloging-in-Publication Data is available

ISBN 978 0 7190 9750 8 *paperback*

First published by Manchester University Press in hardback 2013

This paperback edition first published 2015

Printed by Lightning Source

Contents

Figures and tables

Figures

Tables

Preface and acknowledgements

Civil wars, or intrastate conflicts, have emerged as the most frequent and most deadly form of ethnic violence in the contemporary international system. As these conflicts have proliferated so too have international efforts to resolve them via peace agreements. The vast majority of these political settlements are based on power-sharing solutions in which the key antagonists to the conflict are guaranteed a place in government. Yet, in a growing number of cases, particularly since the 1990s, attempts to resolve these wars have led to the successful establishment of a lasting and peaceful settlement. For example, of the 122 intrastate armed conflicts that have occurred since 1989, Peter Wallensteen (2012) has estimated that two-fifths involved peace agreements, the vast majority of which were successful.

It is now generally accepted that the peace accord which ended the Northern Ireland conflict – the 1998 Belfast Agreement – is an exemplar of this trend. As Martin McGuinness (2012), one of the key negotiators to the settlement and the current deputy first minister in Northern Ireland, put it: 'We are privileged that we are at the helm of one of the most successful peace processes in the world today.' Indeed, since its ratification in 1998, a virtual cottage industry has emerged which seeks to export the Northern Ireland experience as a model for resolving ethnic conflict around the globe. Politicians, journalists as well as a range of academics have toured the world advocating the Northern Ireland peace process as a model for resolving ethnic conflict in violently divided societies. Much of the success of the Northern Ireland peace process has been attributed to the consociational nature of its power-sharing arrangements. Yet, not all political analysts are convinced as to the suitability of this approach. Some scholars argue that rather than resolving the conflict, consociational power-sharing arrangements further entrench and perpetuate ethnic divisions.

Using these differing interpretations as a starting point, this book focuses on the nature and extent of the Northern Ireland conflict as well as attitudes towards the political changes that have taken place since 1998. In doing so, we are fortunate in having a range of academic public opinion surveys stretching as far back as 1968, coinciding with the onset of the most recent phase of the conflict or what has become euphemistically known as the Troubles. These surveys enable us to explain and understand the motivations of the main perpetrators and bearers of the brunt of the conflict – the Northern Ireland people themselves. Since the 1980s, at least one academic survey has been fielded in Northern Ireland each year, sometimes containing as many as 200 or 300 separate questions. The net result is that we possess a huge cumulative database on what the adult population thinks, how they behave, details of their past experiences and information about their hopes, aspirations and predictions for the future of their society. This is a resource that few medium-size countries possess, but it is unique to a region with a population of just under 1.8 million people.

While these opinion surveys have been quoted extensively in books and articles, there has been no systematic attempt to analyse them in order to provide a new perspective on Northern Ireland politics and society. Using the surveys, we extend existing research on Northern Ireland society and politics in two important ways. First, by examining the trends in responses to the same questions repeated in successive surveys, we can determine how much change has taken place and identify the causes of that change. Since there is still considerable disagreement on what lies at the heart of the Northern Ireland conflict, this provides an unrivalled perspective on that debate. Second, by pooling the surveys conducted since 1989, we can generate a very large sample size. This enables us to analyse small groups within the population which would otherwise have too few respondents for any statistically reliable analysis.

Any analysis based on survey research has obvious limitations, particularly when it is applied to a bitter civil conflict. One limitation is the tendency to under-report public support for controversial groups, an example being the significant underestimation of electoral support for Sinn Fein in the surveys. Survey respondents are also often hesitant in indicating their support for controversial policies. Nevertheless, while these are serious limitations, we argue that the surveys represent the most important method available to document and gauge changes in public opinion among the Northern Ireland population over an extended period. Empirical evidence, even with caveats, will always trump informed speculation.

This book makes use of these academic opinion surveys to examine, for the first time, the changes that have taken place in behaviour and attitudes in Northern Ireland over almost half a century. This is a period that coincides with the start of the most recent conflict in 1968 and covers all of the momentous events that have taken place since. These include the establishment of the 1974 power-sharing executive and its collapse just five months later in the face of a loyalist general strike; the 1980–81 hunger strikes when 10 republican prisoners died; the 1998 Belfast Agreement and the effective cessation of violence; and the establishment in 2007 of a power-sharing government dominated by the Democratic Unionist Party and Sinn Fein. These were all momentous events, and the surveys enable us to chart their impact on the population in detail.

Our analysis of this wealth of opinion poll data leads us to one simple conclusion. We argue that the previous intractability of the Northern Ireland conflict and the current problems in establishing a genuine peace stem not from one single division within the society but from a series of reinforcing divisions which encompass politics, social relations and the economy. Any one of these divisions would be difficult, but not impossible, to resolve through one or more public policy measures. A series of such divisions, each reinforcing the other, makes the task of finding a solution hugely more complicated. It is this aspect of the problem that led Richard Rose (1976: 139) to comment in the middle of the first full decade of the conflict that it was an insoluble problem. His conclusion has proved to be too pessimistic, but it still took more than 20 years after his comment to halt the physical violence and reach even a basic accommodation between the parties to the conflict.

The surveys thus offer us a unique window on these political, social and economic processes and how they interact with one another to create a deeply divided society. The surveys also provide some clues as to the measures that are likely to be most effective in reducing the conflict and the expected timescale for these measures to become effective. In most cases, the timescale for change is likely to be measured in decades rather than in years: while political institutions can be created quickly, generating public support for those institutions, and creating the informal rules and conventions that make them work effectively, takes very much longer. In some cases, however, community relations being one example, polarization is actually increasing, thus placing doubt on the trajectory of change.

Following these trends over time also allows us to evaluate the effectiveness of the 1998 Belfast Agreement. While the post-1998 period has been a difficult one, with three suspensions of devolution, it has also been marked by a cessation of violence among the main republican and loyalist protagonists, and it has created a power-sharing executive with a Democratic Unionist leader and a Sinn Fein deputy leader. Such an outcome would have been unthinkable at any time before 1998. Whatever its ultimate fate, the Belfast Agreement represents a watershed and enables us to use the surveys to study the dynamics of a post-conflict society. With the end of the violence, the focus has necessarily shifted away from conflict resolution and towards reconciliation among the former protagonists.

Symbols and labels represent the most visible manifestation of the Northern Ireland conflict. How events and actors are described is therefore very much a matter of dispute. So far as is possible, we use the least contentious labels. For example, we term the 1998 Agreement 'the Belfast Agreement' rather than 'the Good Friday Agreement' in order to avoid any religious overtones. We describe the two communities as 'Protestant' and 'Catholic', respectively, which represents their most distinctive characteristic. We use the term 'Londonderry' rather than 'Derry' to reflect the official title of the city and county.

This book has had a long genesis. Our joint work progressed during the 1990s in the form of journal articles, while the physical conflict was still underway. As these articles accumulated, it became increasingly clear that the body of survey evidence could be marshalled to address fundamental questions about the nature of the Northern Ireland conflict. In particular, the 1998 Belfast Agreement provided an ideal opportunity to compare change before and after this pivotal political event and to evaluate the utility of attempts at political engineering to resolve long-standing conflicts. As the physical conflict receded, new areas of interest, such as the treatment of victims of the violence, have emerged.

Any book that covers such a long time span and is based on a large number of academic opinion surveys necessarily incurs many debts. Our first debt is therefore to all those who have collected the surveys used in this book and who have assisted with providing us with the data sets. Richard Rose collected the benchmark 1968 Loyalty Survey, and Gillian Robinson, Lizanne Dowds and Paula Devine had the foresight to establish the Northern Ireland Life and Times Surveys and to secure continuous funding so they could be conducted in a timely manner and to a consistently high standard. Similarly, a range of academics have been involved in securing funding for various election and national identity surveys conducted since the 1990s. Without the efforts of these individuals, this book would have been impossible.

We are also grateful for the support of a variety of institutions which enabled us to meet at various times over the past decade to progress the research. We would like to express our thanks to Elizabeth Meehan and the Institute of Governance at Queen's University, Belfast, for awarding us a visiting fellowship, and Bernadette Hayes is also grateful to the Research School of Social Sciences at the Australian National University for awarding her two visiting appointments. At various times, friends and colleagues at the University of Ulster, Queen's University of Belfast and more recently at the University of Aberdeen, particularly John Brewer, have provided crucial support. We would also like to acknowledge the help, patience and encouragement of Tony Mason at the University of Manchester Press. Finally, we would like to thank our partners – Marysia Zalewski and Toni Makkai – for their continuing support.

This book is dedicated to the memory of Bernadette Hayes' aunt, Eileen Sadlier.

Bernadette C. Hayes
Ian McAllister

Abbreviations

ACT	All Children Together
DENI	Department of Education, Northern Ireland
DUP	Democratic Unionist Party
EU	European Union
FPTP	First Past the Post
IRA	Irish Republican Army
MLA	Member Legislative Assembly
NIAC	Northern Ireland Affairs Committee
NICIE	Northern Ireland Council for Integrated Education
NICRA	Northern Ireland Civil Rights Association
NILT	Northern Ireland Life and Times Surveys
NIO	Northern Ireland Office
NISRA	Northern Ireland Statistics and Research Agency
OFMDFM	Office of the First Minister and Deputy First Minister
PR	Proportional Representation
PSNI	Police Service of Northern Ireland
RIR	Royal Irish Regiment
RUC	Royal Ulster Constabulary
SDLP	Social Democratic and Labour Party
STV	Single Transferable Vote
UDR	Ulster Defence Regiment
UUP	Ulster Unionist Party
UVF	Ulster Volunteer Force

1

Theoretical and practical perspectives

A common observation in comparative politics is that divisions within a society that cross-cut one another lead to moderation and compromise, while divisions that reinforce one another lead to extremism and conflict. This observation was first made when the stable, moderate, pluralist politics of the Scandinavian democracies was contrasted with the relatively unstable, divisive politics of some European countries, notably Belgium, the Netherlands, Switzerland and Austria (Lipset and Rokkan, 1967). However, it was also noted that in many of these countries, all of which were deeply divided on some combination of language, ethnicity or religion, institutional mechanisms had been put in place to manage the potential conflict these divisions generated. This gave rise to the theory of consociationalism, which is most closely associated with the work of Arend Lijphart[1] and is now commonly applied to societies emerging from deep-seated ethnic conflicts (see Rothchild and Roeder, 2005).

The theory of consociationalism argues that fundamentally divided societies can come together as a result of an elite agreement, whereby executive power is shared between competing groups. The premise is that no single group has a majority and can therefore govern in its own right, so the competing groups are forced to compromise or suffer immobilism. Consociationalism has been subject to widespread criticism since it was first developed in the late 1960s and early 1970s.[2] However, few of its opponents disagree with the basic premise, namely, that reinforcing cleavages are the most difficult divisions to resolve and that they have major polarizing effects on the outlooks and behaviours of the communities that are affected by them.

Consociationalism had immediate attractions for those interested in understanding the nature of the Northern Ireland conflict and designing institutions that had a realistic chance of halting the violence. However, for much of the conflict, it was only one among a number of theories. Moreover, the majority position of the Protestant community and the presence of external actors, such as the Irish and British governments, meant that Northern Ireland did not meet the *prima facie* conditions for consociational institutions to succeed. Indeed, the intellectual debate over the theories that underlie the conflict has been an almost constant though barely visible companion to the physical conflict; John McGarry and Brendan O'Leary (2006a: 44) refer to this intellectual debate as Northern Ireland's 'meta-conflict'.

This chapter examines the theories that have been advanced to explain the conflict and how they have been translated into the design of political institutions. The first section examines the development of the theory of consociationalism and how it has been woven into the intellectual debate about the nature of the Northern Ireland conflict. We also examine the major criticisms of the theory. The various attempts to construct institutions to resolve the conflict are outlined in the second section, leading up to the 1998 Belfast Agreement. The 1998 Agreement and its aftermath is the topic of the third section, with a particular focus on the problems of implementing the main terms of the Agreement. The final two sections outline, respectively, the empirical base for our study and the content of the remaining chapters.

The consociational approach to conflict resolution

Consociational models of government became popular in the 1960s and 1970s as a means of governing deeply divided societies. It was initially developed in reaction to adversarial models of governance, such as those that had evolved from Westminster parliamentary practice, which it was argued exacerbated rather than ameliorated deep-seated conflict.[3] The central principle of the model was that government should proceed through negotiation between the competing groups within the society, rather than through the decisions of the majority. Countries where this form of government was regarded as operating in various forms and at various times have included Austria, Switzerland, the Netherlands, Cyprus, Bosnia and Lebanon (Coakley, 2010). The consociational model is, however, most frequently associated with the work of Arend Lijphart, who developed it in an article in 1969 and in a famous book on the Netherlands, *The Politics of Accommodation* (Lijphart, 1968a, 1969).[4]

Lijphart identified four basic principles that a consociational democracy must adhere to in order to overcome ethnic conflict (Lijphart, 1977: 25ff). These principles have largely been preserved in the scholarly work on the topic. The first principle is that government must be based on power-sharing between the main communities, in what he termed 'government by grand coalition'. The second principle is that each community should have the right to veto any measure that might harm their interests. Third, all key positions in the government and the bureaucracy should be allocated proportionally to members of each community. Finally, each community should enjoy some degree of self-government over matters that do not affect the other communities. This principle is particularly pertinent for linguistically divided societies. While there has been much debate and revision concerning consociationalism since the 1970s, these principles still remain central to the model (see McGarry and O'Leary, 2006a, 2006b).

In the course of a 1975 article, Lijphart developed his ideas on consociationalism and how it might apply to Northern Ireland. However, by that time he noted that several of the key elements had already been integrated into the 1973–74 Northern Ireland Assembly and Executive, the latter based on power-sharing between the communities. As John Coakley (2009) has convincingly argued, power-sharing was identified as essential to any future form of government as far back as 1969, even before the suspension of the Stormont parliament in 1972. It was given further momentum when it was advocated by John Whyte in a 1971 pamphlet which promoted the Swiss system of proportional representation in government as a possible model. The idea subsequently went through several more permutations, first being adopted by the Social Democratic and Labour Party (SDLP) and then the Alliance Party in the 1970s, and then being discussed by various unionist groupings during the 1980s (Coakley, 2010: 12ff). By the mid-1990s, the power-sharing principle had been effectively accepted by all of the major actors in the conflict.

Consociational theory has generated a wide variety of critics since the 1970s, and those questioning its application to Northern Ireland have been particularly visible from the early 1990s onwards. These criticisms have broadly followed three lines of argument. First, it is suggested that power-sharing institutionalizes a conflict through setting quotas or mechanisms by which all groups are represented in government (Brass, 1991; Taylor, 2009a). In other words, the institutional arrangements that are created by the consociational model serve to reinforce the cleavages within the society, making them even more resistant to change. Ian Shapiro (1996: 102) puts it well when he says that rather than resolving the problem, consociationalism further exasperates 'the malady it is designed to treat'. Indeed, even if the conflict were to moderate to such an extent that the power-sharing arrangements were deemed superfluous, path dependency would suggest that it would be difficult to unravel them.

A second line of argument concerns how other divisions within the society are treated and are effectively relegated to second-order issues. The focus on ethnic division often masks social inequalities within the society, such as those that are based on class or gender. It is the negation of these other potential forms of social division in favour of ethnic identity that many scholars see as the main disadvantage of consociational forms of government (see Taylor, 2009a). In defence of the consociational approach, McGarry and O'Leary (2009: 377–8) argue that if liberty and individual choice are maximized, then the risk that ethnic division will be 'frozen' by these institutional arrangements will be reduced.

A third line of argument questions the elite approach to managing divisions which is inherent in the model. A consociational approach assumes that political elites will form a grand coalition including all of the protagonists; such coalition arrangements are, in turn, the product of institutional design. Critics, such as Donald Horowitz (1990, 2000), argue that institutional design has little impact on mass attitudes and values and that a more effective approach is to focus on civil society initiatives and to devote resources to encouraging cross-community interaction. Such a 'centripetal' approach will therefore help to create a shared set of cultural values. Others, such as Rupert Taylor (2009a), have suggested that such elite politics is so divorced from the population's everyday lives that it ignores the underlying nature of the society and has little chance of success. Taylor's approach is to encourage support for civil society organizations which can 'challenge and erode the clash of ethno-nationalisms and create new relationships of mutuality through networking and debate' (Taylor, 2001: 47; cf. McGarry, O'Leary and Simeon, 2008).

Whatever the criticisms of the consociational approach and its application to the Northern Ireland conflict, intellectual opinion and those of the political class had, by the late 1980s, largely agreed that consociationalism offered the best hope for a lasting solution. In moving British and Irish government opinion in this direction, the work of John McGarry and Brendan O'Leary has been particularly influential. In turn, they have recognized that the Northern Ireland experience serves to revise consociational theory in important ways.[5] They point particularly to the constructive role that external actors can play at crucial stages; in the Northern Ireland case, this role was fulfilled by the Clinton administration in the U.S. (Arthur, 2000). They also identify the need to integrate self-determination disputes into the model and to extend institutional design beyond the narrowly political. In the next section, we outline the evolution of political thinking about possible solutions to Northern Ireland in the three decades leading up to the 1998 Belfast Agreement.

The troubled road to peace

For most of the first half century of its existence, the institutions of governance in Northern Ireland were stable, even if they were not supported by the Catholic community. The 1920 Government of Ireland

Act established a devolved legislature, with a cabinet and a prime minister modelled on Westminster. The parliament had the power to legislate on most major aspects of Northern Ireland life, the main exceptions being foreign relations, the armed forces, citizenship and some aspects of taxation.[6] This arrangement suited successive British governments, who were relieved of any direct responsibility for governing the region and the accompanying risk of re-entanglement with the Irish problem. During the half-century life of the Stormont parliament, the British government withheld royal assent to just one piece of legislation – the removal of proportional representation in local elections – and then only temporarily. Devolution in Northern Ireland suited both the Ulster unionists and the British government.

In one important respect, the Stormont parliament did differ from the Westminster model: the Ulster Unionist Party (UUP) was permanently in government. This had a range of negative consequences, the most important being how the government and opposition behaved. The Unionist government was in practice unaccountable for its decisions, and as a result, successive governments engaged in numerous acts of discrimination against the Catholic minority, particularly at the local government level.[7] For its part, the permanent minority position of the nationalist opposition meant that they had no incentive to engage in parliamentary politics as a 'government in waiting' in the Westminster model; as a result, they were often obstructive and even abstentionist in their legislative behaviour.[8] While the devolved government established in 1921 effectively removed the Northern Ireland problem from British politics, its operation was highly dysfunctional. It was less a question of *if* its authority would be seriously challenged than *when* this would occur.

When the challenge came in the late 1960s, it was not in the form of parliamentary opposition from the Nationalist Party, or through a violent campaign orchestrated by the Irish Republican Army (IRA), but through peaceful street demonstrations. These were organized by the Northern Ireland Civil Rights Association (NICRA), a group founded in 1967. Consciously emulating the tactics of the U.S. civil rights movement and Britain's National Council for Civil Liberties, NICRA's role was to document and publicize instances of individual or systematic discrimination against the Catholic minority. The inability of the police to respond effectively to street demonstrations organized by NICRA resulted in widespread violence and, ultimately, to the mobilization of British troops to keep order in August 1969. From that point on, the British government was again directly involved in the governance of Northern Ireland.

The initial British response was to press for reforms to deal with the most overt instances of discrimination. The Unionist prime minister, Terence

Table 1.1 Key dates in the governance of Northern Ireland

1921–72	Northern Ireland Stormont Parliament
1973–74	Northern Ireland Assembly
1974	Northern Ireland Executive
1975–76	Constitutional Convention
1979	Consultation Document
1981	Partial or Rolling Devolution
1982–86	Northern Ireland Assembly
1983–84	New Ireland Forum
1985	Anglo-Irish Agreement
1991	Trilateral Talks
1993	Down Street Declaration
1996	Northern Ireland Forum
1998	Belfast Agreement
1998–	Northern Ireland Assembly
2006	St Andrews Agreement

O'Neill, implemented a series of reforms in November 1968, particularly relating to the contentious issue of the provision of public housing. These reforms were regarded as not far-reaching enough by civil rights activists and as a backdown by many of O'Neill's own supporters. Following a general election in February 1969, when one-third of the unionists who were elected opposed O'Neill, he was forced to resign. Further unsuccessful attempts at reform followed, but the violence escalated. The internment without trial of terrorist suspects was introduced in August 1971, but the policy was botched and the violence increased. In January 1972, 13 civilians were killed by British troops in Londonderry following a civil rights march. 'Bloody Sunday', as it became known, generated worldwide publicity; in March 1972, the Stormont parliament was prorogued, and direct rule from Westminster was introduced.

From 1972 and the introduction of direct rule onwards, the British government assumed full responsibility for designing a system of government for Northern Ireland that would halt the violence and start the long process of reconciliation between the two communities. There have been at least seven separate attempts to establish a devolved, power-sharing government in Northern Ireland; six of these attempts have failed, sometimes after only a few months. The seventh system of government, established under the 1998 Belfast Agreement, remains in existence. These attempts at devolution are summarized in Table 1.1.

Between 1972 and 1985, there were three failed attempts to establish a devolved, power-sharing government in Northern Ireland: the

1973–74 Northern Ireland Assembly and Executive, the 1975–76 Constitutional Convention and the 1982–86 Assembly. Each of these three approaches had two common elements. First, they were designed to marginalize the political extremes within the two communities. The premise was that by isolating the extremists in each community, the success of the new institutions would demonstrate the benefits of compromise to the moderate majority, thereby starving the extremists of the popular support necessary to continue the violence (Horowitz, 2002: 193). The British government judged that by reducing the political violence, the chances of a negotiated settlement between the communities would be greatly enhanced. Second, all three attempts recognized the unionist right to veto any solutions that they did not endorse (Byrne, 2001). In practice, this meant that any form of power-sharing between the communities would not be accepted.

Consociational solutions depend on political elites reaching an overarching agreement and on those elites delivering the consent of their supporters for the settlement. But in each of the three attempts at a solution between 1972 and 1985, either elite consent or popular consent was withheld (McGarry and O'Leary, 1995). The 1975–76 Convention and the 1982–86 Assembly both ultimately failed because of the refusal of the SDLP to participate in the absence of any recognition of the Irish dimension. In the case of the 1973–75 Sunningdale Agreement, which established an assembly and executive, the absence of popular Protestant consent was dramatically exposed in a May 1974 loyalist general strike which brought down the five-month-old power-sharing executive.

While still promoting a consociational approach to resolving the conflict, the 1985 Anglo-Irish Agreement represented a significant turning point. For the first time, it accepted that the Irish government had a legitimate role to play in the affairs of Northern Ireland, beyond economic or security cross-border co-operation, and it institutionalized this principle in a binding international agreement (Arthur, 1999). However, the Agreement also produced a hostile reaction from unionists, and they mounted a major political campaign to halt it (Aughey, 1989). Their tactics included mass rallies and, most dramatically, the resignation of all 15 unionist MPs at Westminster. In the resulting by-elections, all but one of the unionists was re-elected, most with substantially increased majorities. Nevertheless, despite this trenchant opposition, the Anglo-Irish Agreement remained in force. The Agreement represented a new basis for a negotiated settlement, though it would take a further 13 years for this to come to fruition.

Less dramatic discontent also emerged within some sections of the nationalist community. For the first time, the Anglo-Irish Agreement highlighted the distinction between republicans and their more moderate nationalist colleagues in their approach to Irish unity (O'Leary and McGarry, 1993: 222–3). Sinn Fein was deeply suspicious of the initiative, claiming that it had surrendered the Irish Republic's legitimate constitutional claim to the reunification of Ireland and instead delivered *de jure* recognition to Northern Ireland as part of the United Kingdom. In contrast, the leader of the SDLP, John Hume, saw it as the first step in the process of persuading unionists as to the legitimacy of their case and the inevitability of Irish unity (Hume, 1996).

More so than any other factor, it was the response of the paramilitary organizations that signalled a fundamental change in party politics. In January 1987, a group aligned with the Ulster Defence Association issued a strategy document called *Common Sense*, which advocated the return of devolved government to Northern Ireland, based on a model of shared responsibility in government (McMichael, 1999: 24). A similar move towards a more overtly political strategy came from Sinn Fein (see McIntyre, 1995). Although Sinn Fein had made impressive electoral gains since the introduction of its 'Armalite and ballot box' strategy at the beginning of the decade, it still attracted the support of only 1 in 10 Northern Ireland voters. Sinn Fein realized that it had to build strategic alliances with other groups, and in 1988 the Sinn Fein leader Gerry Adams secretly met John Hume, an initiative that sowed the seeds of Sinn Fein's transition to a constitutional party (Murray, 1998: 161–86).

The four attempts at a settlement that have taken place since the 1985 Anglo-Irish Agreement have, in contrast to earlier attempts, included the Irish dimension as an integral part of their approach. The first initiative took place in 1991 when trilateral talks commenced between the British and Irish governments and the main political parties. The talks failed to produce any willingness on the part of the unionists to accept power-sharing, and they were discontinued in late 1992 without any progress having been made. In 1993, the British and Irish governments agreed on what became known as the 'Downing Street Declaration'.[9] It accepted the principle that Northern Ireland would not become part of the Irish Republic without the consent of a majority, and in turn accepted that the Irish government had a legitimate role to play in the affairs of Northern Ireland. These principles were integral to the 1995 Frameworks Documents, which outlined the establishment of an assembly and a power-sharing executive.

The post-1985 efforts to achieve a solution to the Northern Ireland problem differed from earlier attempts in at least four important respects. First, by the mid-1980s, it had become clear to both the British and Irish governments that a consociational solution to the problem would require a long period of adjustment by the political elites in both communities. To achieve this, change would have to be incremental, with both communities taking time to absorb each change before moving to the next stage and starting the negotiations once again. As a result, the negotiations became known as a 'peace process' rather than a 'peace settlement', a title used in numerous books and articles. This process culminated in the 1998 Belfast Agreement.

A second change inaugurated by the post-1985 peace process was that inclusive arrangements were viewed as having a better chance of success than efforts that excluded the main loyalist and republican paramilitary organizations. The inclusion of armed groups in government had always been controversial, particularly for unionists. The loyalist paramilitaries had themselves concluded as long ago as 1987 that Sinn Fein would have to be brought into any future government in order for it to have any chance of success, but general unionist acceptance of the principle took longer to achieve.[10] Such a position made it easier for the UUP to agree to Sinn Fein's inclusion in the 1998 Belfast Agreement, though the Democratic Unionist Party (DUP) rejected it. But even within the UUP it remained controversial, particularly in the absence of conclusive evidence that the IRA had genuinely relinquished its military role.

For their part, republicans were also moving towards a position whereby they could agree to participate in government and achieve the transition from a mainly military to a mainly political organization (McIntyre, 1995; McAllister, 2004). While the 'ballot paper in one hand and the Armalite in the other' strategy had brought significant electoral gains during the early 1980s, the modernizers within the party realized that there was no point in mobilizing mass electoral support only to be sidelined from the political negotiations that followed.[11] As a result, Sinn Fein's abstentionist policy was formally rescinded at their 1986 conference, provoking a walkout by a small minority of delegates.

A third assumption underlying post-1985 thinking about the ingredients of a successful settlement was that the political elites who would be party to any agreement had to deliver the consent of their supporters – the very basis of all successful consociational solutions. In the case of the nationalist SDLP, there was little doubt that their supporters would agree to a compromise, but both the British and Irish governments were concerned that a rapid transition towards an exclusively political strategy would split the republican movement and result in a return to violence carried on by a traditionalist minority. This largely accounts for the 'slow and contradictory shifts in republican rhetoric' (Dixon, 2002: 728) that took place as the IRA leadership attempted to sell participation in government to their supporters without resiling from the traditional goal of Irish unity.

Compared to republicans, delivering the consent of unionist supporters for any agreement represented another level of complexity altogether. Since the collapse of the devolved Northern Ireland parliament in 1972, successive schisms and disagreements over an appropriate strategy to return devolution to the province had weakened unionism. The collapse of the power-sharing executive in 1974 in the face of what amounted to a loyalist rebellion influenced the political outlook of several generations of unionist leaders, making them extremely suspicious of any form of compromise. But equally, there was also an awareness – shared by elites as well as supporters – that the divisions within unionism were undermining their bargaining power and continued fragmentation risked transforming the Protestant community into a political minority. There was also the fear that the longer it took to reach a settlement, the fewer the concessions unionism would win: 'every time unionism walked away from the table, it was offered less than the time before' (Horowitz, 2002: 207; see also Aughey, 1989).

The fourth assumption upon which post-1985 settlements have relied is that a consociational arrangement has to be coercive, by stipulating the inclusive nature of the new institutions as a precondition for their establishment (O'Leary, 1989; O'Leary and McGarry, 1993). Such a prescriptive approach to the composition of political institutions is based on the premise that voluntary consociationalism in divided societies is inherently difficult to achieve. Inevitably, minorities seek guarantees for their position which complicates decision-making and risks immobilism. For their part, majorities wish to retain the right to rule on their own: 'it takes an unusual concatenation of circumstances to induce majorities to part with majority rule in favour of explicitly nonmajoritarian institutions of a consociational sort' (Horowitz, 2002: 197–8). The risk of such coercive arrangements is, of course, that when one party withdraws from the arrangement, the whole enterprise is placed in jeopardy. This is exactly what happened in three of the four suspensions of the assembly and executive between 1998 and 2003, when the Ulster unionists withdrew from participation.

The 1998 Belfast Agreement

These four principles underpinning an eventual agreement – process, inclusion, consent and coercion – were applied progressively to the various post-1985 attempts to devise a solution. Their most visible and important manifestation is in the 1998 Belfast Agreement. The direct origins of the 1998 Agreement rest in the 1993 Downing Street Declaration which eventually paved the way for the establishment of the

Northern Ireland Forum and the start of multiparty negotiations. These negotiations commenced in June 1996, presided over by a former member of the U.S. Senate, George Mitchell. However, it was not until the election of the Blair Labour government in May 1997 that significant progress began to be made. In order to further the talks, the new Labour government deliberately blurred the issue of the decommissioning of paramilitary arms, reasoning that the most divisive issues could be dealt with last. The talks finally concluded with the ratification of the Northern Ireland Agreement on 10 April 1998.

The common theme underlying the Agreement is 'parity of esteem' – the principle of providing full expression to differing identities. In practice, this means that there is recognition for the political rights of both communities and the freedom to express those rights in political institutions.[12] The key parts of the Agreement have been characterized as reflecting 'constructive ambiguity', so that the key details 'could be interpreted in various ways to suit the receiving audience' (Dixon, 2002: 736). For unionists, the Agreement was portrayed as a means of cementing Northern Ireland's constitutional position within the United Kingdom, by delivering reform and, as a consequence, bringing republicans into the political process and stopping the violence. This was a message that the British government emphasized continually to unionists (Dixon, 2001). For republicans, the Agreement was seen as a means of furthering the goal of Irish unity, this time by guaranteeing republicans a formal role in government, a process that they argued would eventually result in reconciling unionists to the inevitability of Irish unity (Mallie and McKittrick, 1997).

This 'constructive ambiguity', so vital in securing the consent of the main parties, has also been the Agreement's major weakness. The unionists believed that Sinn Fein's participation in the Agreement meant that they would disarm and become an exclusively political organization, garnering support through elections. By contrast, republicans believed that they had committed themselves to a phased disarmament, the pace of which would be determined by the degree of political progress that was achieved. The British government themselves suspended the assembly and the executive in February 2000 for four months when there was inadequate progress on the decommissioning of paramilitary arms. In July 2001, David Trimble, the UUP leader, resigned as first minister, also citing lack of progress on decommissioning, and only taking up his position again in November after General John de Chastelain, the Canadian head of an international commission set up to monitor decommissioning, said he had witnessed a 'significant' disposal of arms. Trimble again resigned in October 2002 after allegations that Sinn Fein was continuing to gather intelligence on potential military targets.

The compromises required by the 1998 Agreement were not equally acceptable to all unionists and nationalists alike. No sooner had the Agreement been signed than significant divisions began to emerge within the mainstream unionist groups. In addition to the unionists who had adopted an anti-Agreement stance almost from the very beginning of the negotiations, significant opposition to the Agreement also came from many mainstream unionists (see Aughey, 2000). The major dispute was less over constitutional matters, which had already been debated intensely during the negotiations, but rather over the issues of weapons decommissioning by the paramilitaries, reform of the police and the accelerated release of paramilitary prisoners. These issues consumed much of the debate about the Agreement among unionists.

For many unionists, the concession to Sinn Fein and the two loyalist fringe parties with paramilitary links to introduce a phased early prisoner release programme was unacceptable. The scheme saw all prisoners released within two years and many released within the first six months. Although early release was confined to prisoners affiliated with organizations that had established and maintained an unequivocal ceasefire, this failed to ameliorate unionist concerns. Many unionists reacted with horror to the thought of the release of convicted murderers who might, in some cases, be released after having served less than three years.[13] There was also nationalist concern when it was realized that sectarian murderers would also be eligible for early release.[14]

A related issue was the continuing ambiguity over the decommissioning of paramilitary weapons. Despite British assurances to the unionists that the decommissioning of IRA weapons was a necessary precondition to the inclusion of Sinn Fein in government, much confusion surrounded the issue. Pro-Agreement and anti-Agreement unionists both argued that the immediate surrender of all paramilitary weapons was a necessary prerequisite for their inclusion in government, typified in the slogan: 'no guns, no government'. Republicans adopted a different interpretation; decommissioning remained a necessary but long-term aspiration, whose eventual success should be seen as a consequence of, rather than a precondition for, access to political office.[15] Support for this position was voiced by John Hume, the SDLP leader (see de Breadun, 2001: 195–6).

There was also widespread unionist concern over the proposed Independent Commission on Policing, a key concession to nationalists. Among moderate unionists, it was viewed as a mechanism to undermine the Royal Ulster Constabulary (RUC), and many feared that it would pave the way for the force's eventual disbandment. Nationalists, in contrast, viewed the reform of the RUC as a crucial step in making the police more widely acceptable.[16] They envisioned that not only would the commission recommend the establishment of a new police service that would attract cross-community support but one which would be representative of both communities. The Commission was established in June 1998 under the chairpersonship of Chris Patten, a former Conservative minister. The subsequent report, published in September 1999, contained a total of 175 recommendations, the most contentious of which was to change the name of the RUC to the Police Service of Northern Ireland.[17]

There were also some anti-Agreement nationalist dissenters. While the vast majority of nationalists saw the Agreement as an important advance in meeting their aspirations and demands, many republicans saw the establishment of cross-border bodies and the power-sharing executive as inadequate. They pointed out that not only did the Agreement fail to deliver a united Ireland, but through its principle of majority consent for any future change in the constitutional position of Northern Ireland, it again reaffirmed partition and the unionist veto.[18] Furthermore, they argued that although the Agreement promised a review of policing, it contained no firm commitment to either disband or reform the RUC. Eventually, how-ever, most republicans added their voices to the pro-Agreement camp, no doubt encouraged by the promised prisoner release programme.

The continual instability of the executive together with the issues surrounding decommissioning, prisoner release and the recognition of the police led to a conference in October 2006 in St Andrews, Scotland, between the British and Irish governments and the main political parties. The subsequent agreement committed the DUP to power-sharing with Sinn Fein. For their part, Sinn Fein agreed to recognize the police service and the courts. In May 2007, the DUP leader Ian Paisley was elected first minister and Martin McGuinness from Sinn Fein as deputy first minister. This event was a watershed in Northern Ireland politics; in practice, it represented the point at which all of the major elements of a consocia-tional solution to the Northern Ireland conflict finally fell into place.

By their very nature, consociational arrangements have at their heart the requirement that the warring groups consent to the new institutional arrangements. The 1998 Belfast Agreement, coming after six previous unsuccessful attempts to resolve the conflict, has inevitably benefitted from the lessons of those failures. Based on four main assumptions – incremental change, the inclusion of all groups, the consent of the two communities and coercive participation in the new representative institutions – and depending on the bilateral agreement of two sovereign governments, the consociational arrangements enshrined in the Agreement have perhaps been the most complex of their type ever attempted (Byrne, 2001). This complexity has been an advantage, in allowing different aspects to be presented to different groups in order to secure their support. It has also been a disadvantage, in obscuring the crucial importance of attracting and maintaining the consent of the parties to the new institutional arrangements (Bloomfield, 1997).

The 1998 Belfast Agreement has produced a complex institutional architecture which contains many elements that transcend the simple notion of the 'grand coalition' that lies at the heart of the original idea of consociationalism. It has required the consent of party leaders, as well as community representatives, and concurrent majorities were required in different sovereign jurisdictions before it could be implemented (O'Leary, 1999). The very complexity of the Agreement – through overlapping guarantees and vetoes, and external associations – has tended to obscure the most basic requirement of any consociational agreement: the consent of the conflict-prone communities for the institutional arrangements that will be used to govern them (Horowitz, 2002: 194–5). Although the 1998 referendum which ratified the Agreement produced consent from both communities, Protestant support for the principles of the Agreement has always remained fragile. Many Protestants have interpreted post-1998 events as representing something less than the vision of political stability that they believed had been promised.

The empirical base

The opinion surveys that form the empirical base for this book cover the period from 1968 through to the present day. These surveys are used to test our central proposition: that the previous intractability of the Northern Ireland conflict and the current problems in establishing a genuine peace stem from a series of reinforcing cleavages that cover multiple aspects of the society. We are fortunate in that many of the surveys have sought to replicate findings from earlier surveys and therefore ask the same or at least similar questions, even though their central purpose often differs. For example, the 1973 survey was concerned with social mobility, the 1995 survey with identity, the 2011 survey with victims, and the 1992, 1998, 2003 and 2010 surveys with electoral behaviour. The remaining surveys are mostly general social surveys. The commonality in question wording across the surveys makes the process of tracking long-term trends in attitudes and behaviour more reliable.

The criteria for including a survey are that it was society-wide and sampled the adult population. The 1973 survey was based on a sample of men only, as it was primarily aimed at explaining social mobility (at that time almost exclusively considered a male concern), but we considered it important to include the survey because it fills a gap in the period between the 1968 and 1978 surveys. For several of the analyses of young people, we use the 1998–2010 Young Life and Times Survey, which in the first three years of the survey was based on a sample of persons aged between 12 and 17 years (1998–2000) but subsequently restricted to those aged 16 years (2003–10). These surveys replicate a key set of indicators taken from the adult Life and Times Survey. Since 1989, the excellent Northern Ireland Social Attitudes Survey, and its successor since 1998, the equally excellent Northern Ireland Life and Times Survey, provide a core empirical base for anyone interested in the dynamics of public opinion in Northern Ireland. These surveys are listed in Table 1.2, and the Appendix includes more methodological details about each of them.

In order to overcome the problem of small sample size that has hindered many earlier investigations, particularly those dealing with divisions within the two main religious communities rather than between them, we use a pooled data set. The pooled data set includes representative samples of the adult population in Northern Ireland conducted between 1989 and 2010. It combines 31,417 respondents drawn from the 1989–96 Northern Ireland Social Attitudes Surveys, the 1992 Northern Ireland Election Survey, the 1998 Northern Ireland Referendum and Election Survey, the 1998–2010 Northern Ireland Life and Times Surveys and the 2003 Northern Ireland Election Survey. In addition, to investigate those who experienced a formally integrated education, we use a more restricted version of the pooled data set which includes representative samples of the adult population conducted solely between 1998 and 2010. It combines 22,041 respondents drawn exclusively from the 1998 Northern Ireland Referendum and Election Survey, the 1998–2010 Northern Ireland Life and Times Surveys and the 2003 Northern Ireland Election Survey.

Pooled time-series cross-sectional analysis has a long tradition in quantitative political research. A variety of studies conducted in Britain, the U.S. and elsewhere have used this approach to answer central questions about, for example, the impact of economic conditions on party support or electoral outcomes (see, e.g., Price and Saunders, 1995). The main advantage of the approach is that it solves many of the problems associated with both traditional time-series or cross-sectional methods of investigation, namely, the 'small N' problem. This occurs when there are insufficient cases at any single point in time to undertake a detailed examination of an issue.

This approach is not without its disadvantages. One disadvantage is substantive: pooling respondents interviewed at different points in time assumes that all of them have been affected by the same events; this is very obviously not the case. One way of testing and controlling for any potential bias

Table 1.2 Northern Ireland survey details

Survey	Fieldwork dates	Method	Sample	Number of respondents	Response rate (per cent)
1968 Northern Ireland Loyalty Survey	March–August	Personal interview	Society-wide, age 20 years+	1,291	87
1973 Northern Ireland Social Mobility Survey	January–June	Personal interview	Society-wide, males age 18–64 years	2,416	75
1978 Northern Ireland Attitude Survey	July–October	Personal interview	Society-wide, age 18 years+	1,277	64
1989–96 Northern Ireland Social Attitudes Surveys	February–April each year	Personal interview and self-completion	Society-wide, age 18 years+	786–1,519	62–71 (average 68)
1992 Northern Ireland Election Survey	April–August	Personal interview	Society-wide, age 17 years+	1,947	78
1995 Northern Ireland Social Identity Survey	April–July	Personal interview	Society-wide, age 17 years+	982	63
1998 Northern Ireland Referendum and Election Survey	June–August	Personal interview and self-completion	Society-wide, age 18 years+	950	71

Survey	Timing	Method	Population	Sample size	Response rate (%)
1998–2010 Northern Ireland Life and Times Surveys	October–February each year	Personal interview	Society-wide, age 18 years+	1,179–2,200	58–70 (average 63)
1998–2010 Northern Ireland Young Life and Times Surveys	August–October/November–December	Personal interview	Society-wide, age 12–17 years	627–941	21–46
2003 Northern Ireland Election Survey	November 2003–January 2004	Personal interview	Society-wide, age 18 years+	1,000	62
2010 Northern Ireland Election Survey	May–June	Personal interview	Society-wide, age 18 years+	1,000	63
2011 Northern Ireland Social and Political Attitudes Survey	April–July	Personal interview	Society-wide, age 18 years+	1,500	59

resulting from the impact of different events is to include measures of individual years, or groups of years, in the analyses. If these measures are statistically significant, then we know that time or event effects are present. A second disadvantage is methodological. The pooled time-series cross-sectional design may violate the standard assumptions about the error process in ordinary least squares regression, namely, that all errors have the same variance (homoscedasticity) and that they are independent of each other.[19] As a consequence, the regression estimates may be biased and inefficient when they are applied to pooled data. To allow for this factor, all regression coefficients are estimated using robust standard errors.

Mindful of these two caveats, our use of pooled time-series cross-sectional analysis is both limited and highly restrictive in focus. First, in many cases, it is used simply to illustrate the relationship between two variables at an elementary level, such as the proportion of individuals from within a small religious group who identify with a range of political parties. Second, when the approach is used in a multivariate analysis, it is restricted exclusively to instances where the limited amount of available data on the characteristic of interest at any one period in time, the 'small N' problem, necessitates it. These caveats should be borne in mind when interpreting results from the pooled analysis.

Outline of the book

In the chapters that follow, we use this rich vein of survey data, gathered over almost half a century, to evaluate the changing nature of the Northern Ireland problem from the perspective of the ordinary citizen. Chapter 2 examines the role of religion in the conflict, perhaps the key issue of contention. The survey data confirm the predominant role of religion in Northern Ireland society but also reveal the slow drift towards non-affiliation among many former Protestants and the decline in regular church attendance among many Catholics. The trend towards secularization is being driven by, among other things, generational change and by increasing education. The surveys also show that religion is a strong source of personal identity, more so for Catholics than Protestants. A religious identity is also a strong influence on feelings of prejudice towards the other community. Many of these differences can be traced to a strong theological undercurrent of anti-Catholicism among Protestants and to a sense of victimhood and vulnerability among Catholics. While the Northern Ireland conflict is not about religion, its religious overtones are inescapable.

Chapter 3 examines the competing identities that are held by the two communities. Conflicting identifies is perhaps the hallmark of the

Northern Ireland conflict, but what makes it distinctive is the reinforcement of three identifies, demarcated by religion, nation and politics. Just over a half of Protestants see themselves as British and unionist, while 40 per cent of Catholics see themselves as Irish and nationalist. Perhaps the most salient finding is the infinitesimal proportion who adopt the identity of the opposing community. There has been remarkably little change in these identities over the period of the surveys. To the extent that there has been change, it is in the growth of a Northern Irish identity. Even here, however, it is a label that is more popular among Protestants than Catholics, and its rise represents the re-emergence of ethnic division and conflict in a different form.

The political preferences that individuals hold reflect their ethnic identities. Chapter 4 examines the constitutional preferences of the population since 1968 and their preferences for different forms of government. Constitutional preferences have been remarkably consistent over an extended period, with the vast majority of Protestants wanting to continue the link with Britain. Among Catholics, a long-standing majority in favour of Irish unity has given way most recently to a majority in favour of the union with Britain. Public opinion measured before and after the 1998 Agreement shows that Catholics were very much in support of the Agreement, but Protestant opinion was divided; Protestant support also weakened considerably after 1998. The experience of devolution has not been a happy one, but the relative stability since 2007 has effectively made constitutional preferences a second-order problem, as the public policy concerns of daily government have come to the fore.

Patterns of party competition both reflect and promote the divisions within society (see Chapter 5). In Northern Ireland, this has resulted in a rigid division between the main parties based almost exclusively on religion. Since the start of the conflict, the previously dominant parties representing the two communities have split, and party competition is now as much intra-community as intercommunity. The frequency of elections – almost once a year if local, assembly, Westminster and European elections are counted – places a major burden on parties and imposes a high barrier for new entrants. A particularly notable feature of intra-community competition within the Catholic community has been Sinn Fein's mobilization of the working-class vote. The extensive electoral engineering that began in the 1970s has failed to create a centre ground, but coupled with social and demographic change, has created a new form of politics. Ironically, one consequence is that the centre ground of Northern Irish politics remains as illusive as ever.

The extent and quality of cross-community contacts is a key indicator of the level of polarization in a divided society. Chapter 6 examines the degree of contact between the two communities and public perceptions about community relations. The results lead to pessimistic conclusions. Marital endogamy remains the norm, and there has been little change in this since 1968. Levels of social contact between Protestants and Catholics are also low, and support for increased intercommunal mixing in specific social arenas is, at best, tepid. When asked what they believe community relations will look like in five years' time, the trends show that optimism has been declining in recent years. Perhaps more worryingly, but common in other societies emerging from conflict, these patterns are particularly noticeable among the young.

Chapter 7 focuses on education and its potential role in ameliorating divisions in a post-conflict society. Historically, Northern Ireland has maintained an almost completely separate educational system. In recent years, this has been offset by the introduction of integrated education. From modest beginnings, around 14 per cent of secondary school children now attend an integrated school. Our results, using different surveys and adopting a variety of methods, suggest that attendance at a formally or informally integrated school has positive long-term benefits for community relations. While education cannot on its own solve the problem of ethnic division, it represents an important starting point for any sustained attempt at a solution.

How societies emerging from conflict deal with the victims of violence is often seen as a litmus test of the success of the new arrangements. Chapter 8 charts the impact of the violence on the Northern Ireland population and evaluates the policies that have been proposed for reconciliation. Few people have remained untouched by the violence; one in four of the population regards themselves as a victim of the violence. But victims of violence can also be perpetrators, and many of the early approaches to reconciliation have foundered on this distinction. Nevertheless, there is a recognition that this issue must be confronted and that any lasting reconciliation has to be inclusive and not based solely on a single approach.

Finally, Chapter 9 evaluates the successes and failures of the Northern Ireland peace settlement. The results of this investigation suggest that in relation to many derivative aspects of the settlement – such as the eradication of physical force and the increasing stability of its political institutions – the peace process must be considered a remarkable success. Nevertheless, many issues still remain unresolved, particularly at the individual and community level. Despite the promise of a more equal and inclusive society, Northern Ireland remains bitterly divided along communal lines, with an increasing trend towards segregation. The old adage that 'high fences make good neighbours' continues to inform attitudes to community relations, particularly among the young. Moreover, despite increasing public recognition of the need to address the concerns of victims and the violent legacy of the past, efforts to deal with this issue have been piecemeal, ineffective and highly divisive. Finally, we evaluate the experiences of Northern Ireland – both positive and negative – in terms of their implications for other societies emerging from conflict.

Notes

1 See particularly Lijphart (1968a, 1968b, 1969, 1977, 1999). Another early observer of consociationalism was Gerhard Lehmbruch. The evolution of much of this thinking and its application to Northern Ireland is well described in Coakley (2010).

2 For an overview and evaluation of the criticisms, see Andeweg (2000).

3 Coakley (2010: 7) traces the origins of the term to the work by David Apter in the 1960s, which was subsequently taken up by Gerhard Lehmbruch and Arend Lijphart in separate papers in 1967.

4 Lijphart also developed this theme in his 1977 book, *Democracy in Plural Societies*.

5 See the discussion and extensive references in McGarry and O'Leary (2006a, 2006b).

6 These are outlined in section 4 of the Government of Ireland Act 1920.

7 These have been well documented. See, for example, Darby (1976).

8 See Lynn (1997) for historical accounts of the Nationalist Party.

9 The Downing Street Declaration set out the principles under which a peace process based on an inclusive dialogue between the various political parties in Northern Ireland could proceed. The Framework Documents dealt with proposals for the internal governance of Northern Ireland (strand one), relationships between Northern Ireland and the Republic of Ireland and those between Ireland and Britain (strands two and three). See Wilford (2000) for a comprehensive overview of the terms and proposals contained in the Framework Documents.

10 In January 1987, a group aligned with the Ulster Defence Association issued a strategy document called *Common Sense*, which advocated the return of devolved government to Northern Ireland, based on a model of shared responsibility in government.

11 This is effectively what occurred during the 1970s when IRA violence created the preconditions for major political change, but the SDLP took on the role of negotiating on behalf of the Catholic community.

12 See Wilford (2001) for comprehensive overviews of the terms and conditions of the Agreement.

13 As the 1998 assembly election manifesto of the DUP, in typifying the view of many unionists, bluntly stated: 'All decent people recoil with moral contempt at the prospect of the mass release of those who have murdered and maimed the innocent, whilst the RUC is to be demoralised and disarmed.'

14 The first opinion poll on the early release of prisoners confirmed the greater disquiet among Protestants. Conducted by Market Research Consultancy (MRC) Ireland between 9 and 15 May (*Belfast Telegraph*, 18 May 1998), the results showed that an overwhelming majority of Protestants – 84 per cent – said that prisoners should not be released in two years, compared to 45 per cent among Catholics.

15 Opinion poll data conducted immediately after the ratification of the Belfast Agreement lends further support to this finding. A poll conducted by the Harris Research Centre on 1–2 June (*Irish Times*, 5 June 1998) found that 61 per cent of Protestants believed that decommissioning should begin immediately, before the introduction of any other reforms including the establishment of the Executive, compared to just 31 per cent among Catholics.

16 A poll conducted by MRC Ireland between 9 and 15 May (*Belfast Telegraph*, 18 May 1998) found that an overwhelming majority of Catholics – 79 per cent – said that the RUC needed to be reformed, compared to just 36 per cent among Protestants.

17 These proposed changes produced a 400,000-signature petition in opposition, delivered to Downing Street in January 2000 by the Police Federation of Northern Ireland. Despite both unionist and, to a lesser extent, nationalist opposition, much of the Patten report was finally implemented in November 2000 with the passage of the Police (Northern Ireland) Act.

18 Some senior members of the IRA resigned over republican support for the Agreement and switched their allegiance to the 'Real IRA', a breakaway dissident republican group formed in 1997 in opposition to the IRA ceasefire and Sinn Fein's participation in the peace process.

19 See Sayrs (1989) for a comprehensive discussion of this issue.

2

Religion

It is increasingly accepted that religion is a cause of many of the world's violent conflicts. The vast majority of contemporary conflicts are intrastate conflicts and involve issues of religious, national or ethnic identity. Although religious conflicts in general have been less common in the post-Second World War era than nonreligious conflicts – or ethnonational conflicts where religion plays no role – the proportion of such conflicts has increased significantly since the 1980s, as has their inherent violence when compared to other types of conflict (see Fox, 2004). These include the conflicts in Afghanistan, East Timor, Kashmir and several states in the Middle East. Moreover, religious teachings have commonly been used to legitimize wars and all forms of violence (Appleby, 2000). However, more so than any other factor, the attacks in New York on 11 September 2001 stand out in the popular imagination as evidence for the link between religious fervour and political violence.

In contrast to its role in generating conflict, the contribution of religion to resolving armed conflicts has often been neglected. Most of the focus has been on the work of such groups as faith-based organizations, religious peacekeeping movements, the established churches and religious institutions in general. Yet religion can also play an important role in conflict prevention and resolution.[1] Advocates of this approach point to the crucial role of religious leaders in mediating between political leaders and the mass public in establishing post-conflict peace agreements; indeed, religious leaders have often been active in the prevention of violence before it occurs. As Kofi Annan (2002), the United Nations secretary-general, put it: 'religious organizations can play a role in preventing armed conflict because of the moral authority they carry in many communities'.

The role of religion in conflict transformation has emerged as an important issue in Northern Ireland. It has been argued that religious institutions have long played an important but neglected role in trying to resolve the conflict, particularly by mediating between the main

actors.[2] Scott Appleby (2000) has suggested that religious leaders in
Northern Ireland have been among the most effective in the world in
contributing to conflict transformation, not least by revising the religious traditions on which the dimensions of the conflict are based. In
other words, according to Appleby, a lasting reconciliation cannot be
based on a policy which seeks to undermine religious ties, or what he
refers to as the creation of a 'community beyond communities' (2000:
171). Rather, what is needed is a network of associations that transcend
religious boundaries and emphasize forgiveness and reconciliation rather
than revenge and grievance.

   Not everyone is convinced as to the beneficial role of religious
institutions and leaders in resolving deep-seated conflict. Some have
pointed to the traditional role of religion in perpetuating conflict through
theological convictions and by boundary-maintaining practices such as
opposition to interfaith marriage and insistence on a religiously separated
educational system (see Liechty and Clegg, 2001). Indeed, the high levels
of endogamy within the two communities, as identified by Rosemary
Harris in her 1972 anthropological study *Prejudice and Tolerance in
Ulster*, is often seen as the single most important factor maintaining the
conflict. Similarly, segregated education and the consequent lack of
cross-community contact among the young is often identified as a key
contributor to sustaining division.[3]

   Current debates thus emphasize the role of religion as a mechanism
for both perpetuating and ameliorating social divisions in post-conflict
societies. Using this debate as a starting point, this chapter focuses on
religious identity in Northern Ireland and examines the nature and
extent of religious conviction as well as its role in perpetuating communal division. The first section outlines differing perspectives on the role
of religion in relation to the Northern Ireland conflict, while the second
and third sections focus on the nature and extent of religious differences.
Building on this analysis, the fourth and fifth sections assess the role of
religion in perpetuating or ameliorating communal division.

Religion and the Northern Ireland conflict

Opinions differ markedly as to the role that religion has played in the
Northern Ireland conflict. On the one hand, there are those who argue
that religion has not played any significant role in the conflict and is thus
irrelevant as a solution. Exemplifying this position, John McGarry and
Brendan O'Leary (1995: 213) argue that 'explanations that emphasize the
primacy of religion...need to be exposed to strong light. When that happens, they evaporate, leaving little residue'. According to McGarry and

O'Leary, the conflict is not religious but rather ethnonationalist in nature and thus must be understood primarily as a clash about ethnic identity and contested national territory. The churches themselves have supported this position. In 1972, in the first few years of the Troubles, all four of the main churches released a joint letter which stated that 'the conflict is not primarily religious in character. It is based rather on political and social issues with deep historical roots' (quoted in Darby, 1976: 331).[4] From this perspective, religion is seen simply as an 'ethnic marker', and the terms 'Protestant' and 'Catholic' should be considered nothing more than badges of identity that simply distinguish nationalists and unionists.

The alternative view is that religion has been a crucial influence in both generating and perpetuating the conflict.[5] One of the earliest and leading proponents of this view is Steve Bruce (1986: 249) who has stressed the importance of religion, especially Protestant fundamentalism, in shaping community identities and division and thereby giving the conflict its uncompromising character. Advocates of this view also see other factors, such as economic and social differences, as complementing religious identities.[6] Bruce (1986: 249), in exemplifying this position, puts it well when he says that 'the Northern Ireland conflict is a religious conflict. Economic and social differences are also crucial, but it was the fact that the competing populations in Ireland adhered and still adhere to competing religious traditions which have given the conflict its enduring and intractable quality'.

Recent research by Claire Mitchell (2006, 2008a) lends support to the view that the conflict is essentially religious in nature. While not arguing that the conflict is exclusively religious, Mitchell underlines the importance of religion in contributing to the conflict via its social and political significance. More specifically, not only is religion an essential component in the construction of identity within both communities, but it is also a key factor in constituting social divisions. Mitchell argues that because religious ideas and practices play a central role in the construction of identity in Northern Ireland, they remain a significant factor not only among those who claim a religious identification but also among those who do not.[7] In rejecting the ethnonationalist explanation for the conflict, Mitchell (2008a: 150) argues that 'religion plays an important role in constituting social divisions in Northern Ireland, rather that simply marking them out ... As such, religion is an essential part of identification processes in contemporary Northern Ireland and it is at least as much about the social as about the spiritual'.

Other work has pointed to the under-researched and neglected role of religion in ameliorating communal division. In one of the most recent discussions of this issue, Gladys Ganiel and Paul Dixon (2008) see religiously committed individuals contributing to conflict transformation via their membership of various cross-community organizations as well as through their work in trying to resolve conflict in the interface areas between the two communities. They also emphasize the role of Protestant and Catholic clergy in seeking to end the conflict, most notably in their willingness to engage with paramilitary groups, particularly during the early stages of the peace process and long before it was considered acceptable among the main political parties to do so.[8] A similar conclusion is reached by Brewer *et al.* (2011) who draw attention not only to the important contribution of religiously motivated individuals at the grass-roots level but also the crucial role of the churches in mediating the conflict via facilitating secret communications between politicians and paramilitary organizations. As Brewer *et al.* (2011) put it: 'backchannel political communication was the churches' single most effective achievement'.

Nevertheless, Claire Mitchell (2008b) and others have found that many of the clergy in the traditional churches have eschewed any involvement in community peace groups. In an investigation of the role of the Protestant churches in working-class loyalist areas, Mitchell found that the clergy not only totally dissociated themselves from such organizations, but many believed that they were nothing more than a front for paramilitary activity. Even among the minority of churches who did engage in such activities, their primary purpose was less the transformation of society and more the saving of souls. As Mitchell (2008b: 155) explains: '... most Protestant churches do not engage very much with contemporary loyalism. While some churches ... do attract working-class loyalist congregations, their primary goal is saving souls, and dealing with gritty realities of paramilitarism, poverty and other social issues is usually not a priority'.

The role of religion in relation to the Northern Ireland conflict is therefore both contested and complex. While a number of analysts point to the crucial role of religion in generating and perpetuating the conflict, others reject this view and point to the irrelevance of religion as an explanation for the conflict. There are similarly divided views on the contribution of religious institutions to conflict transformation. While some have stressed the neglected contribution of religiously committed individuals to resolving the conflict, others, while acknowledging their contribution, point to the paucity of such individuals within their respective communities and to their exclusively theological focus. It is with these competing interpretations in mind – the role of religion as both a mechanism for conflict generation and conflict transformation in Northern Ireland – that the following section outlines the nature and extent of religious conviction.

Religious conviction

Previous research on the nature and extent of religious affiliation and behaviour in Northern Ireland suggests that, by any standards, Northern Ireland is a deeply religious society (see Fahey *et al.*, 2006; Mitchell, 2006). Not only do the overwhelming majority of the population continue to identify with one of the two main religious affiliations, but a significant majority believe in the five core beliefs of the Christian faith – God, life after death, heaven, hell and sin – and a significant proportion within both religions attend church services on a regular basis. Even by the late 1990s and contrary to the expectations of secularization theorists, not only was Northern Ireland still a deeply religious society but it had remained exceptionally religious by European standards.[9] As Fahey *et al.* (2006: 54–55) put it: 'At the close of the twentieth century, Ireland as a whole, both north and south, remained among the most Christian parts of Europe and among the most committed to institutionalized religious activity'.

Using census data from 1951 onwards, the results in Table 2.1 demonstrate the high rate of religious belonging, as measured by religious affiliation. In 1951, 95 per cent of individuals claimed to belong either to the Catholic faith or to one of the three main Protestant denominations (Church of Ireland, Presbyterian or Methodist). By 2001, the proportion who self-identified with either of these two religions still constituted an overwhelming majority of 80 per cent. Furthermore, when the 6 per cent who constitute 'Other Christian' denominations are added, the vast majority of whom may be considered Protestant variations,[10] Protestants continue to predominate, although they no longer constitute an absolute majority. There has also been a slow but steady growth in the proportions of Catholics, from 34 per cent in the 1951 census to 40 per cent in 2001.

Table 2.1 Religious affiliation, 1951–2001

	Catholic	Church of Ireland	Presbyterian	Methodist	Non-affiliated
	(Percentages)				
1951	34.4	25.8	29.9	4.9	0.4
1961	34.9	24.2	29.0	5.0	1.9
1971	31.4	22.0	26.7	4.7	9.4
1981	28.0	19.0	22.9	4.0	18.5
1991	38.4	17.7	21.3	3.8	11.0
2001	40.0	15.3	20.7	3.5	13.9

Sources: Northern Ireland Census 1951–2001, available at http://www.nisranew.nisra.gov.uk/census/start.html

The trends in Table 2.1 also show two other important patterns. First, a small but notably increasing group of individuals – the non-affiliated – have emerged in recent years.[11] Changes in the census question on religion from a compulsory to a voluntary one in 1971 make it difficult to trace the growth of this non-affiliated group – the 'not stated' category – with any precision. Nevertheless, the results suggest that the number of individuals who constituted this group rose from just 0.4 per cent of the population in 1951 to 9.4 per cent in 1971.[12] In the 1981 census, the proportion rose yet again to 18.5 per cent of the population. However, when a separate category for those with no religion was introduced in the 1991 census, the non-stated proportion declined to 7.3 per cent, as compared to a further 3.7 per cent who specifically claimed no religious identification – a total of 11 per cent.

A similar pattern to 1991 emerged in the 2001 census; here, the non-stated proportion declined even further to just 4.2 per cent, as compared to 9.7 per cent who specifically claimed no religious identification – a total of 14 per cent overall. Thus, for these two census periods at least, there is empirical evidence to suggest that if individuals in Northern Ireland are allowed to choose between not volunteering any religious affiliation and explicitly stating that they have no religion, the formal disavowal of a religious identification is the dominant outcome. In fact, equivalent data from the 2001 census in England and Wales suggests that the proportion of individuals currently claiming no religious identification in Northern Ireland is now almost identical – 15.5 per cent – to that in Britain.[13] There is, then, some evidence of secularization in Northern Ireland, although the trend remains relatively weak.

A second finding that emerges from Table 2.1 is that the large increase in the 'not stated' category in 1981 was substantially a consequence of Catholics rather than Protestants refusing to state their religion. The increase in the proportion of 'not stated' individuals in that year accounts for most of the drop in the proportion of Catholics. By contrast, the proportions identifying with the three main Protestant denominations show no break in the downward trend.[14] Removing the particular circumstances of the 1981 census from the trend, the results demonstrate that the increase in the size of the non-affiliated group has been almost exclusively at the expense of the main Protestant denominations. The net effect of these changes is that, by 2001, the non-affiliated category was the fourth largest group in Northern Ireland, after Catholics, Presbyterians and Anglicans, and almost the same size as the latter. This is a significant change in the religious map of Northern Ireland.

Survey data enable us to further refine these patterns, by examining in more detail the trends in the period since 1968, particularly in relation to those who claim to have no religious identification.[15] With the exception

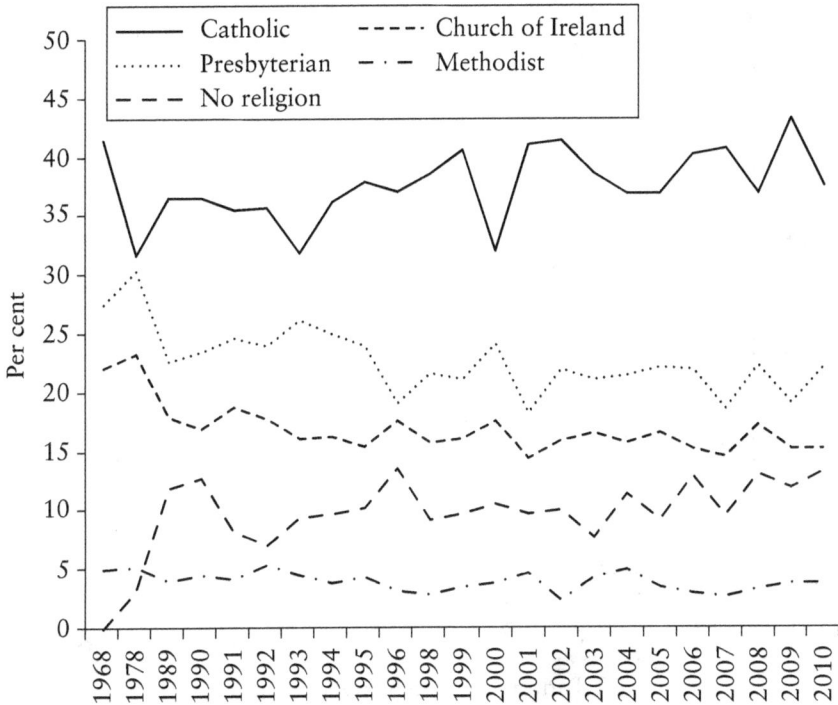

Figure 2.1 Religious affiliation, 1968–2010
Sources: Northern Ireland Loyalty Survey, 1968; Northern Ireland Attitude
Survey, 1978; Northern Ireland Social Attitudes Surveys, 1989–91, 1993–96;
Northern Ireland Election Survey, 1992; Northern Ireland Life and Times
Surveys, 1998–2010

of the period between 1968 and 1978 and some minor fluctuations in the
early 1990s, Figure 2.1 confirms the incremental increase in the proportion of the population identifying themselves as Catholic for much of the
period since 1968. In 1978, 32 per cent of those interviewed identified
themselves as Catholic; in 2007, the same figure was 41 per cent, representing an increase of 0.3 per cent per year. At the same time, there has been
a recent decline among self-identified Catholics – from 41 per cent in 2007
to 38 per cent in 2010.

Two of the main Protestant denominations show the same consistent
decline revealed in the census, although to a lesser degree. Over the
1968–2010 period, the proportions of Presbyterians and Anglicans have
declined by around 6 per cent and 7 per cent, respectively. Perhaps surprisingly given the patterns revealed in the census, the proportion explicitly
claiming no religion has only increased slightly over the period, from

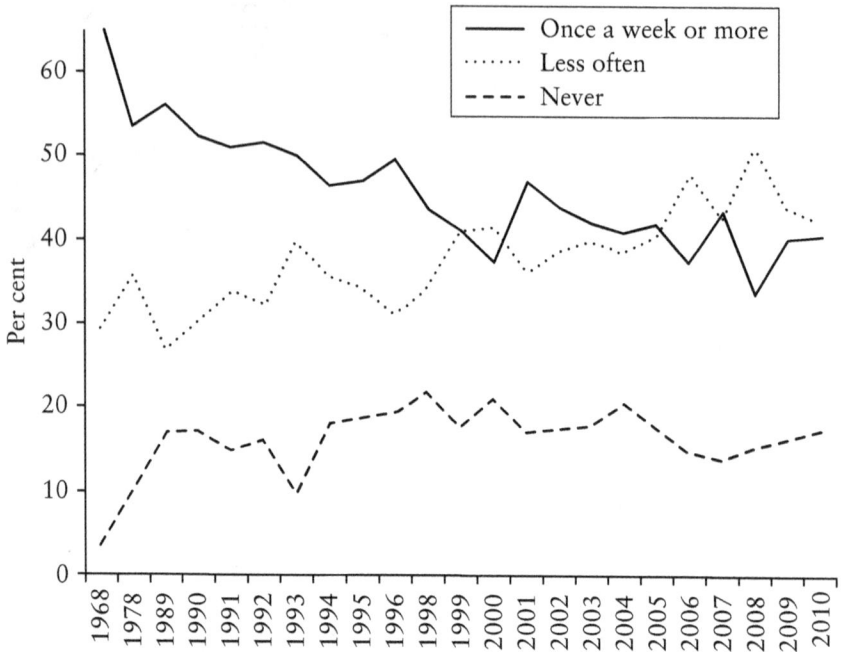

Figure 2.2 Patterns of church attendance, 1968–2010
Sources: Northern Ireland Loyalty Survey, 1968; Northern Ireland Attitude Survey, 1978; Northern Ireland Social Attitudes Surveys, 1989–91, 1993–96; Northern Ireland Election Survey, 1992; Northern Ireland Life and Times Surveys, 1998–2010

around 12 per cent at the beginning of the 1990s to 13 per cent in the most recent survey. Recent survey estimates suggest, however, that the proportion claiming no religious affiliation in Northern Ireland is now equivalent to that in the U.S. but significantly lower than is found in Britain.[16]

Another way in which religion conviction can be gauged is in terms of religious behaviour, which is measured by the frequency of church attendance. Previous research suggests that while levels of religious affiliation remain high in many countries, including Northern Ireland, there has also been a rise in 'nominal' adherents, that is, those who claim a religious affiliation but who do not regularly attend religious services (see Fahey *et al.*, 2006). The data in Figure 2.2 supports this interpretation. In the late 1960s, over two-thirds of the population attended church at least weekly, but by the late 1980s this had fallen to just over half, a significant decline in a relatively short period of time. Since then, the proportion had declined even further, so that currently only around two-fifths of the adult population attends church on at

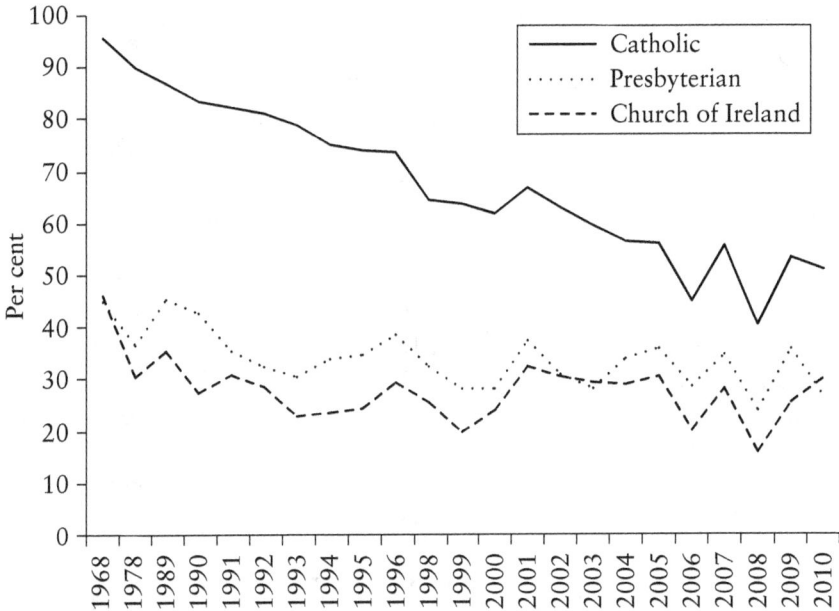

Figure 2.3 Weekly church attendance, main denominations, 1968–2010
Sources: Northern Ireland Loyalty Survey, 1968; Northern Ireland Attitude
Survey, 1978; Northern Ireland Social Attitudes Surveys, 1989–91, 1993–96;
Northern Ireland Election Survey, 1992; Northern Ireland Life and Times
Surveys, 1998–2010

least a weekly basis. The estimates suggest that frequent church
attendance has been replaced by less frequent church attendance, rather
than by complete non-attendance; those attending church less frequently
than once a week have increased from just 30 per cent of the population
to around two-fifths and are marginally higher than the proportion who
attend weekly. By contrast, those never attending church have remained
relatively stable at about one in six of the population.

Which denominations account for the declining frequency in church
attendance? Research in the U.S. and elsewhere shows that during
periods when religion is relatively unpopular, the denominations which
expect less formal commitment from their members are those which experience the greatest decline. By contrast, the denominations which require
greater involvement and commitment from their adherents are more
likely to remain stable or even prosper (Iannaccone, 1994). This accounts
for the rise of many small, evangelical groups, which for the most part
have flourished in the face of decline among their larger, liberal counterparts (Finke and Stark, 2005).[17] The results in Figure 2.3 lend partial
support to this hypothesis in the Northern Ireland context.

Regular church attendance – defined as at least weekly attendance – has declined among the three major denominations, Catholic, Presbyterian and Church of Ireland.[18] However, the decline has been greatest among Catholics, traditionally the most diligent church attenders. For example, in 1968, 95 per cent of Catholics said that they attended church at least weekly; by the mid-1990s, that proportion had declined to 74 per cent – an average decline of 0.8 per cent per year. Since then, the proportion of Catholics who attend church at least weekly has declined by an almost equivalent margin – 0.7 per cent per year – so that currently only just over half attend church on at least a weekly basis. By contrast, regular attendance by Presbyterians has declined by just 18 per cent over the period, and among Anglicans, by 16 per cent. Because the main Protestant denominations have shown significant declines in the proportion of affiliated members, those that are left tend to be more committed. This is much less the case for Catholics, where the proportions of nominal members have actually increased, as Table 2.1 and Figure 2.1 both demonstrate.

These results suggest three conclusions. First, Northern Ireland continues to maintain an internationally high rate of religious belonging. The vast majority of the population self-identify with either the Protestant or the Catholic faith. Second, notwithstanding this finding, there has been the emergence of a significant proportion of the population who disavow any religious identification; these individuals are disproportionately former Protestants. At around 13 per cent of the adult population, they represent a significant new grouping in Northern Ireland society. The distinctive nature of their social and political opinions as compared to their religious counterparts means that their long-term significance for intercommunity relations should not be underestimated (see Hayes and McAllister, 1995, 2004; Fahey et al., 2006).

A third conclusion is that while there is a high rate in religious belonging, this has been accompanied by a dramatic decline in religious practice, especially among Catholics. Although the survey data suggests that, until recently, the proportion of self-identified Catholics has grown over the period of study – from 37 per cent in 1989 to 41 per cent in 2007 – this growth has been accompanied by a significant decline in church attendance. For example, in 1989, 10 per cent of Catholics attended less than weekly, and 3 per cent never attended. By 2010, the same figures were 39 per cent and 10 per cent, respectively – an important change given the Catholic Church's emphasis on regular attendance by its members.

The impact of these factors indicates that two parallel processes are now underway in the Catholic and Protestant churches. Within the Catholic Church, declining religious conviction is reflected in declining church attendance, once the characteristic that set the church apart from the main Protestant denominations. Among members of the Protestant churches, by contrast, the decline in religious conviction is occurring via a formal move away from the churches and by expressing no formal religious attachment. What may explain this decline in religious conviction? The next section tests a variety of explanations for the decline in religious attachment.

The transmission of religious attachment

It has long been suggested that the successful transmission of religious attachment from parent to child is the key mechanism behind the maintenance of religious conviction.[19] It is argued that people grow up in families and that they inherit their religion, along with many other things, from their parents and from the immediate family group. The traditional family cycle sees children leave the family, disengage with religion and then re-engage as they marry and start a family of their own (Roof, 1993). The current decline in religious attachments, or what has been traditionally referred to as secularization, suggests that the process of family socialization into religion may be undergoing change. Moreover, as the proportion of those with no religion in the population increases, this in itself is an important driver of change. This assumes, of course, that those who grow up in a family that has no religion stay that way; in fact, as Hout and Fisher (2002) have demonstrated in the U.S., that rarely holds, and many who grow up without a religion acquire one in later life. As Hout and Fisher also point out, however, this movement back to religion is much reduced among those gaining adulthood from about 1990 onwards, compared to those growing up in earlier periods.

How effective are the various denominations in transmitting religion through the family from parent to child? Table 2.2 addresses this question by showing the religion that the person reported being brought up in and their current religion. As in previous research, the results suggest substantially different levels of transmission between the various groups (see Sherkat and Wilson, 1995). The strongest rate of transmission, as we would expect, occurs among Catholics; of those who reported being brought up as a Catholic, 92 per cent in the combined surveys reported their current affiliation as Catholic; among those who did not inherit their family religion, most (7 per cent) said that they now had no religion.

The second highest level of transmission in Table 2.2, after Catholics, is those who were brought up in families with no religion. No less than 88 per cent of those who were brought up in such households said that they themselves had no religion. Since just 2 per cent of the respondents in the combined data file had been brought up in such a family, the

Table 2.2 The inheritance of religious attachments, pooled sample

(Current religion)	Catholic	Anglican	Presbyterian	Methodist	Other Protestant	No religion
			(Family religion)			
Catholic	92	1	1	*	2	3
Anglican	0	70	5	5	3	2
Presbyterian	0	8	74	8	7	2
Methodist	*	2	2	62	1	1
Other Protestant	1	7	8	11	73	4
No religion	7	12	10	14	14	88
Total	100	100	100	100	100	100
(N)	(10,442)	(5,689)	(7,055)	(1,239)	(1,702)	(585)

An asterisk denotes less than 0.5 per cent
Source: Northern Ireland Surveys, Pooled Sample, 1989–2010

aggregate effect on the total number of those who currently claim no religious affiliation (10 per cent) is relatively small, but it nevertheless demonstrates that being brought up without a religion is a strong predictor of current religious outlooks. In contrast to those from either Catholic families or families with no religious affiliation, the Protestant denominations show varying levels of inheritance. Among the liberal Protestant denominations – Anglican, Presbyterian and Methodist – the lowest levels are found among the Methodists, at 62 per cent, and the highest, 74 per cent, among the Presbyterians. The more fundamentalist Protestant denominations – the other Protestant category – show similar levels of transmission to that of the Presbyterians.

In addition to the religious background of parents, a number of other factors may also affect religious transmission, and this is particularly the case in the movement away from a religious affiliation. There is a growing body of literature to suggest that gender, marital status, age and educational attainment can all significantly influence an individual's chances of remaining within or leaving their religious tradition of origin. Previous research in Northern Ireland and elsewhere demonstrates that religious disaffiliation is most common among males, the better educated and the young (Hayes and McAllister, 1995; Hayes, 2000). Those who are disaffiliated are also less likely to be married and, if they do marry, are more likely to be divorced, separated or involved in a remarriage (Sherkat and Wilson, 1995). Some studies suggest that they are also disproportionally drawn from the ranks of the unemployed and economically marginal members of society, but others suggest that this is not so (see Hayes, 2000).

The results in Table 2.3 lend support to these findings as they relate to age, gender, marital status and education. For both Protestants and Catholics, being younger, male and divorced (compared to being single) are all strongly related to the disavowal of one's religious origins. Education, reflected in the lack of an educational qualification, is also a strong and consistent predictor for both Protestants and Catholics. While there is also a statistically significant effect for a secondary education among Catholics, it is clear that the educational effect is primarily between those who possess a tertiary education and those who do not. Economic status is also a significant determinant among Protestants; Protestants who are employed are more likely than those who are unemployed to disavow their family religion.

To what extent has this reduction in religious conviction led to a decline in the salience of religion as a source of identity? In other words, has the growth in religious disaffiliation as well as the decline in religious conviction been accompanied by any reduction in the importance

Table 2.3 Disavowing the family religion for no religion, pooled sample

	Former Protestants		Former Catholics	
	Est	(SE)	Est	(SE)
Gender (male)	0.36**	(0.05)	0.63**	(0.08)
Age (years)	−0.02**	(0.01)	−0.02**	(0.01)
Marital status (single)				
Married	−0.28**	(0.06)	−0.08	(0.10)
Divorced/separated	0.47**	(0.08)	0.65**	(0.13)
Widowed	−0.44**	(0.13)	−0.09	(0.22)
Education (tertiary)				
Secondary	−0.10	(0.06)	−0.29**	(0.09)
No qualification	−0.23**	(0.06)	−0.52**	(0.10)
Labour active (yes)	0.12*	(0.06)	−0.10	(0.09)
Constant	−0.46**		−0.99**	
Pseudo R-squared	0.05		0.05	
(N)	(15,638)		(10,281)	

Significant at **$p < 0.01$, *$p < 0.05$

Logistic regression analyses showing parameter estimates and (in parentheses) robust standard errors predicting those currently having no religion (scored 1) versus those who claim to be Protestant/Catholic (scored 0) among those brought up as a Protestant or Catholic. Both models include year dummy variables for unobserved heterogeneity. All variables are binary except age, which is scored in single years. Single is the omitted category for marital status and no qualification for education

Source: Northern Ireland Surveys, Pooled Sample, 1989–2010

of religion as a mark of identity at both the individual and societal level? The next section examines this issue using the 2007 Life and Times Survey, which contained specific items designed to measure religious identity.

Religion as a source of identity

Modernization theorists argue that religion has become at best an epi-phenomenal factor in modern life. Because the world has become increasingly secularized, religion, it is argued, is no longer a relevant political or social force. Rising economic standards, growing rates of literacy and education, urbanization and advancements in science and technology have all led to the demise of the influence of religion in modern life.

Rather than being a force for collective action, religion has been relegated from the formal or public sphere to the informal one, or nothing more than a private affair for the individuals involved (see Bruce, 2002). Recent research has questioned this argument. Pointing to the growing feelings of alienation and insecurity associated with modernization, proponents of this perspective argue that not only is religion now of even greater importance in peoples' daily lives than hitherto, but religious differences have become a key source of intrastate armed conflicts (see Fox, 2004; Norris and Inglehart, 2004). As Tanja Ellingsen (2005: 319) argues: 'Religion has and continues to be an important source of identity to people.... There is some evidence that during the last decades we have witnessed a resurgence of the impact of religion on the question of identity, as well as the question of warfare'.

While the exact nature of its contribution to the conflict remains in some dispute, most commentators agree that religion continues to remain an important source of identity in Northern Ireland. As Mitchell (2006) notes, religion not only provides individuals with a sense of belonging, but it also acts as a primary source of differentiation between the two communities. Some commentators suggest that not only do both the Protestant and Catholic communities perceive themselves as independent of each other, but this independence is reinforced by stereotypical views of the other community (see Fulton 2002). Ronald McAllister (2000: 843) puts it clearly when he says that: 'in Northern Ireland, people grow up not only thinking of themselves as either Protestant or Catholic but also thinking *as* Protestants or *as* Catholics'. It is this unambiguous boundary which led Richard Rose (1971: 248), among others, to describe Northern Ireland as a 'biconfessional' society.

The results in the first part of Table 2.4 support the view that religion is an important form of identity for both communities. Among Protestants, just under two-thirds of respondents claimed that being a Protestant is an important reflection of 'who they are', compared to around one-fifth who disagreed with this view. A more pronounced pattern is apparent among Catholics. Around three-quarters of Catholics self-identify with their religion, compared to just 17 per cent who do not. Thus, for both religious communities, their religious affiliation is a key source of identity, and this is particularly the case for Catholics. The greater sense of religious identity among Catholics may be a consequence of their stronger religious commitment. It may also reflect their minority status within Northern Ireland and the consequent need to maintain communal solidarity in order to optimize their bargaining power with Protestants (O'Connor, 1993).

Table 2.4 Religion as a source of identity and division, 2007

	Protestant	Catholic	No religion	Total
Personal identity				
Agree	65	74	na	69
Neutral	13	9	na	11
Disagree	22	17	na	20
Total	100	100		100
(N)	(570)	(477)		(1,046)
Separate peoples in the past				
Agree	70	66	67	68
Neutral	5	7	5	6
Disagree	25	27	28	26
Total	100	100	100	100
(N)	(569)	(467)	(112)	(1,148)
Separate peoples in the future				
Agree	50	38	39	44
Neutral	9	11	13	10
Disagree	41	51	48	46
Total	100	100	100	100
(N)	(569)	(466)	(112)	(1,147)

The questions were: 'Being [Protestant/Catholic] is an important reflection of who I am'. 'In Northern Ireland, Protestants and Catholics *have always been* separate peoples; In Northern Ireland, Protestants and Catholics *will always be* separate peoples'.
Source: Northern Ireland Life and Times Survey, 2007

A more complex picture emerges with regard to the role of religion as a source of social division; these results appear in the second and third parts of Table 2.4. The vast majority of the population believe that Protestants and Catholics have always been 'separate peoples' in the past, and this relationship holds for Protestants and Catholics as well as those with no religious identification. However, only a minority believe that religion will cause future communal division. Moreover, it is Protestants who are the more pessimistic in their views about the future role of religion. For example, whereas exactly half of the Protestant respondents claimed that religion would always be a primary source of demarcation, just under two-fifths of Catholics or those with no religious affiliation endorsed this view.

What explains these differences between the two communities in their views about religion and identity? We would suggest that one factor is the long tradition of anti-Catholicism that exists within the Protestant community (see Bruce, 1986; Brewer and Higgins, 1998; Mitchell, 2006). Previous studies have demonstrated that not only do some Protestants see the Roman Catholic Church as a force that is seeking to destroy true Christianity, but, in some quarters, such as the evangelical Free Presbyterian Church, the Roman Catholic Church is viewed not as a Christian body at all but as a manifestation of the work of the anti-Christ.[20] As Steve Bruce (1986: 224) comments: 'Free Presbyterians differ from most other Protestants in the strength of their anti-Catholicism, which leads them to attribute more power and influence to Rome than would other Protestants. For the Free Presbyterians, Rome is not only totally evil but also extremely efficient'.

Of course, not all Protestants belong to this evangelical tradition or share their views.[21] However, this evangelical tradition does form the basis for the construction of a Protestant community in Northern Ireland. As such, it not only appeals to many Protestants, but it has also provided a theological justification for maintaining a boundary with Catholics. In the words of Claire Mitchell (2006: 82), 'Catholics have consistently been cast as the "other" by Protestants'. This is not the case within the Catholic community where a religious overlay on the communal division has been much less important.[22] It is therefore a strong anti-Catholic tradition based on theological convictions which we suggest explains the more separatist stance adopted by Protestants.

For both Protestants and Catholics, religious affiliation remains an important source of personal identity. This sense of religious identity is particularly strong for Catholics. However, in contrast to their Protestant counterparts, these higher levels of religious identity among Catholics do not translate into a more separatist view of the future role of religion in shaping communal divisions; rather, it is Protestants who stand out as more separatist in their predictions about the future. To what extent are these differences in religious identity also associated with a more prejudiced view of the opposing religious community? In other words, does an attachment to a religious label perpetuate prejudice? The next section addresses this question by focusing on differences in levels of knowledge and respect for the culture and traditions of the two religious communities.

Religion and communal prejudice

As we have argued in this chapter, the place of religion in the Northern Ireland conflict is both complex and contested. While few observers see the conflict as exclusively religious in nature, many point to the role of religion in perpetuating the conflict via its boundary-maintaining practices, such as the insistence on a separate educational system and opposition to interfaith marriages. In turn, being educated within a religious environment and marrying within one's own community serves to strengthen a religious identity, which helps to generate communal enmity and perpetuates the conflict. To what extent does an attachment to a religious affiliation lead to a lack of understanding of and stereotypical views about the opposing community? And what role, if any, does levels of contact between the two communities, particularly within a marriage and educational setting, play in this process?

The 2007 Northern Ireland Life and Times Survey allows us to test the role of religion in shaping views of the opposing community. The survey contained two questions about the respondents' understanding of and respect for 'the culture and traditions' of the two communities. The results in Table 2.5 support the interpretation that religion is an important influence in producing stereotypical attitudes. Among both Protestants and Catholics, the first part of the table shows that there is a significant lack of understanding of the opposing community. For

Table 2.5 Religion and attitudes towards the other community, 2007

	Protestants about Catholics	Catholics about Protestants	No religion about Protestants	No religion about Catholics
Understanding				
A lot	25	30	49	46
A little	58	53	38	38
Hardly any	14	14	11	14
None at all	3	3	2	2
Total	100	100	100	100
(N)	(574)	(479)	(112)	(112)
Respect				
A lot	55	62	62	61
A little	39	32	30	31
Hardly any	5	6	8	8
None at all	1	0	0	0
Total	100	100	100	100
(N)	(573)	(476)	(111)	(110)

The questions were: 'And, how much do you understand about the [Catholic/Protestant] community's culture and traditions?'; 'And how much respect do you have for the [Catholic/Protestant] community's culture and traditions?'
Source: Northern Ireland Life and Times Survey, 2007

example, while only a quarter of Protestants claimed to understand 'a lot' about the culture and traditions of the Catholic community, the equivalent level of Catholic understanding of Protestants is similar, at 30 per cent. In fact, for both groups, a staggering 17 per cent of the respondents answered 'hardly any' or 'none at all' when asked about their understanding of the culture and traditions of the other community.

Those who identify themselves as having no religious affiliation display a different pattern to both Protestants and Catholics. Individuals who report no religious affiliation claim to have a significantly higher level of understanding of the culture and traditions of the two main religious communities. Moreover, this pattern of association holds for the views of either community. For example, whereas nearly half of those who explicitly stated that they had no religion claimed 'a lot' of understanding of the Catholic community, the equivalent proportion who endorsed this view about the Protestant community was only marginally lower at 46 per cent. In fact, individuals who disavow a religion show about twice the level of understanding of Protestants as Protestants show of Catholics. This is a major difference and one that cannot be explained by variations in social background.

There are more positive results with regard to professed levels of respect for each of the religious communities. The second part of Table 2.5 shows that among both Protestants and Catholics, a majority claim to have 'a lot' of respect for the other community. This is particularly the case among Catholics, 62 per cent of whom say they have 'a lot' of respect for the culture and traditions of Protestants; the same figure for Protestants is slightly lower, at 55 per cent. Once again, individuals who claim no religious affiliation emerge as the most consistently positive in their views, with 6 out of 10 saying that they had 'a lot' of respect for the culture and traditions of both communities. Moreover, the views of the religiously non-affiliated towards both communities were almost identical.

Respect for the other community therefore generates much more support than understanding. There are probably two explanations for this finding. First, 'understanding' implies intimacy and personal knowledge, and in Northern Ireland's segregated society with a series of reinforcing cleavages, such contact is rare. Moreover, one of Rosemary Harris's main findings in her book *Prejudice and Tolerance in Ulster* was that on those occasions when such contact happens, 'the greatest efforts were made to prevent any controversial topic from being discussed' (1972: 146). By contrast, 'respect' is independent of understanding or knowledge of the other group and involves a positive sense of esteem which is often regarded as one of the fundamental moral values of a modern society (see, e.g., Rokeach, 1979). A second explanation is more practical:

one of the central tenets of the 1998 Belfast Agreement was 'parity of esteem' between the two communities, or a sense of due recognition of fellow citizens. Thus, it is not unreasonable to expect that as individuals have become more comfortable with the principles of the Agreement, they are more likely to show respect for their fellow citizens.

Previous survey data on public perceptions concerning the Northern Ireland peace process highlights the importance of this issue – the lack of respect for one's fellow citizens – as a key factor in giving rise to the conflict. One perspective is provided by Colin Irwin (2002), who conducted eight surveys of public opinion between April 1996 and May 2000. He found that 69 per cent of the population viewed the lack of respect for the people of the 'other' tradition as either a 'very significant' or a 'significant' cause of the conflict. Catholics, however, were more supportive of this position than Protestants. While just under two-thirds of Catholics pointed to the lack of respect for members of the other community as a 'very significant' factor in contributing to the conflict, only 30 per cent of Protestants shared this view. Catholics were also more likely to prioritize this issue in terms of its significance than Protestants, ranking it fifth out of 19 possible causes of the conflict, as compared to a rank of ninth among Protestants.

Despite public perceptions as to the importance of this issue in terms of the future success of the Northern Ireland peace process, both respect and understanding between the two main communities have remained stable since 2005, although reported levels of respect continue to significantly outstrip those of understanding (see Figure 2.4). A total of 58 per cent of Protestants and 59 per cent of Catholics claimed to have 'a lot' of respect for the culture and traditions of the opposing community in 2005; by 2010, the proportion reporting such views was just two percentage points higher at 60 per cent and 62 per cent, respectively. There is a similar stable pattern for levels of understanding between the two religious communities. Thus, whatever the expressed aspirations of supporters of the Belfast Agreement, it appears that levels of enmity between the two communities have not diminished in its wake.

Views of the other community may, of course, vary not only with religious identity but also with life experiences and skills, such as age, education and participation in the labour force as well as levels of contact between the two communities, via marriage and the education system. In order to take account of these various factors, a multivariate analysis was conducted to predict understanding and respect for the other community. The independent variables are the respondents' socio-demographic background, levels of contact between the two communities through marriage and school, and religious identity. The

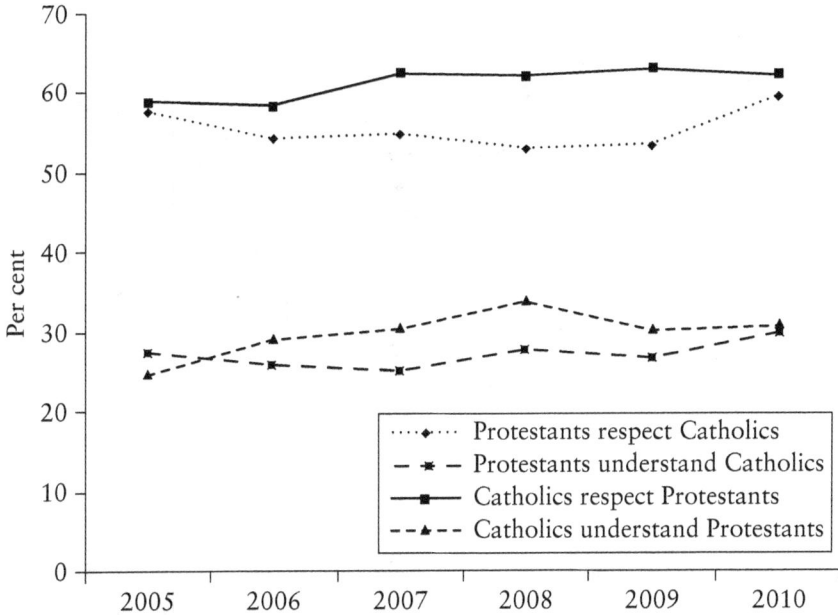

Figure 2.4 Attitudes towards the other community, 2005–10
See Table 2.5 for question wording. Estimates are for those saying 'a lot'.
Source: Northern Ireland Life and Times Surveys, 2005–10

results in Table 2.6 show that religious identity remains a significant influence on understanding and respect for both communities, even after controls are added to the analysis. The most consistently important influence is a sense of religious identity at the societal level – views about whether or not the two communities will remain separate peoples in the future – and this has a greater and more consistent impact on the level of respect for the other community than on the level of understanding.

The analysis also confirms the key differences between the two communities in terms of the impact of religious identity on levels of understanding and feelings of respect towards the opposing religious community. Perceptions of religious identity at both the personal and societal level emerge as important for Protestants, while for Catholics, the sole predictor of attitudes is religious identity at the societal level. These results confirm the view that for Catholics, the personal importance of a religious identity may be understood as a private or individual matter and this in turn does not lead to a more negative view of the culture and traditions of the opposing community.

Table 2.6 The salience of religion and cross-community attitudes, 2007

| | (Protestants) | | | | (Catholics) | | | |
| | Understanding | | Respect | | Understanding | | Respect | |
	Est	(SE)	Est	(SE)	Est	(SE)	Est	(SE)
Socio-demographic controls								
Gender (male)	-0.26	(0.21)	-0.18	(0.19)	-0.14	(0.22)	-0.37	(0.21)
Age (years)	0.01	(0.01)	0.02**	(0.01)	0.03**	(0.01)	0.04**	(0.01)
Education (no qualification)								
Tertiary	1.47**	(0.29)	1.17**	(0.25)	1.49**	(0.32)	1.04**	(0.30)
Secondary	0.41	(0.31)	0.59*	(0.25)	0.89**	(0.32)	0.68*	(0.29)
Religious homogamy								
Single-faith marriage	-0.15	(0.22)	-0.39*	(0.20)	0.18	(0.24)	0.13	(0.23)
Segregated school	-0.31	(0.30)	0.05	(0.28)	-1.19**	(0.34)	-0.34	(0.36)
Religious identity								
Personal level (important)	-0.76*	(0.35)	-0.61*	(0.30)	-0.18	(0.37)	0.60	(0.35)
Societal level (divisive)	-0.67	(0.38)	-1.51**	(0.33)	-1.15**	(0.39)	-1.87**	(0.38)
Constant	-0.97		-0.15		-1.43*		-0.75	
Nagelkerke R-squared	0.13		0.15		0.17		0.19	
(N)	(554)		(553)		(424)		(422)	

Significant at **$p < 0.01$, *$p < 0.05$

Logistic regression analyses showing parameter estimates and standard errors predicting understanding and respect scored 1 (lot) or 0 (other). All variables are binary except age (years) and religious identity (7-point scale scored from 0 to 1). No qualification is the omitted category of comparison for education

Source: Northern Ireland Life and Times Survey, 2007

In addition to religious identity, a range of other factors also predict cross-community attitudes. Education, reflected in the possession of a university degree, is a strong and consistent predictor for both Protestants and Catholics. Individuals who possess a tertiary education are significantly more likely to claim higher levels of respect and understanding of the culture and traditions of the opposing community than those who do not. Age has a positive effect for both Protestants and Catholics; older individuals are significantly more likely to claim both higher levels of respect and understanding of the culture and traditions of the opposing community than their younger counterparts. There are less consistent effects for single-faith marriages and for segregated schooling: the former leads to Protestants showing less respect for the other community, while the latter leads to Catholics showing less understanding. However, the inconsistency in the patterns makes firm conclusions difficult.

These results suggest two conclusions. First, religious identification is an important source of communal division. Individuals who see themselves as religious demonstrate less understanding and, to a lesser degree, reduced respect for the opposing community than those who disavow a religious affiliation. This pattern is stronger among Protestants than Catholics. Second, the impact of religious identity on attitudes towards the opposing religious community differs for Protestants and Catholics. While perceptions of the salience of religion at the personal and societal level are a negative predictor of views among Protestants, for Catholics the sole predictor of attitudes is the perceived salience of religion at the societal level. Thus, in further confirmation of earlier research, for Catholics at least, their antipathy towards the Protestant community is less rooted in theological convictions than in feelings of victimhood, vulnerability and negative stereotypes of Protestants. As Mitchell (2006: 114–115) puts it: 'Protestant political culture has become infused with religious ideology. For Catholics this relationship has been less pronounced...Theology is less socially salient for Catholics'.

Conclusion

One feature of the post-cold war era is the rising prominence of intra-state conflicts based on religious, national or ethnic identity. This view is most closely associated with the work of Samuel Huntington (1996), who predicted that most post-cold war conflict would be based on a clash of culture or civilization, and most conflict would have religion as either the main or complementary element. While Huntington's thesis generated a major debate, it does appear to be the case that not only can the vast majority of contemporary conflicts be classified as intrastate in nature, but a sizeable proportion involves disputes surrounding religious identity (see Fox, 2004). Contrary to the expectations of social scientists who had predicted the inevitable decline of religion through modernization, religion has now emerged as an important source of conflict. Moreover, religious conflicts are often more durable and intense than other conflicts because they are zero-sum, thereby making a negotiated settlement more difficult (see Ellingsen, 2005).

Religion not only generates conflict, but it can also help to resolve it. The prominence of religion in Huntington's thesis and conflict research generally has tended to obscure the important role that religion plays in mitigating conflict. Religion can also play an important role in preventing conflict in the first place by bringing the leaders of opposing groups together in pursuit of compromise and by fostering grass-roots organizations that transcend a society's divisions. In fact, it has been argued that a first step in resolving any conflict that has a religious dimension is the explicit recognition that religious differences are central to the solution (see Appleby, 2000). Nevertheless, it is fair to say that we know more – and observe more – about the role of religion as a generator rather than as a resolver of conflict.

This conclusion is aptly born out in evaluating the role of religion in the Northern Ireland conflict. While some point to the role of religion in perpetuating the conflict, others have stressed its irrelevance either as a source or as a solution to the conflict. In contrast, others highlight the contribution of members of religious organizations to resolving the conflict. Across all of these disparate views, however, a common theme is that the conflict is not inherently religious in nature. Rather, religious leaders and institutions play a central role in sustaining the conflict via their various boundary-maintaining practices. Indeed, the social consequences of religion as a marker of communal division are often identified as being the main role of religion in the conflict.

This chapter has used the survey data to examine the role of religion in maintaining the boundaries between the two communities. We find ample support for this proposition. First, despite some recent declines in religious affiliation and behaviour, by international standards Northern Ireland remains a deeply religious society. The overwhelming majority continue to identify with one of the two main religious affiliations, and a significant proportion attend church services, albeit on an increasingly irregular basis. At the same time, and in common with other advanced societies, a growing proportion of the population – currently, around 13 per cent – explicitly disavow any religious identification.

A second finding is that religious affiliation remains an important source of personal identity; this is particularly the case among Catholics.

In contrast to Protestants, this higher level of Catholic religious identity does not translate into a more separatist view of the future role of religion in demarcating communal division. As the results also clearly demonstrated, there is evidence that religious identification is an important source of communal prejudice and division. Unlike their non-affiliated counterparts, those with a religious affiliation display a significant lack of understanding of and, to a lesser extent respect for, the culture and traditions of the opposing community. This pattern is particularly marked among Protestants. These differences in findings between the two religious communities remain even when the salience in religious identity and a variety of background characteristics, including levels of contact in both a marriage and educational setting, are taken into account.

Finally, the results show that the impact of religious identity on attitudes towards the opposing religious community differs for Protestants and Catholics. For Protestants, religious identity is a marker of intercommunal division at both the personal and societal level; for Catholics, the sole predictor of attitudes was religious identity at the societal level. For Catholics, the importance of religion may be understood as a private matter which does not translate into negative and ill-informed beliefs towards the opposing community. This is not the case among Protestants, whose theologically rooted anti-Catholicism continues to underpin and inform their views. It is this factor – the strong anti-Catholic tradition within the Protestant community – which we suggest explains the impact of religious identity on enmity towards the Catholic community at both the personal and societal level.

Although the conflict in Northern Ireland has not primarily been about religion, its religious overtones are inescapable. Despite declines in observance, religious belonging remains strong and is structured around the traditional Protestant/Catholic cleavage. Moreover, religious identity continues to inform social outlooks and to structure relations between the two communities. Even among those who claim only nominal religious attachment, religion continues to act as the main point of reference in determining their views and with whom they interact socially. Rather than negating the influence of religion, the conflict has heightened its social importance as a key mechanism in structuring social life.

Religion also continues to influence the tone, and in some cases even the substance, of Northern Ireland politics. The churches exercise an unofficial moral authority that is reflected in policy and in political life generally. Various Protestant religious leaders remain active in politics, and it is no coincidence that prominent church leaders from both communities have been involved directly in various peace initiatives, such as the decommissioning of paramilitary weapons. Indeed, the conflict appears to have deepened rather than diminished these public dimensions of religion. Religious institutions also continue to play a key role in the organization of daily life, which remains highly segregated. It is the role of the churches in structuring social as well as religious life that has led to the deep-seated antipathy that exists between the two religious communities. As Morrow *et al.* (1991: 20) conclude: '[it is here] that the extent of the churches' involvement with the politics of the conflict is most visible'.

While some of the most prominent religious figures in politics, such as Ian Paisley, have retired from politics, many politicians remain deeply committed in both religious belief and religious practice. Martin McGuinness, the deputy first minister, is a devout Catholic,[23] while Peter Robinson, the first minister, describes himself as a committed Christian and has publicly voiced his Christian convictions to justify his moral views.[24] Religion therefore underpins much of the political debates in Northern Ireland, not just about constitutional matters but about social and economic policy as well. While politics may be the substance of the Northern Ireland conflict, religion very much determines its form.

Notes

1 For examples of this work, see Lederach (1997), Appleby (2000) and Brewer *et al.* (2011).
2 See Brewer (2003a), Ganiel (2008) and Ganiel and Dixon (2008).
3 We examine the relationship between community relations and both single-faith marriages and education in Chapters 6 and 7, respectively.
4 See also McAllister (1982), Rose and McAllister (1983) and Coulter (1999).
5 See Bruce (1986), Brewer and Higgins (1998), Fulton (2002) and Mitchell (2006).
6 For a similar and multifaceted interpretation, see Whyte (1990) and Ruane and Todd (1996). As John Whyte (1990: 111) in his excellent overview of the literature on the interpretations of the conflict up to 1990 concludes, as the sharpness of the divide differs from place to place, so too 'the mix of religious, economic, political, and psychological factors which underpines it varies from one place to another'.
7 Ongoing empirical research, however, calls into serious question this assumption. Hayes and McAllister (1995, 2004) not only found that individuals who did not claim a religious affiliation were different from the religious affiliated in terms of their socio-demographic background and religious beliefs, but they were also significantly more likely to reject sectarian party allegiances and to disavow traditional constitutional preferences in favour of the political centre ground.

8 Examples include the role of the Catholic Church in facilitating the dialogue between Sinn Fein and the Social Democratic and Labour Party (SDLP) during the early stages of the peace process. As Mitchell (2008b: 156) notes: 'From Father Alex Reid and Father Aidan Troy to the Revered Ken Newell and the Reverend Sam Burch there has always been a significant body of both Catholic and Protestant clerics who have been prepared to take risks for peace'.

9 See Bruce (1999: 23–26) for a comprehensive discussion of this issue.

10 These include just over 1 per cent of Baptists and under 1 per cent of Free Presbyterians and Bretherns. There are also over 80 additional smaller denominations that can be classified as Protestant, all of which number less than 0.5 per cent of the population. Many of them have memberships of less than 100 people (see Northern Ireland Census, 2001, Key Statistics Tables, KS07c).

11 There is no consensus on how to label those with no religious affiliation, and they have been called inter alia 'secularists', 'nones', 'apostates' and 'independents'. For consistency, we use the terms 'non-affiliated' or 'no religion'. See Hayes and McAllister (1995) for a detailed discussion of this issue.

12 Hitherto, this increase in the 'not stated' category has been attributed to the voluntary nature of the question; fearing intimidation, it was thought that most were people who would in other circumstances have volunteered a religion (Compton, 1985).

13 There are some important variations on this issue. For example, according to the 2001 census, about 30 per cent of people in Scotland claimed to have no religious affiliation. Moreover, recent survey data suggests that the proportion of individuals in Britain who are willing to say that they do not regard themselves as belonging to a religion has risen from 31 per cent in 1983 to 43 per cent in 2008 (see Voas and Ling, 2010).

14 Although we do not examine it in detail here, there has been an increase in the size of the smaller, fundamentalist Protestant denominations, such as the Free Presbyterians and the Brethern (see Brewer, 2003b).

15 There are obvious difficulties in comparing survey data to the census with regard to religion. In the census, for the reasons discussed in the text, we define the non-affiliated group as those who explicitly answered 'none' to the religion question as well as those who were 'not stated'. In the surveys, we identify this group as those with 'no religion' and include only those who explicitly answered 'no religion'. Those who said 'don't know' or who refused to answer are systematically excluded from this and all future analyses.

16 For example, in 2008, whereas just 15 per cent of adults in the U.S. were willing to say that they did not regard themselves as belonging to a religion, the equivalent figure in Britain was 43 per cent (see Voas and Ling, 2010).

17 There is, however, much debate about this assumption, and traditional secularization theorists remain unconvinced (see Bruce, 2002).

18 Irregular church attendance is not necessarily as reliable an indicator of nominal adherence among Protestants as it is among Catholics, since frequent church attendance is a less formal requirement in Protestantism than in Catholicism.

19 See, for example, Voas and Crockett (2005).

20 Perhaps more so than any other factor, this view is typified by the founder and ex-leader of the Free Presbyterian Church, Rev. Ian Paisley, who throughout his leadership not only repeatedly emphasized that the Roman Catholic Church was not a Christian Church but also claimed that it was responsible for much of the violence in Northern Ireland (see Bruce, 1986).

21 Most recent estimates suggest that the number of evangelicals now constitute up to one-third of the population (Mitchell and Tilley, 2004).

22 This is not to suggest a lack of anti-Protestant sentiment among Catholics. Rather, such sentiments are rarely articulated in theological terms but more frequently expressed in feelings of victimhood and sacrifice as well as some religiously based stereotypical views of the Protestant community (see Mitchell, 2006: 91–116, for a comprehensive discussion of this issue).

23 See the interview with James Macintyre in the *New Statesman*, 17 February 2010.

24 A recent example being his public defence of his wife's (Iris Robinson) homophobic views when he said that: 'It wasn't Iris Robinson who determined that homosexuality was an abomination, it was the Almighty'.

3

National identity

Competing identities within nation states are commonplace in the modern world. Only about 1 in 10 of today's nation states is ethnically homogeneous (Haymes, 1997), leaving considerable scope for ethnic political conflict. Since 1990, ethnonationalist conflict has been particularly intense in the postcommunist states of eastern Europe and central Asia, where ethnic divisions have provided an enduring source of conflict for many centuries (see Petersen, 2002). The collapse of communism and the removal of a strong, uniting state have paved the way for the re-emergence of ethnic divisions, expressed most dramatically in the wars of the Yugoslav succession and later in the conflicts in Chechnya and Nagorno-Karabakh. Nor have the advanced democracies escaped the rise of ethnonationalism; even in Britain, there are divided national loyalties in Scotland and Wales, and in both nations only a minority of the population see themselves as British (Curtice, 2006).

Northern Ireland continues to be an exemplar of a state with divided identities. Historically, the nature of the conflict was reflected most visibly in the identities that the two religious communities use to describe themselves, a situation which, as this chapter illustrates, continues to this day. At one level, the conflict is about differing territorial allegiances, with Protestants seeing themselves as British and Catholics seeing themselves as Irish. At another level, the conflict is concerned with constitutional and political preferences, with Protestants wanting to remain part of the United Kingdom and Catholics wanting to become part of the Irish Republic. It is the reinforcement of these two divisions over an extended period of time, with religion being used as a boundary marker, that has led many observers to view the Northern Ireland conflict as an ethnonationalist one.[1] John McGarry and Brendan O'Leary (1995: 356), for example, see the presence of two competing ethnonationalist groups within the same territory as being the essential endogenous cause of the conflict.

In this context, the pattern of national identities in Northern Ireland is not unique, except for two important differences. First, in Northern

Ireland national identity has a much greater influence on political preferences and outlooks than is the case in, for example, other parts of the
United Kingdom. Identities continue to shape party preferences and
political attitudes to a much greater degree than is found elsewhere.
Second, in Northern Ireland three divisions reinforce one another: religious
affiliations, territorial allegiances and constitutional preferences. It is
this reinforcement of identity, together with the influence of identity on
a range of other behaviours and outlooks, that makes Northern Ireland
different from most other divided societies. And it is the reinforcement
of these divisions that has traditionally made the conflict so intractable,
since a range of divisions have to be dealt with simultaneously, rather
than a focus on a single division. It is this aspect of the problem that led
Richard Rose (1976: 139) to comment in the middle of the first full
decade of the conflict: 'Many talk about a solution to Ulster's political
problem but few are prepared to say what the problem is. The reason is
simple. The problem is that there is no solution'.

Ethnonationalism in Northern Ireland is fuelled, then, perhaps more
than in any other society, by its multifaceted and complex nature. It is
much more than a simplistic clash between Protestants and Catholics,
pitching those with a British identity against those with an Irish identity,
or unionists against nationalists, or even those who support the link
with Britain against those who wish to see both parts of Ireland reunited.
Rather, it is grounded in significant intra- as well as intercommunity differences based not only on differences in ethnic and national identity but
also on conflicting views concerning the very legitimacy of the state and
its boundaries. At a conceptual level, according to Joseph Ruane and
Jennifer Todd (1996), it is reinforced by three 'sociocultural dimensions
of conflict' – religion (Catholicism versus various strands of Protestantism),
ethnicity (Gaelic-Irish versus English and Scottish) and colonialism
(native versus settler). At a practical level, ethnonationalism is reinforced
by the primary agents of socialization that are to be found in any modern
society: parents, family, education and social networks.

This chapter examines the identities that the two communities hold,
focusing on ethnic or national identity (principally British or Irish) and
political identity (principally unionist or nationalist). These we refer to
as 'traditional' ethnonationalist identities. The first section examines
how far these identities continue to reinforce one another and emphasizes the disinclination of both communities to move away from their
traditional allegiances. The second section covers the changing patterns
of national identities apparent in both communities over more than
40 years, while the third section examines trends in political identity over
the same period. The fourth section evaluates some of the explanations

to account for the changes that have occurred in traditional identities, while the fifth section provides an in-depth analysis of the importance of the rise in the Northern Irish identity. The sixth and final section assesses the prospects for change in ethnonationalist identity based on the patterns highlighted in the chapter.

Reinforcing identities: religion, nation and politics

A common finding in studies of comparative politics is that cross-cutting cleavages within a society lead to moderation and compromise, while reinforcing cleavages lead to extremism and conflict. This conclusion, which is most frequently associated with Arend Lijphart's book, *Patterns of Democracy* (1999), led to the development of the theory of consociationalism, by which fundamentally divided societies could come together as a result of an elite agreement. Consociationalism has been subject to widespread criticism since it was first developed in the 1970s, as we outlined in the first chapter. However, few of its opponents disagree with the basic premise, namely, that reinforcing cleavages are the most difficult divisions to resolve. In this section, we outline, in summary form, the basic divisions in national and political identity and demonstrate how each reinforces the other.

The strong overlap between religion and national identity is demonstrated in Table 3.1, which shows the relationship between national identity and religious denomination using the 1989–2010 pooled data file. Around 7 out of every 10 Protestants see themselves as British, followed by 16 per cent who see themselves as Anglo-Irish or Northern Irish and 9 per cent who identify themselves as Ulster. Only 3 per cent of

Table 3.1 Religion and national identity, pooled sample

	Protestant	Catholic	Other	No religion	Total
British	70	10	58	44	45
Ulster	9	1	8	5	5
Anglo-Irish/N Irish	16	23	21	28	20
Irish	3	63	6	17	26
Other	2	3	8	7	3
Total	100	100	100	100	100
(N)	(13,926)	(10,825)	(2,102)	(2,995)	(29,848)

The question was 'Which of these best describes the way you think of yourself?'
Source: Northern Ireland Surveys, Pooled Sample, 1989–2010

Protestants see themselves as Irish. By contrast, among Catholics, nearly two in every three see themselves as Irish, followed by 10 per cent who regard themselves as British; just 1 per cent see themselves as having an Ulster identity. Among those who do not have a religion, just under half opt for being British, but the second largest group, 28 per cent, prefer the label 'Anglo-Irish' or 'Northern Irish', which encompasses elements of the two competing identities.

Protestants therefore remain strongly committed to a British identity, and their support for that identity is greater than Catholic support for identifying themselves as Irish. Moreover, around one-third of Catholics see themselves as having some form of identity which implicitly or explicitly recognizes the link with Britain, either as being British, Anglo-Irish or Northern Irish. These patterns contrast sharply with those recorded in 1968, on the eve of the conflict, when an Ulster identity was almost as popular as a British identity among Protestants; 33 per cent saw themselves as Ulster, compared to 39 per cent who saw themselves as British. An Irish identity was also mentioned by 20 per cent of Protestants. In 1968, Catholics were less divided than Protestants on their identity; 76 per cent regarded themselves as Irish. For Protestants, the 1960s, with its relative economic prosperity and burgeoning sense of cultural independence, was clearly a period when an Ulster identity reflected their distinctiveness within the United Kingdom.

In view of their differing histories and experiences, there are surprisingly few variations between the main Protestant denominations in the preferred national identity of their members. For example, additional analysis of the pooled data set suggests that there is a slight tendency for Free Presbyterians to see themselves as British (75 per cent compared to 70 per cent for Protestants as a whole) or Ulster (16 per cent compared to 5 per cent) and to avoid the Anglo-Irish label with its connotations of class and privilege (8 per cent compared to 16 per cent). Presbyterians are also slightly more likely than the other denominations to see themselves as Ulster; 10 per cent of Presbyterians identify themselves this way, compared to, for example, 7 per cent of Church of Ireland members. In general, however, the differences between the Protestant denominations are relatively minor. Whatever the differences between the Protestant denominations on party politics, this is not replicated in national identity.

The relationship between religion and political identity – unionist or nationalist – is shown in Table 3.2. Once again, a large majority of Protestants see themselves as unionist, with less than 1 per cent regarding themselves as nationalist. The remaining quarter of Protestants do not see themselves as either unionist or nationalist. In terms of identity preferences, then, Protestants are, if anything, actually more united in

Table 3.2 Religion and political identity, pooled sample

	Protestant	Catholic	Other	No religion	Total
Unionist	74	1	52	24	41
Nationalist	*	58	2	7	22
Neither	26	41	46	69	37
Total	100	100	100	100	100
(N)	(13,298)	(10,383)	(1,939)	(3,086)	(28,706)

An asterisk denotes less than 0.5 per cent. The question was 'Generally speaking, do you think of yourself as a unionist, a nationalist or neither?'
Source: Northern Ireland Surveys, Pooled Sample, 1989–2010

their political identity than in their national identity. By contrast, Catholics are slightly less united around political identity compared to national identity. Although almost 6 out of 10 Catholics see themselves as nationalist, the remainder reject either of the two labels. As is the case with national identity, the majority of those with no religion take an intermediate position between the two competing political identities, and 69 per cent reject both the unionist and nationalist labels.

How close is the relationship between national and political identity, and also how strongly are these identities linked to religion? The correlation between national and political identity in the 1989–2010 pooled data set is 0.68 ($p < 0.00$) suggesting that if there is not a complete overlap, then the overlap is certainly very close. Moreover, over the period of the 1989–2010 surveys, the correlation between the two identities has been consistently strong, never falling below 0.57 (in 1989) and never exceeding 0.71 (in 2001). This suggests that for both communities, national and political identity and the way in which the two reinforce one another is enduring and central to the nature of the conflict.

Adding religion to the relationship between national and political identity in Table 3.3 shows that over one-half of Protestants see themselves as both British and unionist and 4 out of 10 Catholics see themselves as Irish and nationalist. So while the relationship between religion and the two identities is by no means absolute, particularly among Catholics, the fact that the three attributes are so strongly related makes the Northern Ireland conflict internationally distinctive. Moreover, even more important than those who follow the dominant identities of their community is the minute proportion who do not: among Protestants, just 0.1 per cent opted for the identity of the opposite community, and among Catholics, just 0.5 per cent. While not all of the members of each community adopt the traditional identity set for them by history, hardly

Table 3.3 The reinforcement of religion and identity, pooled sample

	Protestant	Catholic	Other	No religion
British, unionist	55	*	17	17
Irish, nationalist	*	40	5	5
Other	45	60	78	78
Total	100	100	100	100
(N)	(14,415)	(11,226)	(2,151)	(2,151)

An asterisk denotes less than 0.5 per cent. British includes Ulster and Other includes British-Irish, Anglo-Irish and Northern Irish
Source: Northern Ireland Surveys, Pooled Sample, 1989–2010

any are prepared to take the radical – and almost unthinkable – step of adopting the identities of the opposing community.

The extent of the reinforcement between religion, national identity and political identity is, by any standards, remarkable and attests to the importance of the cleavage in Northern Ireland. But perhaps even more remarkable is the almost universal resistance for someone from one religion taking on the identity of the opposing religion. This is dramatic evidence of the depth of the divisions within Northern Ireland and implies the difficulties that any government will encounter in trying to mitigate these divisions. While there is a sizeable group within each community who are prepared to take a middle path, no-one is prepared to move from one group to the other. In the next two sections, we see if these patterns of identity have changed over time and, if so, in what direction.

Changing patterns of national identity

The preceding section has demonstrated a strong reinforcement between religion, and national and political identity. To what extent have the patterns of national identity remained stable during the period of the surveys? The experience of most countries is that long-term political stability will be reflected in a stable national identity among the mass population, since the territorial boundaries of the state are contiguous with the shared identity of the population. Where there is political instability and/or dispute about the territorial boundaries of the state, then national identity, too, becomes a disputed concept. In these circumstances, national identity may change as a result of political decisions or specific events, or it may be subject to longer-term change as a result of broader society-wide changes, such as population movement or intergenerational change.

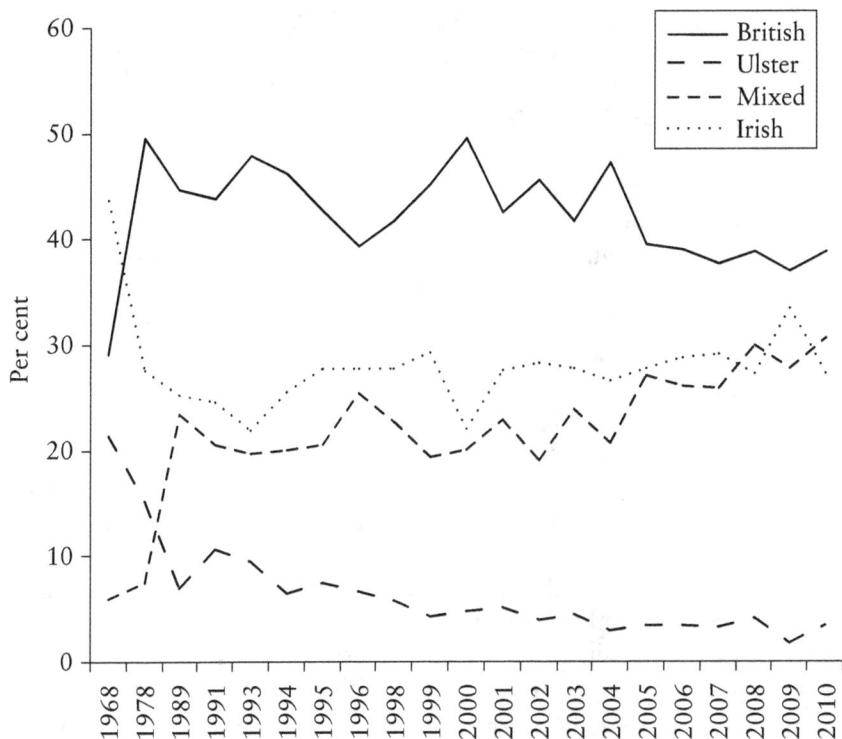

Figure 3.1 Trends in national identity, 1968–2010
See Table 3.1 for question wording for the 1989–2010 surveys. In 1968 and
1978, 'mixed' refers to Anglo-Irish, in 1989–96 to 'British-Irish' and 'Northern
Irish' and in 1998–2010 to 'Northern Irish' only
Sources: Northern Ireland Loyalty Survey, 1968; Northern Ireland Attitude
Survey, 1978; Northern Ireland Social Attitudes Surveys, 1989, 1991,
1993–96; Northern Ireland Life and Times Surveys, 1998–2010

The trends in national identity across the population between 1968
and 2010 are shown in Figure 3.1. Support for a British identity peaked
at nearly half of the population in 1993 and has declined thereafter,
falling to 39 per cent in 2010, the lowest figure since 1968. An Ulster
identity, which attracted support from about one-fifth of the population
in 1968, has gradually declined in significance, and 2007 represents the
lowest point in the series, when just 3 per cent of the population described
themselves in that way. Apart from a peak in 1968, there has been com-
paratively little variation in the proportions describing themselves as
Irish; the lowest figure was 22 per cent in 1993 and the highest 29 per cent
in 2007. The main change has been in the proportions describing

themselves in some other way – 'British-Irish', 'Anglo-Irish' or 'Northern Irish'. Representing just 6 per cent of the population in 1968, this group has increased in size during the 1990s and 2000s and currently self-describes just under one-third of the population or 31 per cent in 2010.

One explanation for the decline in the popularity of the Ulster label and the increasing popularity of a mixed label is undoubtedly a desire among some sections of the population to eschew what they regard as traditional labels which they see as fostering the conflict. However, another explanation is methodological and relates to the way in which the questions are asked in the surveys. In the 1968 and 1978 surveys, the main mixed option was 'Anglo-Irish', a term which has connotations of class and patronage dating back to the nineteenth and early twentieth centuries. In the post-1989 surveys, 'Northern Irish' was offered as an option (either on its own or alongside 'Anglo-Irish'), and this has become a particularly popular identity for many who might otherwise have described themselves as Ulster. A Northern Irish identity is undoubtedly seen as a less contentious alternative to an Ulster label. As Edward Moxon-Browne (1991: 28) notes, 'the attractiveness of a Northern Irish identity lies in its ambiguity; for Catholics, it avoids any legitimation of the border, which is implied in either British or Ulster; for Protestants, it is seen as having a natural association with "Northern Ireland"'.

The patterns of national identity among Protestants since 1968 in Figure 3.2 show a remarkable level of consistency in support for a British identity. Between 1978 and 2010, this never dropped below 60 per cent of the Protestant population and peaked at 75 per cent in 2002. The main change has been the decline in the proportions who see themselves as Ulster and the rise in popularity of the 'mixed' label, which since 1997 has been exclusively a Northern Irish identity. In 1978, for example, four years after the Ulster Workers' Council strike and the collapse of the power-sharing executive – the high point of unionist influence during the Troubles – almost one in five Protestants saw themselves in terms of an Ulster identity. By 2010, this had declined to just one in 20. By contrast, in 2010 and after successive political compromises with the Catholic community, one in four Protestants regarded themselves as Northern Irish.

There is a parallel consistency in the views of Catholics over the four decades of the surveys, this time with the large majority regarding them-selves as Irish (see Figure 3.3). In 1968, three in every four Catholics saw themselves as Irish, a figure which declined to 60 per cent by 1989 but which has remained remarkably consistent ever since. In 2010, 64 per cent of Catholics opted for an Irish identity, a figure that is little changed from the late 1980s. Like Protestants, the main change for Catholics has been the increasing proportions who see themselves as Northern Irish, which has stood at around one-quarter since 1998. This

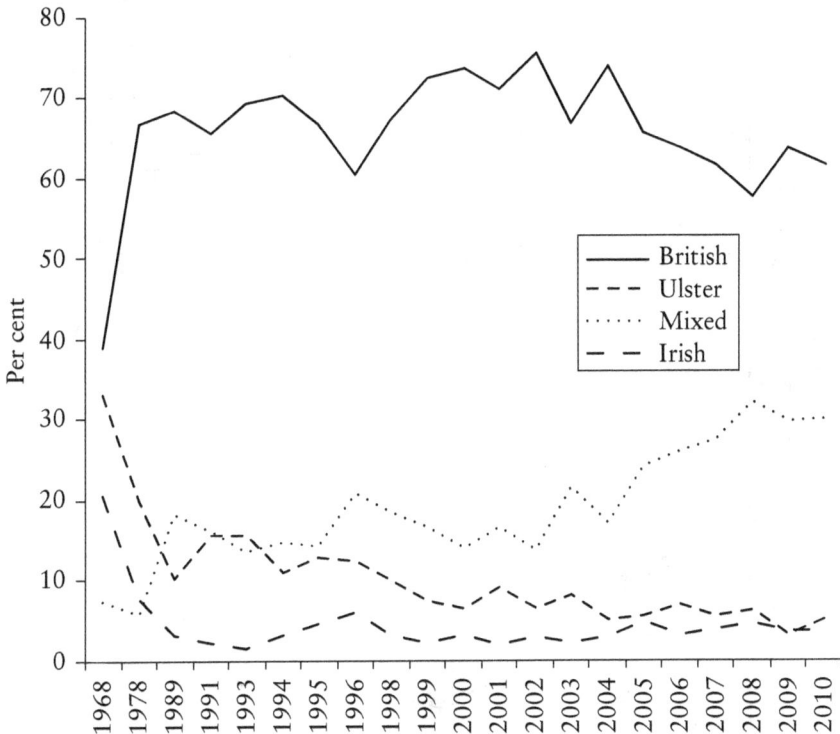

Figure 3.2 Trends in national identity among Protestants, 1968–2010
See Table 3.1 for question wording for the 1989–2010 surveys. In 1968 and
1978, 'mixed' refers to Anglo-Irish, in 1989–96 to 'British-Irish' and 'Northern
Irish' and in 1998–2010 to 'Northern Irish' only
Sources: Northern Ireland Loyalty Survey, 1968; Northern Ireland Attitude
Survey, 1978; Northern Ireland Social Attitudes Surveys, 1989, 1991,
1993–96; Northern Ireland Life and Times Surveys, 1998–2010

has been partly at the expense of those identifying themselves as British,
but it is also the case that Catholics have historically had a higher proportion opting for one of the mixed identities, and the popularity of the
Northern Irish identity continues this trend.

Among those who identified themselves as having no religion, Figure 3.4
shows that the majority saw themselves as having either a British or a
mixed identity, the latter being mostly composed of those with a Northern
Irish identity in the 1990s and 2000s. Indeed, in three separate years – in
1998, 2005 and 2010 – this group was the largest of the four identities.
From 1978 until the early 1990s, British was the most favoured identity,
and in 1989 they made up 55 per cent of all those with no religion. Not
surprisingly given its loyalist overtones, an Ulster identity was least

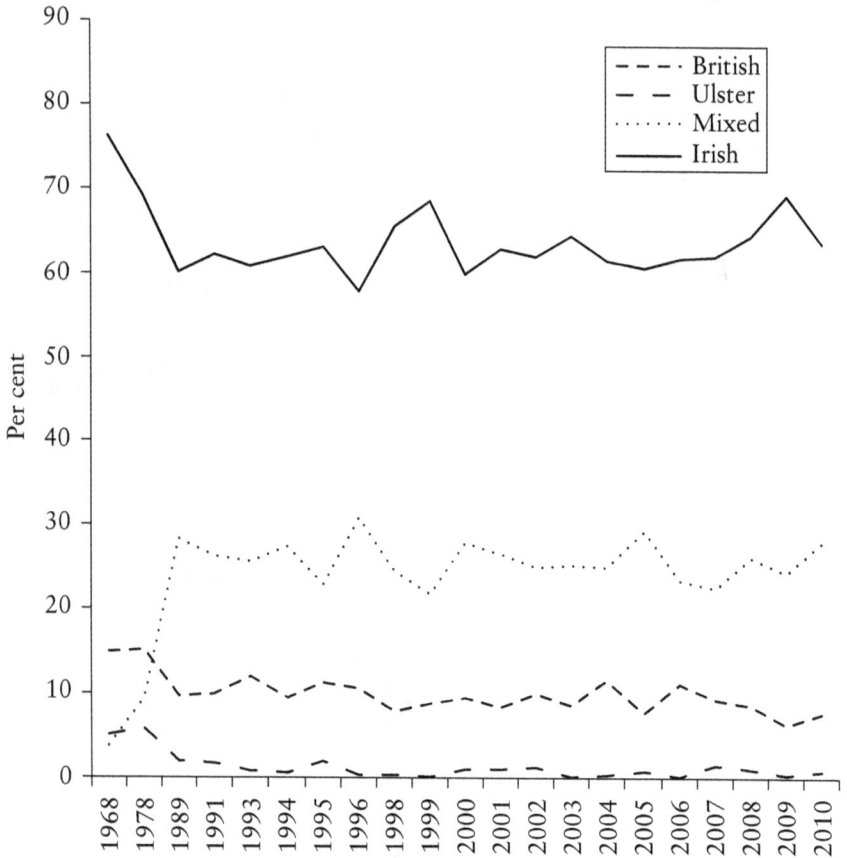

Figure 3.3 Trends in national identity among Catholics, 1968–2010
See Table 3.1 for question wording for the 1989–2010 surveys. In 1968 and 1978, 'mixed' refers to Anglo-Irish, in 1989–96 to 'British-Irish' and 'Northern Irish' and in 1998–2010 to 'Northern Irish' only
Sources: Northern Ireland Loyalty Survey, 1968; Northern Ireland Attitude Survey, 1978; Northern Ireland Social Attitudes Surveys, 1989, 1991, 1993–96; Northern Ireland Life and Times Surveys, 1998–2010

popular among this group, accounting for 6 per cent or less for most of the period of study and falling to just 1 per cent in 2007.

These patterns suggest great stability in national identity, in spite of the major social, economic and – not least – political change that Northern Ireland has experienced since the late 1960s. The findings confirm the enduring nature of the conflict and the importance of territorial markers in identifying in-groups and out-groups. Two points in the

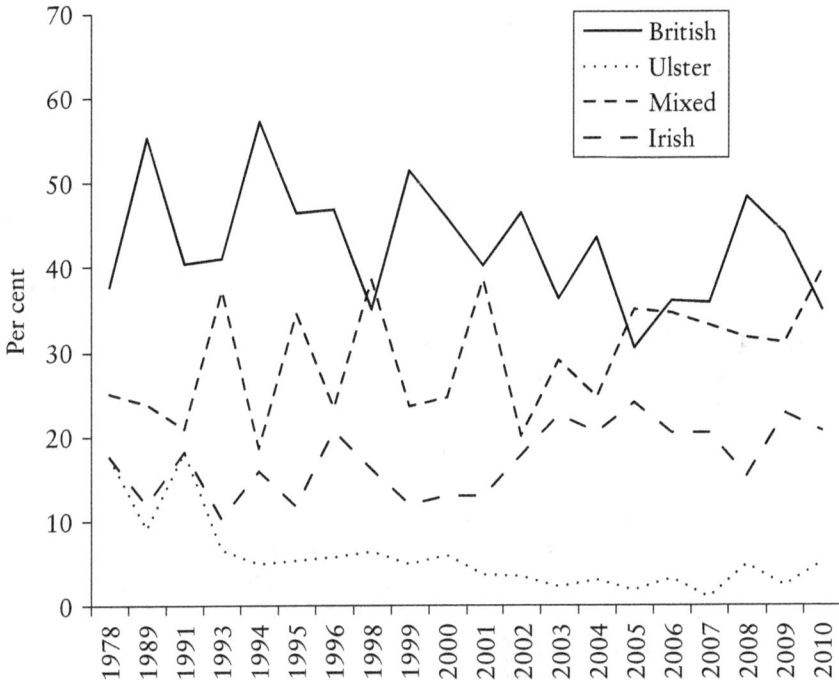

Figure 3.4 Trends in national identity among the non-affiliated, 1978–2010
See Table 3.1 for question wording for the 1989–2010 surveys. In 1978, 'mixed' refers to Anglo-Irish, in 1989–96 to 'British-Irish' and 'Northern Irish' and in 1998–2010 to 'Northern Irish' only. There were too few respondents in 1968 without a religion for reliable analysis
Sources: Northern Ireland Attitude Survey, 1978; Northern Ireland Social Attitudes Surveys, 1989, 1991, 1993–96; Northern Ireland Life and Times Surveys, 1998–2010

graphs do, however, provide some qualification to this conclusion. The first is the fact that on the very eve of the conflict, national identities were biased towards Ulster for Protestants and towards Irish for Catholics. Once the conflict had begun, Protestants were most likely to see themselves as British, and there was a decline in the proportion seeing themselves as Irish. This may reflect an association by some between the Ulster and Irish labels and tacit support for violent conflict and, as a result, a disinclination to identify themselves in that way. The second qualification is the growth in a Northern Irish identity after the signing of the Belfast Agreement in 1998, particularly among Protestants. We examine this phenomenon in more depth later in the chapter. The next section examines trends in political identities.

Changing patterns of political identity

Historically, the political identities of the two communities reflect their territorial aspirations, in the case of Protestants a desire for union with Britain and for Catholics the reunification of Ireland. Since these aspirations are susceptible to changes in the prevailing political climate and are generally less rooted in childhood and adolescent socialization, we would expect them to fluctuate to a greater extent over the period of the surveys in comparison to national identity. Moreover, during the post-1968 period, there have been numerous attempts at political compromise, major changes in the party system with consequent changes in party fortunes and other political changes which should have complicated perceptions of political identity.[2]

Across the population, a majority regard themselves as either unionist or nationalist, and that proportion has averaged 62 per cent over the 1989–2010 period (see Figure 3.5). Most notable has been the increasing proportion during the course of the 1990s who have identified themselves as nationalist, from a low of 16 per cent in 1989 to a peak of 29 per cent in 2002; since 2003, the figure has been stable at around 23 per cent. There has been a drop in the proportion who see themselves as unionist, but the change has been relatively small; 39 per cent saw themselves as unionist in 1989 compared to 34 per cent in 2010. The second largest group over the period is those who eschew both unionist and nationalist labels; they represent about 4 in 10 of the total population.

Disaggregating these patterns by religion produces a sharper focus on how these changes have taken place within the two communities. Among Protestants, Figure 3.6 shows a high degree of stability over the period. Around three-quarters of Protestants regard themselves as unionist, the lowest figure being 65 per cent in 2010 and the highest 77 per cent in 1994. Overall, the variations are generally modest and suggest that the major events of the period have had only a minor effect on how Protestants see themselves politically. The same is the case for those seeing themselves as neither unionist or nationalist, which varies little, and, of course, never more than 1 per cent of Protestants regard themselves as nationalist.

In contrast to the pattern of general stability among Protestants, Figure 3.7 reveals considerable fluctuations in political identities among Catholics. At the beginning of the period, up to 1996, nationalists were either outnumbered or equal in size to those who eschewed both a unionist and nationalist identity. Since 1996, nationalists have consistently outnumbered the latter, with the sole exception of 2008. Indeed, in 2001 and 2002, there were twice as many nationalists as those who rejected

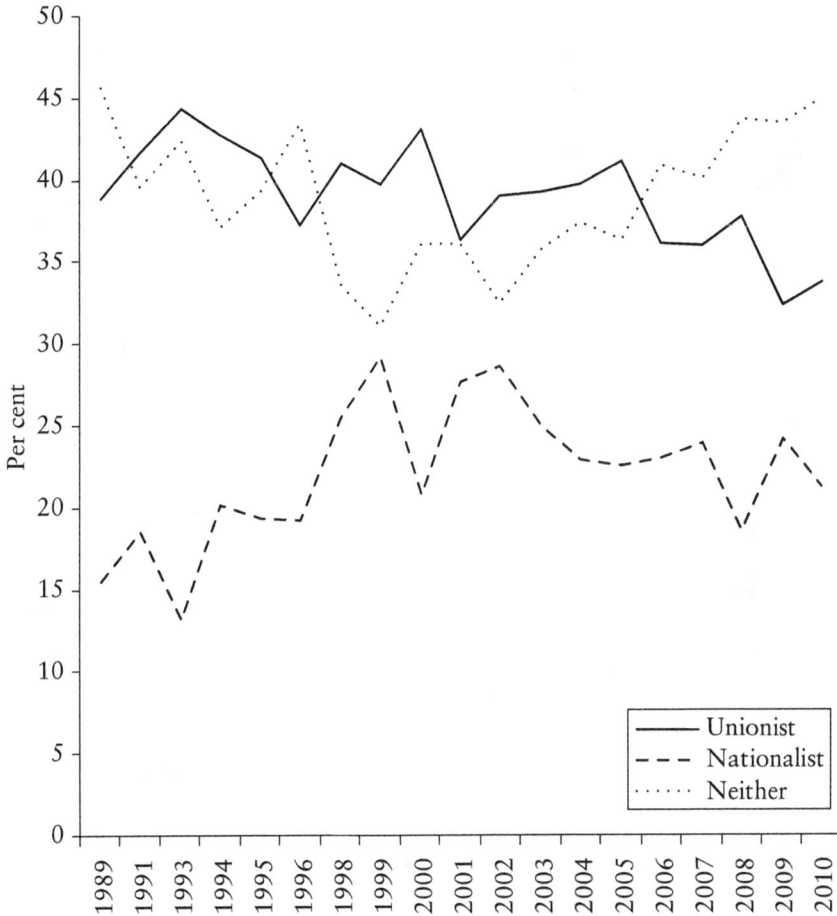

Figure 3.5 Trends in political identity, 1989–2010
See Table 3.2 for question wording
Sources: Northern Ireland Social Attitudes Surveys, 1989, 1991, 1993–96;
Northern Ireland Life and Times Surveys, 1998–2010

either a nationalist or unionist label. Since then, there has been a gradual decline in the proportion of nationalists, and a concomitant increase in those eschewing a nationalist identity. The timing of the resurgence in nationalist identity is hardly accidental; the 1998 Belfast Agreement was regarded as a major political step forward for nationalists through the creation of a power-sharing government and the establishment of the principle of 'parity of esteem' between the two communities. The popularity of the Agreement among Catholics – reflected in their almost

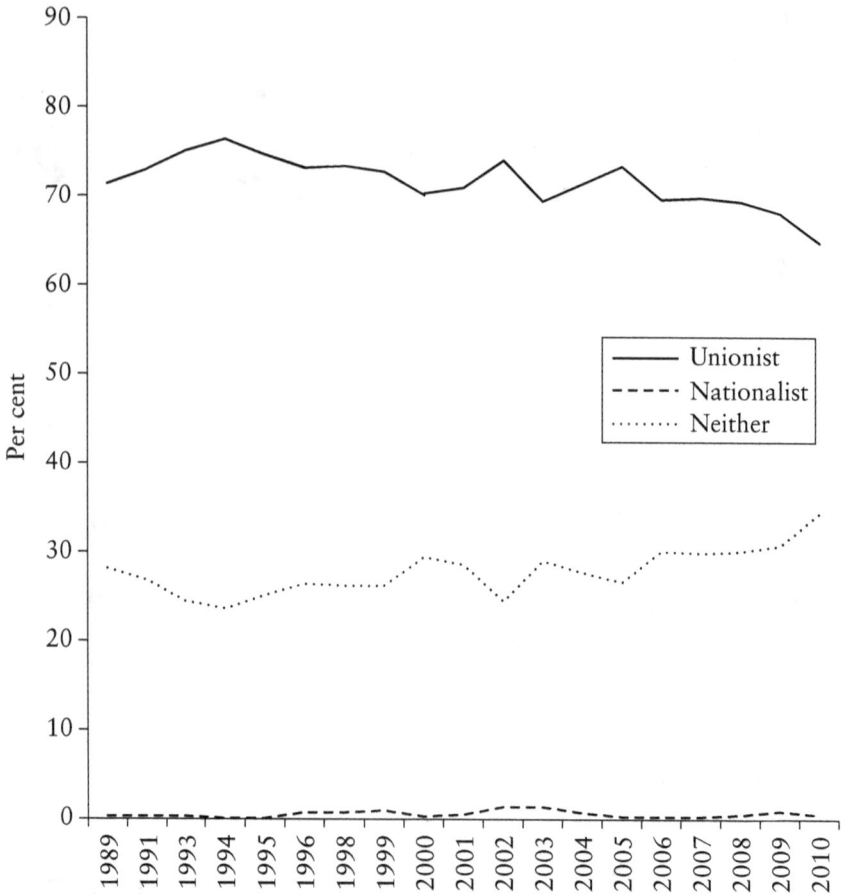

Figure 3.6 Trends in political identity among Protestants, 1989–2010
See Table 3.2 for question wording
Sources: Northern Ireland Social Attitudes Surveys, 1989, 1991, 1993–96;
Northern Ireland Life and Times Surveys, 1998–2010

unanimous endorsement in the May 1998 referendum (Hayes and McAllister, 2001a: Table 2) – underpins the resurgence of a nationalist identity, fostered by political changes which almost all Catholics have supported enthusiastically.

As we might expect, rejecting both unionist and nationalist identities is consistently most popular among those with no religion. Figure 3.8 shows that the popularity of adopting a third 'neither' identity was at its second highest level – 74 per cent – in 2001, shortly after the 1998 Agreement, and has climbed steadily since 2004. In 2010, 85 per cent of those with no religion saw themselves as neither unionist nor

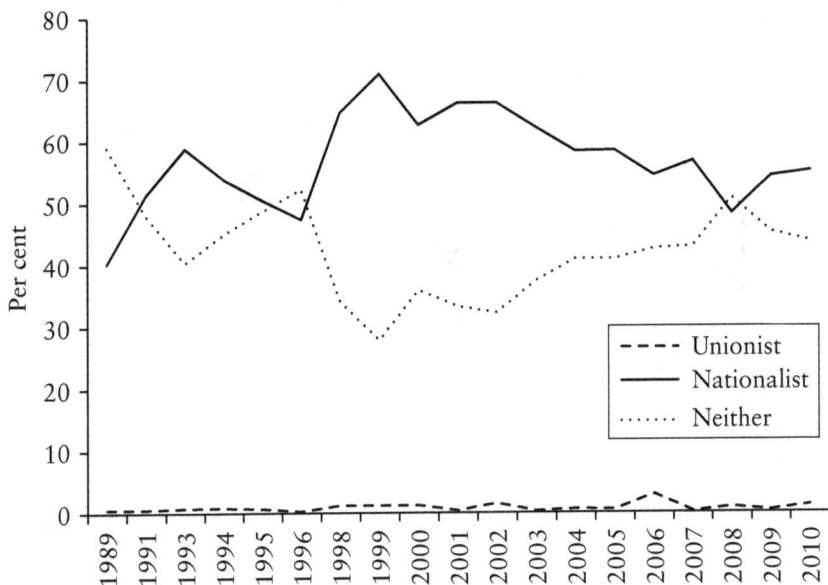

Figure 3.7 Trends in political identity among Catholics, 1989–2010
See Table 3.2 for question wording
Sources: Northern Ireland Social Attitudes Surveys, 1989, 1991, 1993–96;
Northern Ireland Life and Times Surveys, 1998–2010

nationalist, the highest figure recorded to date. A nationalist identity has been least popular; it peaked at 12 per cent in 1996 and reached its lowest point, 4 per cent, in 2009.

These results suggest a remarkable upsurge in confidence among Catholics, as evidenced by the increase in the proportion of nationalist identifiers between 1989 and 1999. The increase was as a result of the political changes brought about by the 1998 Agreement. It is perhaps notable that there has been no contrary trend among Protestants, and their political identities have remained unchanged throughout the period of the surveys. This is despite the serious opposition that the Agreement faced in its early years from Protestants, who regarded it as skewed towards satisfying the demands of nationalists, particularly by bringing Sinn Fein into government without securing the decommissioning of IRA weapons as a precondition (Hayes *et al.*, 2005). The reason for the consistency in the unionist identity among Protestants rests in its political overtones. The vast majority of Protestants wish to remain part of Britain, and to ensure that continuing link, only the unionist label can express that preference.

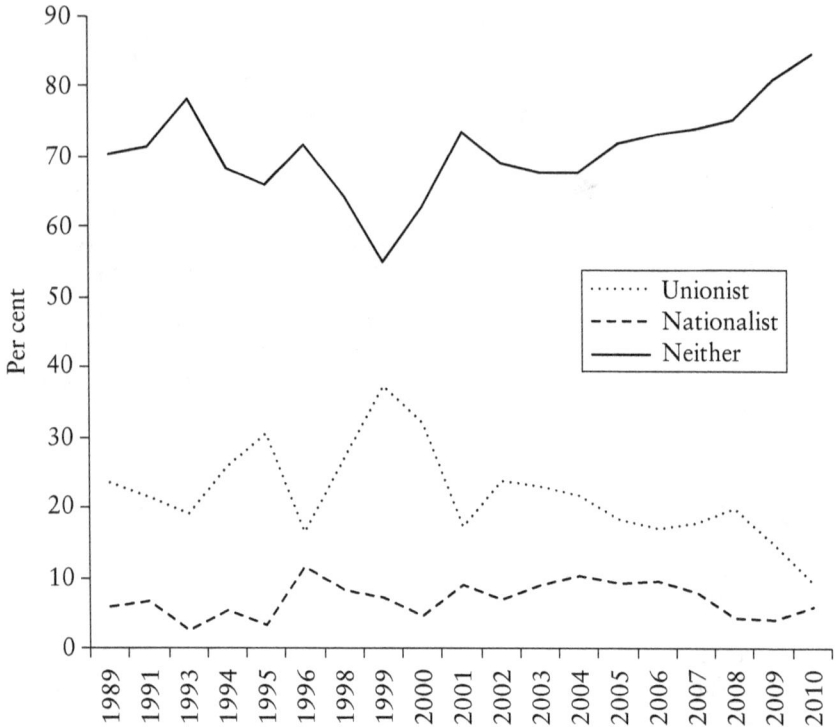

Figure 3.8 Trends in political identity among the non-affiliated, 1989–2010
See Table 3.2 for question wording
Sources: Northern Ireland Social Attitudes Surveys, 1989, 1991, 1993–96;
Northern Ireland Life and Times Surveys, 1998–2010

Explaining changes in national identity

Much of the ethnic conflict in modern society arises because of the lack of congruence between ethnonationalist identity and the state. Although these terms are often used interchangeably, they are very different concepts. Ethnic identity refers to the collective memory and consciousness which is shared by a group and is passed from generation to generation through childhood socialization (Gillis, 1994). It is often reinforced by an ascriptive characteristic such as language, race or, in the case of Northern Ireland, religion, but shared symbols and a common history and traditions also serve to underpin it. Not all of those who share an ethnic identity seek the same national goals; central and eastern Europe, for example, is littered with ethnic groups who identify themselves with bordering nation states and oppose the authority of the state within which they reside. The lack of congruence

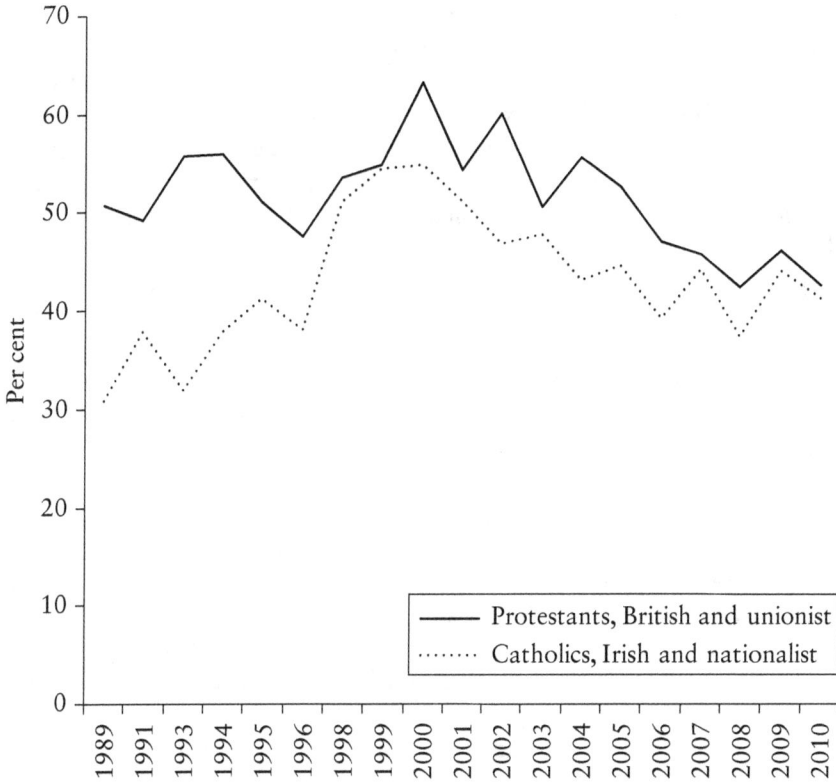

Figure 3.9 The congruence between ethnic and national identity, 1989–2010
Sources: Northern Ireland Social Attitudes Surveys, 1989, 1991, 1993–96;
Northern Ireland Life and Times Surveys, 1998–2010

between ethnonationalist identity and the state is at the heart of most of the conflict within the region.

The stereotypical Protestant is someone who sees oneself as British and unionist, and the corresponding Catholic is someone who sees oneself as Irish and nationalist. As we saw in Table 3.1, two-thirds of Protestants fit this stereotypical image, while just under half of all Catholics do. Our interest in this section is to trace how these images have changed during the period of the conflict and, to the extent that there has been change, to identify the drivers of that change.

For Protestants, being British and unionist has been a consistent preference for a majority during the period up to 2005 and dipping slightly thereafter (see Figure 3.9). In 2010, 43 per cent of Protestants identified themselves in this way. The high point occurred in 2000, when 63 per cent of Protestants fulfilled both these criteria in their self-identification. Overall, the changes over the period have been relatively minor. This is certainly not the case among Catholics; in 1989, 31 per cent regarded themselves as Irish and nationalist, the lowest figure during the period, increasing to the high point of 55 per cent in 1999 and 2000, just after the Belfast Agreement when Catholic self-confidence was at its highest point. While the post-Agreement trend has been for a slight decline, in 2010 more than 4 out of 10 Catholics regarded themselves as Irish and nationalist.

One explanation for these changes is, as we have just noted, the new post-1998 institutional arrangements which have particularly shaped the outlooks of Catholics. However, another explanation is the progressive modernization of the society. Early versions of modernization theory, as advanced by Karl Deutsch (1953) and others during the 1950s, argued that as societies became more materially affluent and mass communications more ubiquitous, ethnonationalist divisions will become less relevant and gradually fade away. This assimilationist explanation was largely discounted by the rise of ethnonationalism during the late 1960s in the advanced societies – the ones that Deutsch and others would have predicted to be at the forefront of assimilation. More recently, Inglehart and Welzel (2005) have adapted modernization theory by including mass culture as a driver of change, and they have argued that modernization has been expressed through value change and the broadening of choice, which in turn has underpinned the unprecedented progress to democracy around the world.[3]

To test the importance of modernization against political events – in this case the Belfast Agreement – in shaping reinforcing ethnic and political identities, Table 3.4 shows the results of a logistic regression analysis, estimated separately for the two communities. For Protestants, the dependent variable is whether or not the person said that they were British and unionist and, for Catholics, if they said that they were Irish and nationalist. The independent variables representing modernization include education, employment, age and marital status.[4] The influence of political events on reinforcing identities is measured by whether or not the person was interviewed in the four key transitional periods: before the signing of the Belfast Agreement (1989–96), immediately after the Agreement was signed (1998–2002), during the last sustained period of the suspension of the Assembly (2003–06) or when devolution was restored (2007–10).

The results suggest that modernization is the major influence on identities, although the Belfast Agreement is important for both communities, with an Irish and nationalist identity increasing consistently after 1998 for Catholics, and a British and unionist identity also increasing after 1998

Table 3.4 Modernization and reinforcing identities, pooled sample

	Protestant		Catholic	
	Est	(SE)	Est	(SE)
Gender (male)	0.18**	(0.04)	0.50**	(0.04)
Age	0.01**	(0.00)	−0.01*	(0.00)
Married	0.14**	(0.04)	−0.07	(0.04)
Church attendance	0.42**	(0.04)	0.55**	(0.06)
Education (tertiary)				
Secondary	0.44**	(0.05)	−0.03	(0.06)
No qualification	0.64**	(0.05)	0.22**	(0.07)
Employed	0.13**	(0.04)	−0.16**	(0.05)
Political event (pre-Agreement)				
Agreement/immediate aftermath	0.38**	(0.04)	0.72**	(0.05)
Direct rule	0.30**	(0.04)	0.58**	(0.06)
Restoration of the Assembly	−0.08	(0.05)	0.48**	(0.06)
Constant	−1.68**	(0.11)	−1.19**	(0.10)
Pseudo R-squared	0.04		0.04	
(N)	(14,943)		(10,353)	

Significant at **$p < 0.01$ level; *$p < 0.05$
Logistic regression analyses showing parameter estimates and (in parentheses) robust standard errors predicting Protestants who are British and unionist and Catholics who are Irish and nationalist (both scored 1) against all others (scored 0). Age is scored in single years and church attendance on a scale from 0 (never attends) to 1 (attends once a week or more); all other variables are scored zero or one. Tertiary educated is the omitted category for education, and surveys undertaken in the pre-Agreement period (1989–96) is the omitted category for political events.
Source: Northern Ireland Surveys, Pooled Sample, 1989–2010

for Protestants, albeit only up until the restoration of the Assembly in 2007. For Protestants, the most important factor is education, with those possessing either a secondary or no formal educational qualifications being more likely to see themselves as British and unionist than the tertiary educated. Educational qualifications are also important for Catholics, although of a less consistent and lesser magnitude than for Protestants. These results concerning the importance of education confirm the findings of Karen Trew (1996) who found that, irrespective of religious background, the Irish and British labels were more widely adopted by the less educated and particularly by those with no educational qualifications.

Church attendance, gender, age and employment status are also important for both communities in shaping traditional identities. Regular church attenders are more likely to adopt traditional labels to describe themselves than irregular attenders, suggesting that both sets of churches may operate a reinforcing effect on the ethnonationalist identities of their adherents. Men are more likely to label themselves in a traditional way than women, an effect that is more marked among Catholics. Within the Catholic community, this reflects the integration of Sinn Fein into democratic politics, which has traditionally attracted disproportionately more male than female support (McAllister, 2004). In contrast to church attendance and gender, both age and employment status work differently for the two communities, with both the employed and older Protestant respondents adopting traditional labels but with the pattern reversed for Catholics, with younger Catholics and the unemployed being more likely to see themselves in this way. The increased Catholic self-confidence that has emerged since 1998 has affected both younger and unemployed Catholics to a greater extent than their older or employed counterparts. Marital status is also an important determinant for Protestants but not for Catholics.

In contrast to the socioeconomic effects of modernization on reinforcing identities, the impact of the Belfast Agreement, particularly within the Protestant community, is more modest. Among Protestants, those interviewed before the Agreement was signed are more likely to adopt a traditional label compared to those interviewed after 1998, albeit only up the restoration of devolution in 2007. The impact, while statistically significant, is however relatively small. By contrast, Catholics interviewed after 1998 are substantially and consistently more likely to describe their identity in traditional terms. Our conclusion from this analysis is that modernization is indeed important in shaping ethnonationalist identities in Northern Ireland, although political events have also played a role, albeit a more modest one, among Protestants as compared to Catholics.

To many outsiders, the conflict in Northern Ireland appears to reflect an archaic struggle between two groups identified by religious labels – Protestants and Catholics. While there is no doubt that religious affiliation serves as an important boundary marker in identifying the two protagonists, as we argued in the previous chapter, the conflict cannot be reduced to religious terms. Rather, as McGarry and O'Leary (1995) suggest, the conflict in Northern Ireland can best be understood in terms of a dispute over two contested national identities, unionism versus nationalism, and it is these two differing interpretations of ethnonational identity which lie at the heart of the present conflict. The results presented here show that the conflict is not totally bipolar. Among those who see themselves as British, a significant minority do not describe themselves as unionist, and, similarly, neither do all Catholics identify themselves as nationalist. Moreover, identities do appear to be shaped to some degree by the prevailing socioeconomic and political circumstances of the time, giving hope that gradual changes in the broader society can serve to ameliorate the conflict.

The rise of a 'Northern Irish' identity

One trend that holds out hope for the future of community relations in Northern Ireland, which was mentioned briefly in the first section, is the increasing popularity of 'Northern Irish' as a form of self-identification. The term first came into popular currency in 1976, when it was used by the 'Northern Irish Peace People', the movement formed by Mairead Corrigan and Betty Williams to campaign for an end to the violence (McKeown, 1984). At that time, the label was seen to be the only one that was inclusive of both communities; Catholics could accept it because it included 'Irish' in the label, and Protestants were less threatened by the inclusion of 'Northern', which explicitly recognized their separate identity within Ireland as a whole. However, the term did not gain widespread popularity until the late 1990s, when it became particularly popular among Protestants. The use of the label is disproportionately concentrated among the better educated and the young, who regard it as a more positive way to identify themselves by avoiding the stereotypical images of the past (Trew, 1998; see Fahey et al., 2006: 60–64).

The popularity of the Northern Irish identity among the young has been a particular focus of study. While the vast majority of adolescents define themselves as Protestant-British or Catholic-Irish, there is a minority in both communities who reject the long-standing national identity of their religious community and endorse a Northern Irish label. In a detailed study of college students, Karen Trew (1994) found that although 70 per cent of Catholics and 55 per cent of Protestants selected a traditional identity, 38 per cent of Protestants and 24 per cent of Catholics embraced a Northern Irish identity. Later research by Paula Devine and Dirk Schubotz (2004) supports these findings. Using the 2003 Young Life and Times Survey, they found that one-quarter of all respondents described themselves as Northern Irish and that Protestants were again more likely than Catholics to endorse a Northern Irish identity. It has been argued that ambiguity surrounding the meaning of a 'British' identity for many Protestants has made them more susceptible than their Catholic counterparts to adopt the Northern Irish label (Muldoon et al., 2007).

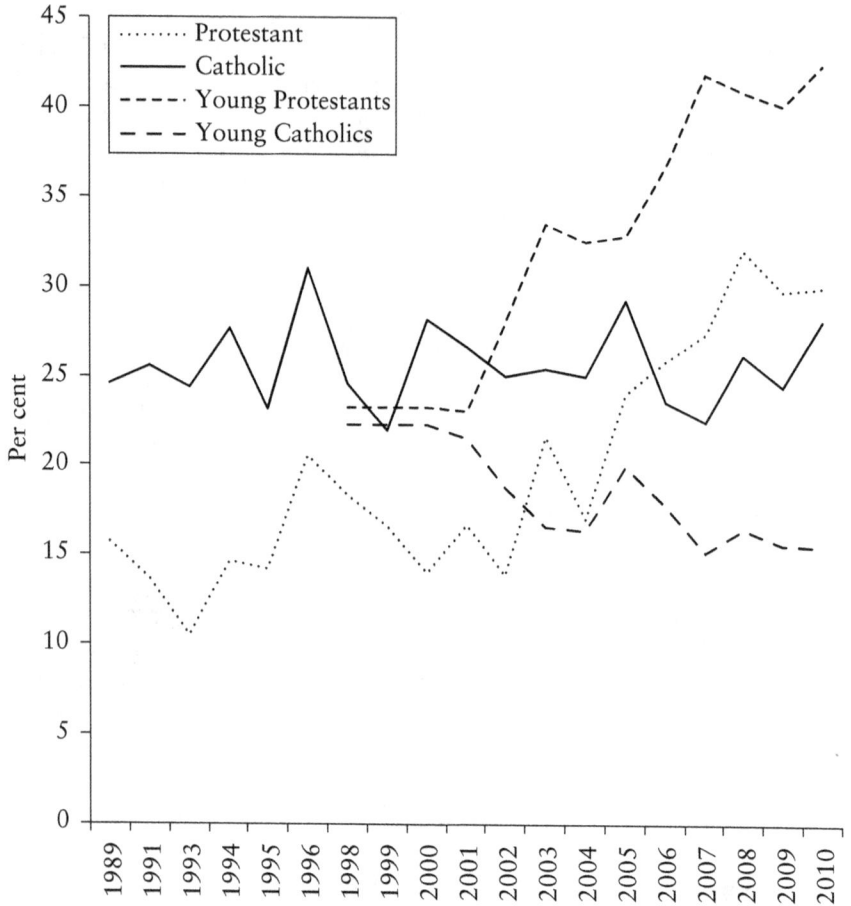

Figure 3.10 Northern Irish identity among adults and adolescents, 1989–2010
The young adult surveys are based on respondents aged 12–17 years old from
1998 to 2000 and aged 16 years from 2003 to 2010
Sources: Northern Ireland Social Attitudes Surveys, 1989, 1991, 1993–96;
Northern Ireland Life and Times Surveys, 1998–2010; Northern Ireland
Young Life and Times Surveys, 1998–2000, 2003–10

The increasing popularity of a Northern Irish label is shown in
Figure 3.10, which shows the proportions of adults and adolescents
who are prepared to describe themselves as Northern Irish.
Among adults, the Catholic figure has remained relatively stable over the
1989–2010 period at around one in four of the community, reaching a
high point of 29 per cent in 2005. By contrast, the Protestant proportion has increased significantly, from 11 per cent in 1993 to 30 per cent

Table 3.5 Northern Irish identity and education among Protestants,
1999–2010

	British	Ulster	Northern Irish
Degree	10	7	21
Postsecondary	16	15	24
Secondary	26	26	25
No qualifications	48	52	30
Total	100	100	100
(N)	(6,218)	(591)	(1,731)

Source: Northern Ireland Life and Times Surveys, Pooled Sample, 1999–2010

in 2010, its highest point. Among adolescents, the trends are more marked. For Catholic adolescents, there has actually been a slight decline in the popularity of the label, from 24 per cent in 2000 to 16 per cent in 2010. Among Protestant adolescents, the label has become highly popular; in 1998, similar proportions of the two community choose the label, but by 2010 there were more than twice as many Protestant than Catholic adolescents – 42 per cent versus 16 per cent – who used the term to describe themselves.

The post-Belfast Agreement popularity of the Northern Irish label is underpinned by education, and as Karen Trew (1998) and others have found, those with tertiary education are more likely to use the label, while those with no qualifications are more likely to use traditional identities. In the post-1998 adult surveys, among Protestants 21 per cent of those choosing a Northern Irish identity had a university degree, compared to 10 per cent who chose a British identity and 7 per cent who saw themselves as having an Ulster identity (see Table 3.5). Almost half of those with no qualifications said that they were British, compared to one in three of those who opted for describing themselves as Northern Irish. Education is, then, along with youth, a major driving force behind the popularity of the Northern Irish label.

The apparent willingness to reject traditional identities has not led to a radical shift in national identity. In the main, as we found in Table 3.1, Catholics still reject a British or an Ulster identity and Protestants eschew an Irish identity, and the changes that have taken place in these allegiances over the past quarter of a century have been relatively minor. In effect, those who adopt a Northern Irish identity may be seen to represent the 'middle ground' in Northern Ireland politics. They represent the furthest a person can go within their own community without crossing the political divide and effectively risking being ostracized by their peers.

The gradual adoption of a Northern Ireland label is an important step towards reconciliation. However, despite the expectations of McGarry and O'Leary (2009: 83) that it would eventually become a unifying force if the current institutions endured, there are three main reasons why it is unlikely to lead to a radical shift in political outlooks. First, although both Protestants and Catholics claim to be Northern Irish, previous research indicates that this similarity coincides with very different political allegiances between the two communities (see Trew, 1996, 1998). Among both Protestants and Catholics, Northern Irish identifiers share the same constitutional preferences as those expressed by other members of their own community. Second, while there is evidence to suggest that Northern Irish identifiers are proud of their identity, they do not see it as an important part of their self-identification; this is particularly the case among Protestants (Cassidy and Trew, 1998). Third, Northern Ireland identifiers tend to be weaker in their commitment than other identifiers.[5]

Despite these caveats, the increasing prevalence of a Northern Irish identity remains an important development for community relations. Indeed, it has been argued that it is precisely because of its lack of clarity in status and intercommunity ambiguities in meaning that it has become so popular. As a result, its increasing use has much to offer in breaking down traditional allegiances and in facilitating the emergence of a shared national identity in Northern Ireland. As Karen Trew (1998: 67) has put it: 'This could be the potential strength of the Northern Irish identity, which unlike any other identity, can offer a basis for a shared identification by some Catholics and Protestants while not threatening the ideological commitments of either'.

Conclusion

Social categorization represents an important shortcut by which people can interpret and become familiar with their environment. In turn, loyalty to and membership of a social group can provide important physical and psychological resources which facilitate everyday interactions within a society. However, as Henri Tajfel (1978) has observed, the danger is that if memberships do not overlap and/or there is no possibility of moving from one group to another, the risk is that the groups will come into conflict. When this occurs, social categorization is zero-sum and becomes self-perpetuating, being handed down from generation to generation and reinforced by the perceived threats emanating from the opposing groups within the society.

The Northern Ireland conflict was a stereotypical example of the dangers of social categorization. The conflict was reflected as much in identity and labels as it was in direct physical confrontation between the opposing communities. Religious affiliation, ethnic identity, national identity and territorial allegiance were all intertwined in a complex way, reinforcing one another and creating exclusive social categories within which individuals remained bound for the course of their lives. It is these interlocking and reinforcing facets that not only defined the ethnonationalist basis of the conflict but also gave rise to its reinforcing and recurring nature. As the results presented here have shown, identities and the labels that reflect those identities not only were, but continue to be, readily used by Protestants and Catholics, and while not every member of a community uses exactly the same label, hardly any will use a label that is associated with the opposing community. And, despite the 1998 Belfast Agreement, nor have there been any significant changes in these patterns since the Troubles began in 1968.

The only change of any significance during the almost half-century period of the surveys has been the increasing endorsement of a Northern Irish identity, particularly among younger Protestants. The 1998 Belfast Agreement, with its prospect of reconciliation, appears to have been instrumental in legitimizing this label. Indeed, other research has shown that individuals who endorse a Northern Irish identity are significantly more likely to be optimistic about community relations than their more politically entrenched counterparts and to act out their views in daily social behaviour (Hayes and McAllister, 2009a). However, the abandonment of traditional allegiances in favour of a Northern Irish identity among young Protestants will not eradicate national identity as a source of division. Rather, what is occurring is the re-emergence of ethnic division in a different form. Given the continuing centrality of national identity to social divisions in Northern Ireland, our results suggest that any recourse to a Northern Irish identity as a vehicle to promote tolerance would be unlikely to achieve the desired results.

Notes

1 The term is relatively new and was first coined by Walker Connor in the 1960s (Connor, 1973).

2 Unlike national identity, political identity was not asked in the 1968 and 1978 surveys. We have, therefore, just a 21-year trend between the 1989 and 2010 surveys which necessarily limits the conclusions we can draw from the survey evidence.

3 Nevertheless, affluence remains a potent explanation for reducing the intensity of the conflict (see Rose and McAllister, 1983).

4 We are necessarily limited by the variables that are available in the dataset.

5 For example, among Protestants who see themselves as Northern Irish in the 1989–2010 pooled data file, 11 per cent describe themselves as 'very strong' identifiers compared to 18 per cent among those who see themselves as British. Among Catholics who see themselves as Northern Irish and Irish, 'very strong' identifiers are 5 per cent and 15 per cent, respectively.

4

Constitutional preferences

Modern states are based on the premise that legal and political boundaries are congruent with territorial boundaries in what Miles Kahler (2006: 2) has termed 'jurisdictional congruence'. For most of the twentieth century, it was assumed that examples of jurisdictional incongruence – where politics and geography are not aligned – would fade away into irrelevance, either through economic modernization or by virtue of globalization. Such predictions have proved to be unduly optimistic. Not only have territorial disputes remained salient across many advanced societies, but they have emerged in many newly democratizing countries where they had been held in check by their authoritarian rulers. As a result, territorial disputes now dominate the politics of many countries in the former communist states of southeast Europe and central Asia, as well as the Middle East and East Asia.

For most of the twentieth century, the issue of jurisdictional incongruence was at the heart of the Northern Ireland conflict. Between 1969 and 1998, when the Belfast Agreement was signed, the conflict defied all efforts by the British and Irish governments to solve it. While the post-1998 period has also been one of occasional drama, with suspensions of the power-sharing executive and numerous accusations of underhand tactics between the competing parties, territorial issues have become less prominent in political debate. Moreover, as we show in this chapter, there has been an important shift in Catholic opinion towards an acceptance of devolution and, along with it, the principle that Northern Ireland should remain within the United Kingdom.

Although Northern Ireland has long been considered an integral part of the United Kingdom, the constitutional position has been the topic of recurring debate since partition in 1920. Following the 1920 Government of Ireland Act, British policy was dominated by a desire for noninvolvement in the domestic affairs of the region (O'Leary and Arthur, 1990; Hadfield, 1992). This policy was accomplished by the establishment of a Northern Ireland parliament at Stormont which left successive Ulster Unionist governments 'masters in their own house', with all the trappings of self-government (Hadfield, 1992: 3). Although these political arrangements changed with the introduction of direct rule from Westminster in 1972, the governance of Northern Ireland still remains distinct from that of any other region within the United Kingdom. When powers have been devolved – as in 1973–74, 1999–2002 and since 2007 – it has been based on power-sharing between the two communities, a principle that does not apply anywhere else in the United Kingdom.

Historically, the territorial question has been complicated by the position of the Republic of Ireland. Despite the Republic's introduction of a constitutional territorial claim over Northern Ireland in 1937 (articles 2 and 3 of the Irish constitution, subsequently removed after a referendum in 1998), prior to the 1970s the Republic of Ireland and Northern Ireland cultivated what 'was essentially a political and economic non-relationship' (Hertz, 1986: 135). Not only were the two parts of the island perceived to have very little in common but, until the 1965 Stormont meeting between Sean Lemass, the Irish Taoiseach, and Terence O'Neill, the Northern Ireland Prime Minister, there had been little or no contact between either their elected representatives or their respective citizens. Peter Mair (1987: 87) puts it well when he comments that for successive Irish governments, 'the national aim was the achievement of social and economic self-respect in the 26-county state, rather than the achievement of territorial self-respect in a new 32-county state'. It was not until the signing of the Belfast Agreement in 1998 that the Irish government attempted to address the territorial issue, by holding a referendum with a view to removing its constitutional claim to Northern Ireland.

This chapter examines the trends in public opinion towards constitutional preferences, which reflect territorial aspirations. The first section examines the broad trends in constitutional preferences from 1968 to the present, but with a specific focus on the period since 1989. The second section examines the 1998 Belfast Agreement, without doubt the most successful attempt at a constitutional settlement, while the third section deals with patterns of post-1998 public opinion and specifically the erosion of consent among the Protestant community. The fourth section examines opinions towards devolved government since 1998 and tests the hypothesis that the two communities have become more enamoured of devolution. The final section examines the potential for change and the extent to which the two communities would accept a democratically expressed preference for Irish unity.

The territorial question

Given the traditional centrality of territory and constitutional preferences to the Northern Ireland conflict, it is not surprising that this has been a continuing theme in public opinion surveys, going back as far as Richard Rose's 1968 Loyalty Survey. On the eve of the conflict, the Loyalty Survey found that two-thirds of Protestants approved of the constitutional position of Northern Ireland, while one-third of Catholics disapproved (see Table 4.1). These figures display a much reduced level of polarization on the constitution than is evident in the post-1969 surveys and reflect the fact that while there were deep divisions over constitutional preferences at the time the survey was conducted, there was little immediate threat to the current institutional arrangements. Indeed, one in five Protestants and almost one in three Catholics did not have an opinion on the issue.

The 1968 Loyalty Survey also asked about attitudes to the border, a more pertinent physical expression of the prevailing constitutional arrangements. There was a surprisingly high level of agreement between the two communities on the prospects for any change in the border in the next decade; 33 per cent of Protestants and 35 per cent of Catholics

Table 4.1 Religion and constitutional preferences, 1968

	Protestant	Catholic	All
Approve of constitution			
Approve	69	34	55
Disapprove	10	35	20
Don't know	21	31	25
Total	100	100	100
(N)	(746)	(520)	(1,269)
Changes to border			
Yes	33	35	34
No	51	45	48
Depends/don't know	16	20	18
Total	100	100	100
(N)	(751)	(532)	(1,287)

The questions were 'There has always been a lot of controversy about the constitutional position of Northern Ireland, on balance, do you approve or disapprove of it?' and 'Do you think that in the next ten years or so there will be any big changes in the situation concerning the border?'
Source: Northern Ireland Loyalty Survey, 1968

said there was some prospect of change, but most thought there would be no change or had no opinion. Overall, these opinions reflect the relatively settled nature of the constitutional arrangements that existed in 1968, a situation that would change within just a few short years.

The polarizing effects of nine years of conflict on public opinion towards the constitution can be seen in Table 4.2, which shows the results from the 1978 Northern Ireland Attitude Survey. By 1978, opinions had shifted markedly; around 9 out of 10 Protestants favoured Northern Ireland remaining part of the UK, though preferences for institutional arrangements within that framework were divided between devolution based on majority rule to form the executive and devolution with power-sharing arrangements. The collapse of the power-sharing

Table 4.2 Religion and constitutional preferences, 1978

	Protestant	Catholic	All
Preference			
Remain part of UK, devolution with majority rule	38	1	26
Remain part of UK, devolution with power-sharing	35	39	36
Remain part of UK, direct rule	16	9	14
(Total remain part of UK)	(89)	(49)	(76)
Irish unity	1	25	9
Federal system in Ireland	4	14	7
Independence	3	3	3
Joint control	2	8	4
Don't know	1	1	1
Total	100	100	100
(N)	(772)	(402)	(1,267)
Will border disappear			
Yes	49	68	56
No	48	29	41
Don't know	3	4	3
Total	100	100	100
(N)	(772)	(402)	(1,267)

The questions were 'There has been a lot of talk about solutions to the present problem in Northern Ireland. Now I want you to leave aside what you would like to see in an ideal world, and tell me which of the following is the most workable and acceptable to you as a solution'. 'Leaving your hopes to one side, do you think the border will eventually disappear?'
Source: Northern Ireland Attitude Survey, 1978

executive in May 1974 had divided Protestant opinion on the best means of ensuring a return to devolution and created an enduring split in unionism which has remained up until the present.

The Catholic community had no such equivocation about power-sharing. Around half of the Catholics interviewed in the 1978 survey favoured remaining part of the UK, with their overwhelming preference for some form of power-sharing arrangement between the two communities. Irish unity attracted the support of one in four Catholics, while the proposal for a federal system across the whole island of Ireland – the *Eire Nua* plan first advocated by the Provisional IRA in 1971[1] – attracted the support of 14 per cent of Catholics. The figures in Table 4.2 are also notable – particularly when compared to the results for 1968 in the previous table – for the very small number who did not express an opinion on the constitution. Clearly, the widespread political violence and the accompanying political debate about how to stop it had galvanized opinions.

The first years of the conflict also had a significant effect on the public's views of the likelihood of a change in the border. While 33 per cent of Protestants thought there would be some change in 1968, the same figure in 1978 is much higher, at 49 per cent. Among Catholics, the proportion seeing some change in the border as likely almost doubled between 1968 and 1978.[2] Once again, the proportions expressing no opinion on the issue are very small and are just one-sixth of the proportion with no opinion about the border in 1968. The first decade of the conflict had rapidly polarized public opinion and focused the public's mind on how best to resolve the problem.

The Northern Ireland Social Attitudes Surveys and its successor, the Northern Ireland Life and Times Surveys, which have been conducted more or less annually since 1989, allow us to examine constitutional preferences in more detail and to judge the potential for change across different political scenarios. Across the population as a whole, Figure 4.1 shows that a majority has consistently opted for continued union with Britain; in 1989, 70 per cent of the survey respondents opted for this choice, slightly down from the 76 per cent recorded in the 1978 survey. However, the results show a steady decline in the proportion favouring the union, especially in the immediate post-1998 period, with the lowest figure – 50 per cent – being recorded in 2001. The institutional arrangements introduced by the Belfast Agreement had a significant impact on public opinion in making the union with Britain appear a less attractive option in the years immediately after the ratification of the Agreement. Since then, support for the union has rebounded so that, by 2010, 72 per cent of the survey respondents opted for this choice.

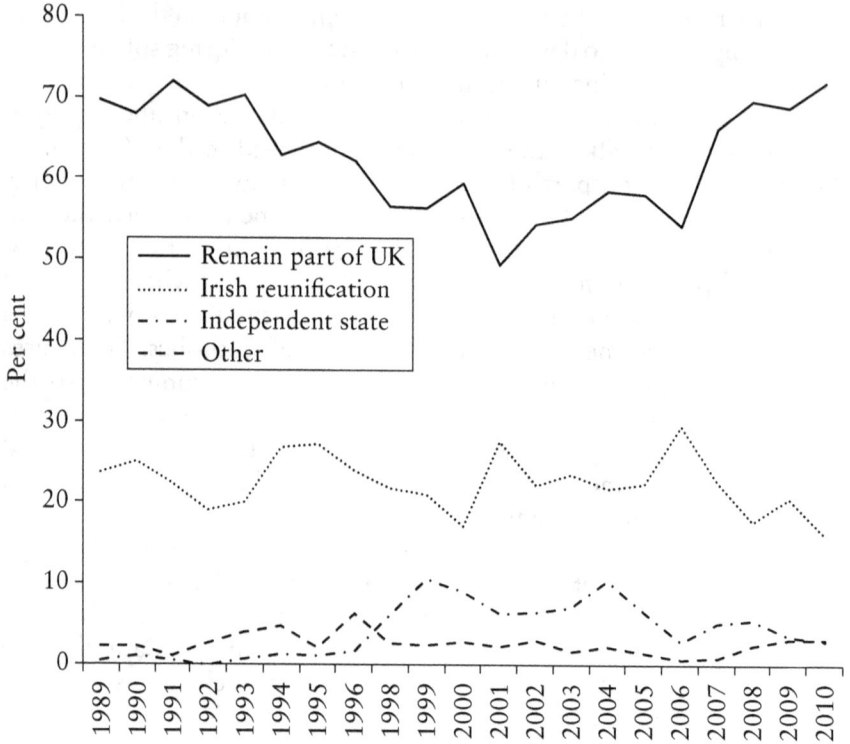

Figure 4.1 Constitutional preferences, 1989–2010
The question was 'Do you think the long-term policy for Northern Ireland should be for it to remain part of the United Kingdom, or to reunify with the rest of Ireland?' From 2007, the option 'to remain part of the UK' was divided between 'to remain part of the UK, with direct rule' and 'to remain part of the UK, with devolved government'
Sources: Northern Ireland Social Attitudes Surveys, 1989–91, 1993–96; Northern Ireland Election Survey, 1992; Northern Ireland Life and Times Surveys, 1998–2010

The fluctuation in the proportions supporting the union has not led to an increase in those supporting Irish unity, which has remained reasonably constant over the period of the surveys, at between 20 and 25 per cent of the population. Rather, those moving away from a preference for union with Britain have moved to a position of expressing no opinion: in the 10 years prior to 1998, don't know responses stood at an average of 6 per cent; in the 12 years following the Belfast Agreement, they increased markedly to an average of 9 per cent. Other options, aside from the two main ones, have rarely attracted any significant support. Support for

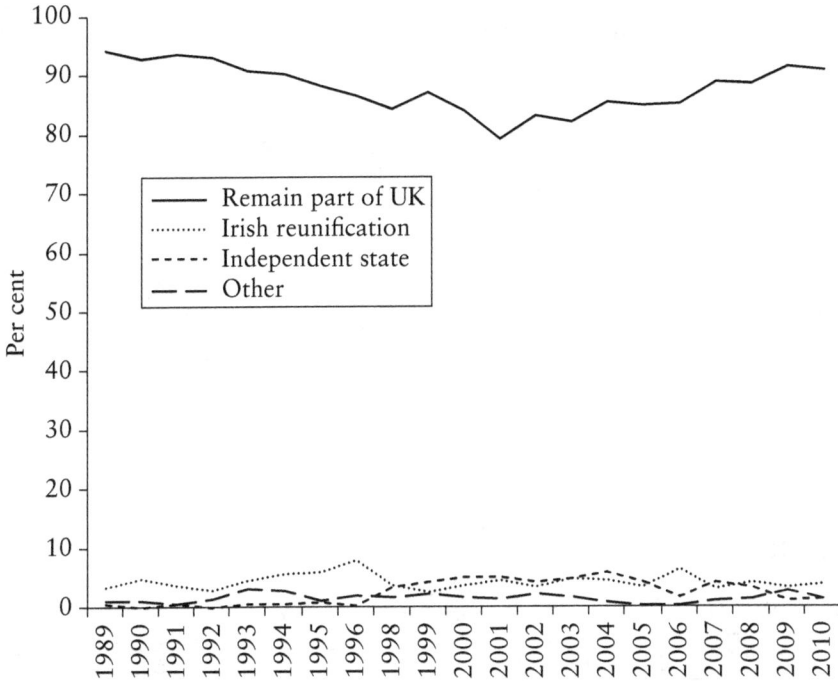

Figure 4.2 Constitutional preferences among Protestants, 1989–2010
See Figure 4.1 for question wording
Sources: Northern Ireland Social Attitudes Surveys, 1989–91, 1993–96;
Northern Ireland Election Survey, 1992; Northern Ireland Life and Times
Surveys, 1998–2010

political independence for Northern Ireland peaked at 1 in 10 of the survey respondents in 1999 but has averaged only 4 per cent over the period, similar to the figure recorded in the 1978 survey.

Estimating the constitutional preferences for the two communities separately sheds important light on what has motivated the changes that are apparent across the whole population. Among Protestants, Figure 4.2 shows that union with Britain enjoys overwhelming support, as we would expect; in 1989, 94 per cent of those interviewed chose this option, compared to just slightly less, 91 per cent, in 2010. However, there was a noticeable decline in support for the union after the Belfast Agreement, dropping to 79 per cent in 2001 but recovering soon afterwards. The overall trend suggests strong and relatively stable support for the union among Protestants, and the trend is remarkably consistent with the data reported in Table 4.2 for 1978. The various institutional changes in

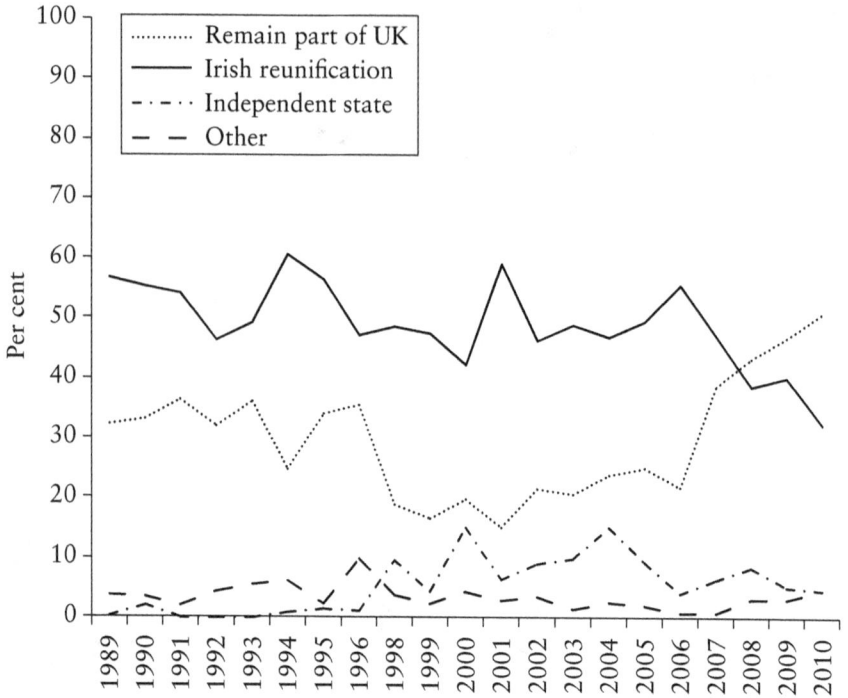

Figure 4.3 Constitutional preferences among Catholics, 1989–2010
See Figure 4.1 for question wording
Sources: Northern Ireland Social Attitudes Surveys, 1989–91, 1993–96;
Northern Ireland Election Survey, 1992; Northern Ireland
Life and Times Surveys, 1998–2010

governance in Northern Ireland would appear to have had relatively little impact on the Protestant community's desire for continued union with Britain, with the exception of some relatively short-term changes such as a decline in the immediate post-Agreement period. This is a by-product of the highly unstable and dysfunctional nature of the Assembly, particularly during the first two periods of devolved government between 1999 and 2002.[3] This period of devolution has been characterized as little more than a 'war by other means' (see Wilford and Wilson, 2000, 2001).

In contrast to the unanimity among Protestants in their preference for union with Britain, Catholics are more divided in their preferences (see Figure 4.3). About half favour Irish unity, with the highest level of support, 60 per cent, occurring in 1994, just after the Downing Street Declaration of December 1993, which gave the Irish government a formal role in seeking a solution to the conflict. The lowest figures in support of Irish unity occur from 2008 onwards, following the formation of the DUP–Sinn Fein Executive; the installation of the staunch unionist Ian Paisley as first minister obviously made many Catholics feel that Irish unity was a less viable option than it had been immediately earlier. In 2010, just one in three Catholics favoured Irish reunification. However, the post-1989 trends show much higher levels of Catholic support for Irish unity than is found in 1978, when just one in four Catholics favoured it.

The trends also show that a majority of Catholics now favour union with Britain. Until 2007, the proportions favouring this option were much lower than the 49 per cent who favoured it in 1978. Around one in three Catholics favoured union with Britain prior to 1998; following the Agreement, that figure dropped to around one in five. There has been a significant upward trend since 2007; in 2010, 51 per cent supported the union, the highest proportion in any of the surveys. Also notable is the relatively large proportion of Catholics who express no opinion on the constitution, which was as high as one in five in the early 2000s. Over the period of the surveys, 'don't know' responses have averaged 11 per cent for Catholics, around three times the rate for Protestants over the same period, suggesting a much higher degree of indecision among Catholics than Protestants about what constitutional arrangements they would most prefer.

Among those with no religion, remaining part of the UK is the main preference, but Figure 4.4 shows that, up to 2006, support for this option was in long-term decline. In 1989, 83 per cent supported remaining part of the UK, but this had almost halved, to 46 per cent, by 2006. The formation of the power-sharing executive in 2007 had a major impact on the preferences of this group, and in 2007 support increased to 71 per cent. Since then, it has fallen back considerably so that support for remaining part of the union now stands at just 60 per cent among those with no religion. Support for Irish reunification, never strong, is the second most favoured option among those with no religion. It reached 30 per cent in 2006 at a time when, in the light of difficult and protracted negotiations which eventually led to the St Andrews Agreement in October 2006, it looked as if the difficulties in forming a devolved government were insurmountable (see Wilford and Wilson, 2008). Since then, support for Irish unity has declined considerably; currently, only 18 per cent of those with no religion endorse this view. By contrast, the proportion of those with no religion rejecting explicitly all three options – the 'other' category – has steadily increased over the same period, from just 2 per cent in 2006 to 7 per cent by 2010.

It is possible to add a further layer of analysis to the public's constitutional preferences by examining what form of government is preferred by those who wanted to remain part of the UK. In 2007, the

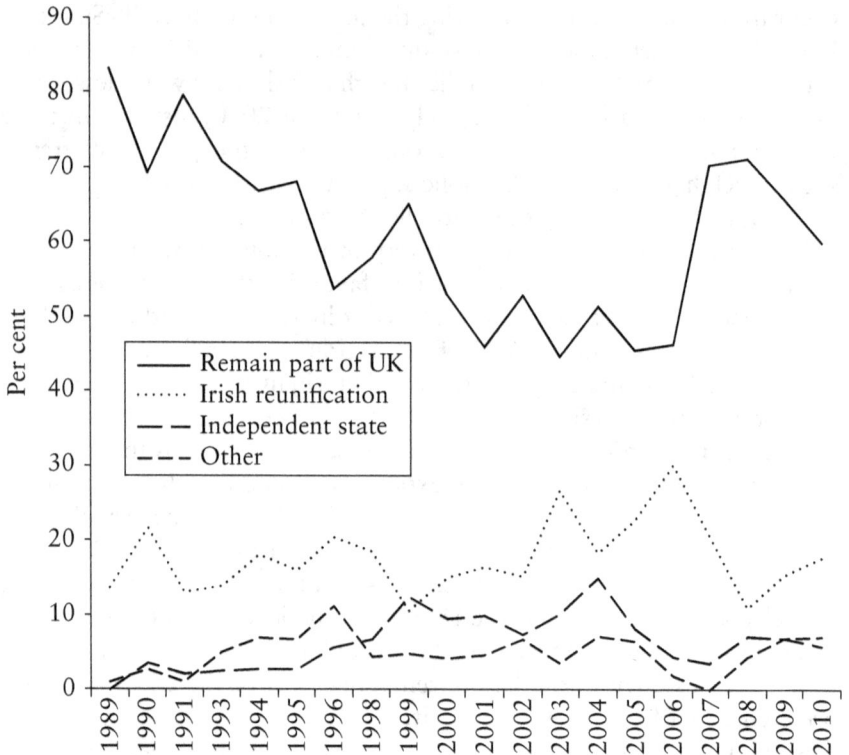

Figure 4.4 Constitutional preferences among the non-affiliated, 1989 –2010
See Figure 4.1 for question wording
Sources: Northern Ireland Social Attitudes Surveys, 1989–91, 1993–96;
Northern Ireland Election Survey, 1992; Northern Ireland Life and Times
Surveys, 1998–2010

wording of this option changed so that the respondents could choose
between remaining part of the UK under direct rule from Westminster or
remaining in the UK with devolved government. The results in Table 4.3
show that devolved government is by far the preferred choice for all
three groups, Protestants, Catholics and those with no religion. However,
there is an important diverging trend, with Protestants showing less
support for devolution after 2007 and Catholics more support. This
probably reflects the differing responses of the two communities to the
experiences of the power-sharing government formed in 2007, with
Catholics responding more positively than Protestants. It also accounts
for the sharp increase in Catholic support for remaining in UK which
we observed in Figure 4.3.

Table 4.3 Preferred form of governance within the UK, 2007–10

	(Percentages)				
	2007	2008	2009	2010	2007–10 change
		(Direct rule)			
Protestant	17	25	27	22	+5
Catholic	4	7	8	6	+2
No religion	10	17	20	14	+4
All	11	17	18	15	+4
		(Devolved government)			
Protestant	72	64	64	69	−3
Catholic	35	37	39	45	+10
No religion	61	54	46	46	−15
All	55	53	51	57	+2

See Figure 4.1 for question wording
Source: Northern Ireland Life and Times Surveys, 2007–10

Public opinion in Northern Ireland on the most central of issues, the constitution, therefore shows several important patterns when measured over the whole period of the post-1968 conflict. The first pattern is relative stability in opinions between the communities in their preferred options, with 9 out of 10 Protestants favouring continued union with Britain and one-half of Catholics favouring Irish unity. Second, while there are some variations in these patterns due to changes in the prevailing institutional arrangements – or discussions about future arrangements – the variations are relatively small and often revert back to trend. Third, there is more variation and indecision on constitutional preferences among Catholics than among Protestants. One explanation for this may be that while Protestants can comfortably opt for the constitutional status quo, Catholics' preferred choice, Irish unity, involves change and therefore introduces a degree of uncertainty in opinions. Nevertheless, the experience of power-sharing government has met with a positive response from Catholics, particularly after 2007 with the election of Ian Paisley and Martin McGuinness and the good working relationship that was established between them.[4]

Attitudes to the 1998 Belfast Agreement

Of all the various attempts at a constitutional settlement in Northern Ireland, starting with the 1973 Sunningdale Agreement which gave rise to the 1974 power-sharing executive, the 1998 Belfast Agreement has

easily been the longest lasting and most effective. As Chapter 1 emphasized, the Agreement was a milestone for being the first explicit attempt
to draw the paramilitary organizations into the political debate, a
change that had long been recognized as a precondition for any lasting
resolution of the conflict, but one which has been difficult to implement. The Agreement also represented an organic evolution in the
thinking of the British and Irish governments, based on what the
Taoiseach John Bruton termed 'strategic continuity' (quoted in Dixon,
2001: 340). In effect, the Agreement represented the end product of
many years of strategic thinking among the numerous parties to the
conflict. And not least, of course, it reflected changes in public opinion
within both communities.

When it was signed on 10 April 1998, the Belfast Agreement involved
a series of compromises which were not equally acceptable to all sides
(see Hayes and McAllister, 2001a). Many of the more contentious issues,
such as the accelerated release of paramilitary prisoners, the decommissioning of paramilitary weapons and reform of the police, were
deliberately blurred by the British government in the belief that they
could be dealt with at a later stage. No sooner had the Agreement been
signed than significant divisions began to emerge within the mainstream
unionist groups. There were also some anti-Agreement nationalist
dissenters who viewed the establishment of cross-border bodies and the
power-sharing executive as an unacceptable compromise. As Bernadette
Sands-McKevitt, sister of Bobby Sands, the first person to die in the
republican hunger strikes of 1981, put it: 'Bobby did not die for cross-
border bodies with executive powers' (quoted in Tonge, 2004).[5]

The contentious nature of many of the Agreement's principles, combined with the need to ratify it in a referendum, generated considerable
uncertainty about whether or not the Agreement would ever be implemented. The referendum to ratify the Agreement was scheduled for
22 May with an assembly election taking place a month later if the referendum proposal was passed. The Agreement received differing recep-
tions within the two Northern Ireland communities. The Ulster Unionist
Party supported the Agreement, with a significant minority opposed,
including several of its Westminster MPs. The DUP, led by Ian Paisley,
pledged to oppose the Agreement; the party chairperson, Nigel Dodds,
saw the Agreement as creating 'a Northern Ireland in transition to a
united Ireland' (cited in Aughey, 2000: 69). There were fewer divisions
among nationalists, with both the SDLP and Sinn Fein welcoming the
Agreement. A special Sinn Fein conference held in Dublin on 10 May
voted overwhelmingly to support the Agreement and to permit members
to take their seats in the proposed assembly.

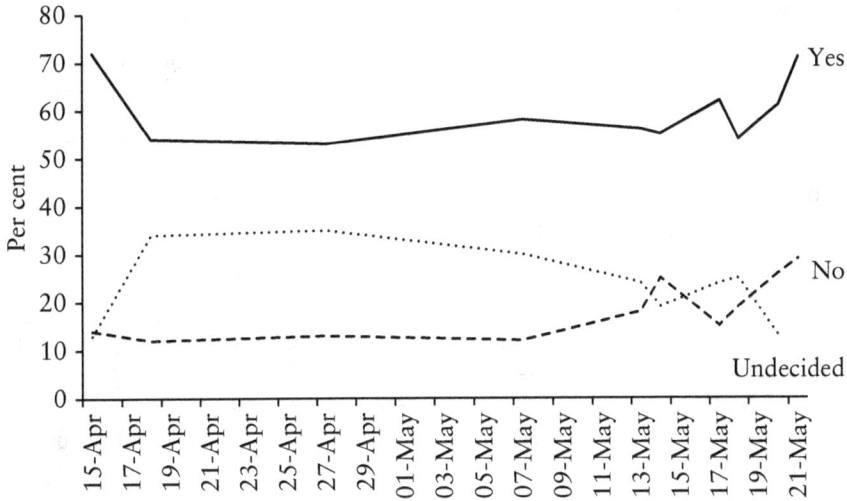

Figure 4.5 Intended referendum vote, April–May 1998
Estimates exclude non-voters
Source: Hayes and McAllister (2001a: Figure 1)

The initial popularity of the Agreement and the positive media attention that it attracted ensured that early public reactions were very favourable. The first poll to test public opinion, conducted in mid-April, showed
that almost three out of every four voters said that they intended to vote
yes, with just 14 per cent saying no and even fewer, 13 per cent, saying
that they were undecided (see Figure 4.5). As unionist leaders articulated
more concerns about how the Agreement would work, Protestant fears
grew; as a result, overall support dropped markedly, to between 50 and
60 per cent. It remained at this level throughout the campaign, even
dropping to 52 per cent according to one survey just five days before
polling day. By the end of the campaign, the final polls showed that
among Protestants, the yes and no groups were almost equal in size. By
contrast, Catholic support for the Agreement never dropped below
76 per cent; Catholic 'no' voters never numbered more than 4 per cent
of all Catholic voters (Hayes and McAllister, 2001a: Figure 2).

The result of the referendum in Northern Ireland was a yes vote of
71.1 per cent and a no vote of 28.9 per cent, based on a turnout of
81.1 per cent (see Table 4.4). The turnout was the second highest in
Northern Ireland in the post-war years, confirming the importance
placed on the issue by the electorate. In the Irish Republic, the result
was even more decisive: on a turnout of 56.3 per cent (similar to the
turnout in other referendums, though significantly lower than in general

Table 4.4 The results of the Belfast Agreement referendums, 22 May 1998

	Northern Ireland		Irish Republic	
	N	Per cent	N	Per cent
Yes	676,966	71.1	1,442,583	94.4
No	274,879	28.9	85,748	5.6
Total valid votes	951,845	100.0	1,528,331	100.0
Spoiled votes	1,738		17,064	
(Turnout)		(81.1)		(56.3)

In Northern Ireland, the question was 'Do you support the agreement reached in the multiparty talks on Northern Ireland and set out in Command Paper 3883?'; in the Irish Republic, 'Do you approve of the proposal to amend the Constitution contained in the undermentioned Bill, the Nineteenth Amendment of the Constitution Bill, 1998?'
Source: Hayes and McAllister (2001a)

elections), 94.4 per cent voted yes and just 5.6 per cent no. There were, however, ten times more spoiled votes in the Irish Republic than in Northern Ireland, indicating some republican dissatisfaction with the Agreement's explicit recognition of the constitutional position of Northern Ireland. Nevertheless, the result in the Irish Republic was never in doubt since all of the major parties campaigned for a yes vote.

Although the referendum result produced a decisive yes vote, it also laid bare the deep divisions that existed among unionists. The Northern Ireland Referendum and Election Study shows that 57 per cent of Protestants voted yes, while 43 per cent voted no (see Table 4.5). The survey provides little evidence of differential turnout across all three religious groupings; one of the government's concerns had been that a low turnout, particularly in the Protestant community, might undermine the result. So concerned was the British government about the inability of political leaders, particularly from within the unionist community, to deliver the consent of their various constituencies in the run up to the referendum that the Northern Ireland Office (NIO) proposed to secretly target middle-class unionist voters, women and first-time voters in an effort to persuade them to support the Agreement.[6]

Closer inspection of the voting patterns confirms that there was considerable fragility in the Protestant vote. The final part of Table 4.5 shows that just over a quarter of Protestants said that they had considered changing their vote (most from a yes to a no vote) during the

Table 4.5 Religion and the 1998 referendum vote

	Protestant	Catholic	No religion	All
Voted	85	84	79	84
(N)	(472)	(335)	(70)	(927)
Vote choice (voters only)				
Yes	57	99	79	75
No	43	1	21	25
Total	100	100	100	100
(N)	(371)	(277)	(70)	(737)
Vote choice (non-voters only)				
Yes	49	83	44	62
No	26	3	19	15
Don't know	25	14	37	23
Total	100	100	100	100
(N)	(72)	(58)	(16)	(158)
Considered changing vote				
Yes	26	7	34	20
(Yes voters considered no)	(16)	(7)	(26)	(14)
(No voters considered yes)	(10)	(0)	(9)	(6)
No	71	91	62	78
Don't know	3	2	4	2
Total	100	100	100	100
(N)	(371)	(277)	(53)	(737)

The questions were 'Talking to people, we found that some people did not manage to vote. How about you, did you manage to vote in the referendum?'; 'How did you vote?'; (non-voters only) 'If you had voted, would you have voted yes to the Agreement or no to the Agreement?'; and 'Was there any time during the referendum campaign when you considered voting in a different way?'
Source: Northern Ireland Referendum and Election Study, 1998

course of the campaign, compared to just 7 per cent of Catholics. If all of these wavering voters (irrespective of the direction of the change) had actually changed their final vote, Protestant opinion would have been equally divided on the Agreement, with exactly half voting in favour and half voting against.[7] Indecision among Protestants therefore came close to altering the referendum outcome and undermining the legitimacy of the result.[8]

What aspects of the Belfast Agreement were Protestant voters most unhappy with? The Agreement set out three dimensions as a basis for a settlement. The first dimension, devolution, had three components: an assembly, a power-sharing executive and north–south consultative bodies; Table 4.6 shows that the last two of these three institutions failed to attract majority support among Protestant no voters. The second dimension, the decommissioning of paramilitary weapons, had been a major source of dispute, and both Protestant yes and no voters supported its phasing with the creation of new institutions and prisoner releases. Finally, the Agreement also dealt with territorial issues: Northern Ireland remaining part of the UK and the Irish Republic removing its claim to Northern Ireland attracted overwhelming support from both sets of Protestant voters.

Protestant opponents of the Agreement were, therefore, particularly concerned about the political institutions that would be created under the new arrangements, compared to Protestants who favoured the Agreement. But another aspect to the Agreement was more subjective: the idea that it represented a 'new beginning'. The prolonged conflict has seen many cathartic events which have temporarily galvanized public opinion against violence. The Belfast Agreement appeared to fit this perception of 'a new beginning'; the frantic all-night talks before the deadline and the religious symbolism of Easter all fostered the belief that the Agreement might indeed represent a fundamental break with the past and deliver a lasting peace. The last part of Table 4.6 suggests that this explanation has some validity for Protestants. A majority of Protestant yes voters believed that the Agreement represented a new beginning in three of the four statements, the exception being that only one in three believed that it would result in a lasting peace.

Although the referendum was passed and a majority of Protestants – 57 per cent – supported the Agreement, there was considerable indecision and unease right up to the referendum vote itself. Indeed, if those who reported considering changing their vote had done so, unionist opinion would have been equally divided, and the Agreement would most probably have collapsed. Unionists were motivated in their support for the Agreement by the belief that it represented a 'new beginning' and by support for the political institutions it proposed, particularly devolution. By contrast, for nationalists the territorial provisions in the Agreement were most important. The desire for a 'new beginning' among Protestants explains the difficulties in implementing the Agreement. In the absence of widespread agreement on fundamental political principles, such an aspiration represents an insecure basis for a permanent settlement. While unionists wanted a 'new beginning', there was little support for reviewing the role of the police or for releasing paramilitary prisoners. In the next section, we examine public opinion in the post-Agreement period.

Table 4.6 Protestant referendum vote and support for aspects of the
Belfast Agreement, 1998

	Referendum vote	
Per cent Protestants who support	Yes	No
Devolution		
Establish Northern Ireland Assembly	97	65
Power-sharing in new Executive	83	48
Create north–south bodies	71	24
Decommissioning		
Paramilitaries decommission before enter government	86	88
Prisoners only released after decommissioning	83	87
Territorial		
NI remain part of UK	98	98
Removal of Republic's claim to Northern Ireland	81	85
'A New Beginning'		
All parties make Assembly success	98	69
Agreement brings economic prosperity	67	29
Agreement breaks political deadlock	61	21
Agreement leads to lasting peace	34	7
(N)	(257)	(173)

The questions were as follows. (Devolution) 'Now I would like to ask you about your own views on some of the proposals contained in the Belfast Agreement. Choosing your answer from this card, could you tell me how you feel about ... 'the setting up of a NI Assembly ... the requirement that the new Executive is power-sharing ... the creation of North-South bodies ... (Territorial) The guarantee that NI will remain part of the UK as long as a majority of the people in NI wish it to be so ... the removal of the Republic of Ireland's constitutional claim to Northern Ireland'. (Decommissioning) 'Can you tell me if you agree or disagree with the following statements? Nobody with links to paramilitaries that still have weapons should be allowed to be a government minister ... Prisoners should not be released until the paramilitaries have handed in their weapons'. (A new beginning) 'Can you tell me if you agree or disagree with the following statements? All parties elected to the Assembly should try and make it a success even if they were opposed to the Agreement.... . The Agreement will bring economic prosperity to NI ... The Agreement has finally broken the political deadlock in NI ... The Agreement will lead to a lasting peace in NI'. Estimates are for Protestant voters only. Ns for individual items vary slightly due to missing data
Source: Northern Ireland Referendum and Election Study, 1998

Post-Agreement political attitudes

Given the political instability in the immediate post-Agreement period, it is not surprising that Protestant opinion exhibited a slow decline in support for the political institutions embodied in the Agreement. Although the referendum on the Agreement was supported by 71.1 per cent of voters in Northern Ireland, this public endorsement masked major differences between the two communities. While Catholics (and to a lesser extent the religiously non-affiliated) were almost universally in favour, Protestants were deeply divided; as we showed in the previous section, just 57 per cent of Protestants voted for the Agreement, compared to 99 per cent of Catholics and 79 per cent of those with no religion. There was, then, less than wholehearted support for the Agreement among Protestants.

Weak Protestant support for the Agreement persisted well into the 2000s. The surveys conducted between 1999 and 2010 show that while the vast majority of Catholics and those with no religion continued to favour the Agreement, Protestant support slowly eroded through to 2005 and then rose sharply to 73 per cent in 2006, when the survey question was changed to reflect support for the 2006 St Andrews Agreement. When the question was changed back to the Belfast Agreement, support again fell back to 53 per cent in 2010 (see Figure 4.6).[9] There was a particularly steep decline in the two years immediately following the referendum; in 1999, it stood at 52 per cent and in 2000 at just 46 per cent. It would appear that the early experiences of devolution were negative for many Protestants, while more recent experiences have tended to be positive.

The changing proportions willing to vote 'yes' since 1998 are underpinned by fluctuations in support for the principles of the Agreement. Each of the three strands in the Agreement – the new political institutions, the north–south relationship and the British–Irish relationship – represents a trade-off between unionist and nationalist aspirations. In return for nationalist demands for the creation of cross-border bodies, nationalists and republicans endorsed the return to devolved government and the creation of an elected assembly. To make the creation of cross-border bodies more acceptable to unionists, the north–south dimension was complemented by an east–west dimension via the establishment of a British–Irish Council. For nationalists, in return, the elected assembly was to be based on the principle of proportionality with a power-sharing executive composed of all groups within the assembly, chosen by the d'Hondt procedure.

What specific parts of the Agreement did Protestants object to, and how has this changed since 1998? Of the seven main aspects to the

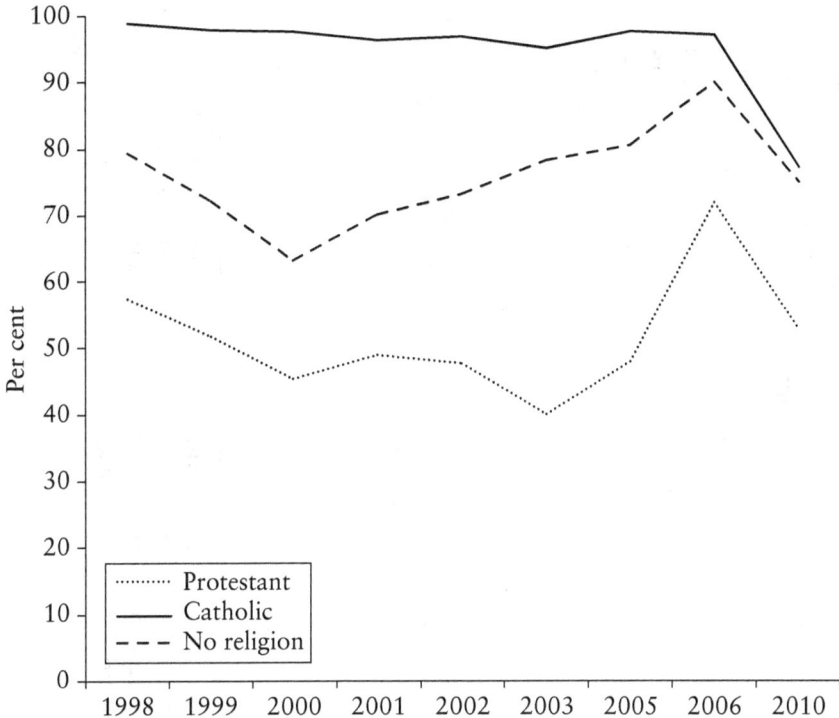

Figure 4.6 'Yes' vote if Agreement referendum repeated, 1998–2010
Estimates of the 'yes' vote exclude non-voters and don't knows. The questions
were (1998) 'Talking to people, we found that some people did not manage to
vote. How about you, did you manage to vote in the referendum?' and 'How
did you vote?'; (1999) 'If the vote on the Belfast Agreement was held again
today would you still vote the same way that you did last May?' and 'How did
you vote last May?'; (2000–05, 2010) 'If the vote on the Belfast Agreement
was held again today, how would you vote?' and (2006) 'And how do you
think you would vote in 2007 if a referendum on the St Andrew's Agreement
were held'.
Sources: Northern Ireland Referendum and Election Survey, 1998; Northern
Ireland Life and Times Surveys, 1999–2006; Northern Ireland Election
Survey, 2010

Agreement, the first column of Table 4.7 shows that, in 1998, the early
release of prisoners was least popular, with just 7 per cent supporting it,
followed by the establishment of north–south bodies which was supported by half of the respondents. Power-sharing was also not as popular
as other parts of the Agreement, gaining support from two-thirds of the

Table 4.7 Support for principles of the Agreement, 1998–2011

Per cent who support	1998	2000	2003	2011	1998–2011 change
			(Protestants)		
Northern Ireland remain part of UK	98	92	94	93	−5
North–south bodies	50	40	53	54	+4
Northern Ireland Assembly	83	67	78	68	−15
Removal of claim to Northern Ireland	83	78	77	69	−14
Decommissioning	95	96	99	—	—
Early release of prisoners	7	3	—	8	—
Power-sharing executive	66	44	79	79	+13
(N)	(479)	(983)	(534)	(669)	
			(Catholics)		
Northern Ireland remain part of UK	75	53	72	55	−20
North–south bodies	91	83	90	79	−12
Northern Ireland Assembly	94	86	90	70	−24
Removal of claim to Northern Ireland	49	27	26	16	−33
Decommissioning	87	81	95	—	—
Early release of prisoners	38	33	—	29	—
Power-sharing executive	93	82	97	83	−10
(N)	(343)	(573)	(381)	(611)	

The questions were 'Now I would like to ask you about your own views on some of the proposals contained in the Good Friday Agreement (1998) Choosing your answer from this card (2003: 'Looking back at some of the proposals contained in the Belfast Agreement), could you tell me how you feel about (2010: Can you tell me how you feel about the following issues) ... the setting up of a NI Assembly ... the requirement that the new Executive is power-sharing ... the creation of North-South bodies ... the decommissioning of paramilitary weapons ... the early release of paramilitary prisoners ... the removal of the Republic of Ireland's constitutional claim to Northern Ireland ... the guarantee that NI will remain part of the UK as long as a majority of the people in NI wish it to be so'. Numbers of respondents vary due to missing data

Sources: Northern Ireland Referendum and Election Study, 1998; Northern Ireland Life and Times Survey, 2000; Northern Ireland Election Survey, 2003; Northern Ireland Social and Political Attitudes Survey, 2011

respondents. At the other end of the scale, almost all Protestants supported the link with Britain and the decommissioning of paramilitary
weapons. There was, then, very divergent support within the Protestant
community for the various components of the Agreement.[10]

Over the course of the next 13 years, the remaining columns in Table 4.7
show a consistent decline in support for three of the seven principles for
which complete 1998–2011 data are available. For example, 83 per cent
of Protestants in 1998 supported the principle of a Northern Ireland
Assembly; by 2011, that support had declined to 68 per cent. The average decline across the three principles is a substantial 11 percentage
points. By contrast, support for the power-sharing executive has increased
substantially, from 66 per cent in 1998 to 79 per cent by 2011, or an
increase of 13 percentage points in just over a decade.

The second part of Table 4.7 shows the proportions of Catholics who
supported the same seven Agreement principles. The distribution of
support shows similar fluctuations as is evident among Protestants,
although for different aspects of the Agreement. If we take broad
Protestant–Catholic agreement as support which does not vary by more
than 25 per cent in each community, only three of the seven principles –
remaining part of the UK, the Assembly and the decommissioning of
paramilitary weapons – met this test in 1998. The greatest difference was
on removing the Irish Republic's claim to Northern Ireland, which was
supported by 83 per cent of Protestants but just 49 per cent of Catholics.
The pattern of support for the principles since 1998 represents the same
pattern of decline observed for Protestants, although the decline is
substantially greater, with an average of 20 percentage points. The most
substantial decline is in support for removing the Irish Republic's territorial claim, which is supported by just 16 per cent of Catholics in 2011
compared to 49 per cent in 1998, a decline of 33 percentage points,
followed by support for the Northern Ireland assembly, with a decline of
24 percentage points.

Apart from the differing views of the institutional arrangements
defined by the Agreement, there were also major differences in how the
two communities interpreted its implications for the constitutional
future. In reaching these interpretations, the Agreement itself was viewed
as less important than how Protestants interpreted it in the context of
events since the abolition of the Northern Ireland parliament in 1972.
Many saw the various attempts to reach a solution as yet another stage
in a process whereby the British government would edge them closer to
a united Ireland. Opinion poll data from the 2003 Northern Ireland
Election Survey lends support to this conclusion. When asked 'Does eve-
rything that has happened since the Good Friday Agreement was signed

make it more likely that Northern Ireland will eventually join the Irish Republic', 47 per cent of Protestants agreed with the statement as compared to 38 per cent of Catholics. The view that these institutional changes were just one more step in the road to Irish unity was certainly a major element in unionist reactions to the Anglo-Irish Agreement (Dixon, 2002). The inclusion of Sinn Fein in the power-sharing government established by the Agreement was viewed, once again, as another step down this path.

What accounts for post-1998 Protestant disillusionment with the Agreement, or, to put it differently, what occurred to alienate the lukewarm support that existed among a sizeable proportion of the unionist community? Expressed simply, most Protestants believed that the Agreement had disproportionately benefited nationalists at the expense of unionists. When the survey respondents were asked which community benefited most from the Agreement, or whether the benefits were equally shared, a large majority said that nationalists were the net beneficiaries. In 1998, Figure 4.7 shows that 59 per cent of Protestants believed that nationalists benefitted most from the Agreement; just 4 per cent of Protestants believed that unionists benefited more than nationalists.

From 1998 until 2003, the trend towards Protestants seeing nationalists as benefiting more from the Agreement increased consistently; by 2005, just over three-quarters took this view. This increase was at the expense of those who interpreted the Agreement as being of equal benefit to both communities, which declined from 37 per cent in 1998 to nearly half that figure in 2003. The 2008 figure (which is based on a slightly different question wording) shows a substantial decline in the proportion of Protestants who believed that the Agreement benefited nationalists more than unionists, but by 2010 the distribution of opinion had returned to the patterns evident immediately after the 1998 referendum. It would appear that the IRA's decommissioning of weapons in September 2005 and the formation of the power-sharing executive in May 2008, including the DUP and with Ian Paisley as first minister, had influenced Protestant opinions in a positive direction, although the impact was only temporary.

Despite the recent fluctuations, these patterns of negative Protestant opinion about the Agreement are substantial and go a long way towards explaining Protestant disillusionment with the Agreement. Even among Catholics, Figure 4.8 shows that very few believed that unionists had benefited more than nationalists; most believed that the two communities were benefiting equally or that nationalists benefited more than unionists. As with the patterns for Protestants, the most recent figures for 2008 and 2010 show a softening of opinions about

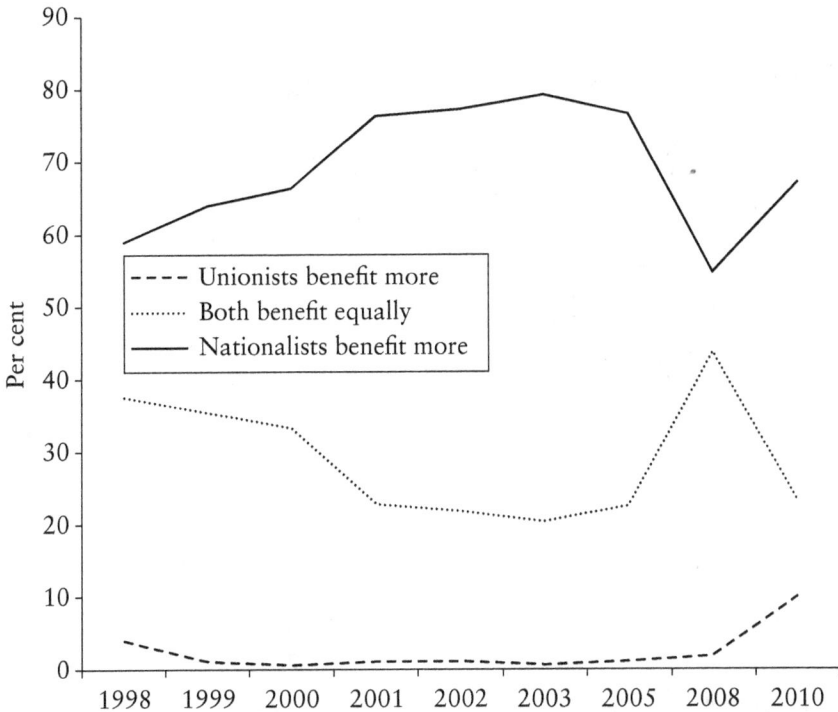

Figure 4.7 Protestant views about community benefits from
the Agreement, 1998–2010

The questions were (1998–2005) 'Thinking back to the Belfast Agreement
now, would you say that it has benefited unionists more than nationalists,
nationalists more than unionists, or that unionists and nationalists have
benefited equally?'; (2008) 'And thinking about all the political changes that
have taken place in Northern Ireland since 1998, would you say that they have
benefited Catholics more than Protestants, Protestants more than Catholics
or have Protestants and Catholics benefited equally?'; and (2010) 'Thinking
about the Northern Ireland peace and political process, would you say that
overall it has benefited unionists more than nationalists, nationalists more
than unionists, or that unionists and nationalists have benefited equally?'
Sources: Northern Ireland Referendum and Election Study 1998; Northern
Ireland Life and Times Surveys, 1999–2008; Northern Ireland Election
Survey, 2010

who has benefited from the Agreement, with 72 and 75 per cent,
respectively, saying that both communities have benefited equally, the
highest figures since 2000. The Agreement thus generated different
feelings within the two communities. For Protestants, the firm view
was that it has disproportionately benefited Catholics, and that view

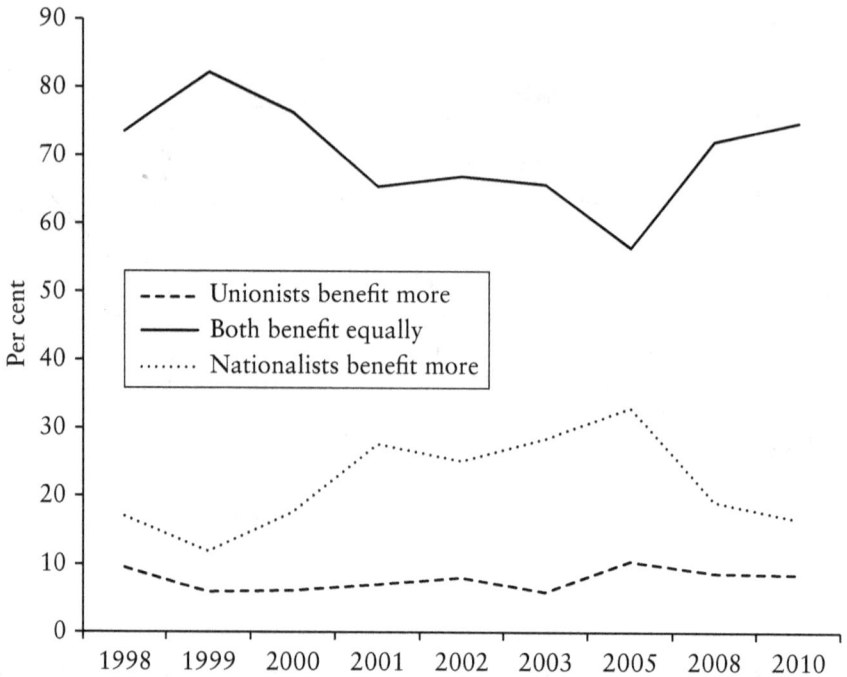

Figure 4.8 Catholic views about community benefits from the Agreement, 1998–2010

See Figure 4.7 for question wording

Sources: Northern Ireland Referendum and Election Study 1998; Northern Ireland Life and Times Surveys, 1999–2008; Northern Ireland Election Survey, 2010

increased significantly after 1998, peaking in 2003. Among Catholics, a majority have consistently believed that the Agreement has benefitted both communities equally.

By any standards, there is less than broad support for the principles embodied in the Agreement and in who benefitted or was disadvantaged by it. Perhaps most tellingly, while support for the Agreement's principles has declined since 1998 across both communities, it has done so most substantially among Catholics, initially the staunchest supporters of the Agreement. These patterns reflect the difficulties in crafting a compromise solution that would provide a minimum willing coalition for the Agreement. It also shows the difficulties in maintaining support for what has often been a dysfunctional institution in its day-to-day operation. In the next section, we expand on this theme by examining public opinion towards the post-1998 institutions of government.

Attitudes towards devolved government

As the previous section made clear, the history of the Belfast Agreement since 1998 has been marked by a steady erosion in Protestant support in the face of a dysfunctional devolved government. Although there has been some reversal of the trend in recent years, the Agreement and the principles underpinning it remain deeply unpopular with unionists. One explanation for this decline is the difficulties involved in convincing a majority to relinquish their political influence by entering into non-majoritarian arrangements. This is reflected in the widespread belief that nationalists benefited more from the Agreement than unionists. A more immediate explanation is the failure of the devolved political institutions to bolster popular consent. These institutions, if they had been seen to have functioned in the manner of a classic consociational 'grand coalition', might have generated popular support for the Agreement and helped to ameliorate communal conflict. Their failure to operate efficiently for much of the post-1998 period has been a major underlying cause of Protestant disillusionment.

Since 1998, the Assembly has been suspended four times. While two of the suspensions (10 August and 22 September 2001) were for only 24 hours, the remaining two periods were more substantial, the last of the four occurring between October 2002 and May 2007 and was caused by allegations of intelligence gathering on behalf of the IRA by Sinn Fein's parliamentary support staff. During this period, devolution was suspended and government was conducted by direct rule from Westminster. The impact of these events on the public's perception of how well the Assembly operated is clearly seen in Figure 4.9. Between 2002 and 2003, there was a consistent decline across all groups in the proportions believing that the Assembly had achieved 'a lot'. For example, 38 per cent of Catholics took this view in 2002; in 2003, the same proportion was just 23 per cent.

Public support for the Assembly recovered in 2007, with the end of the lengthy suspension, but support again dissipated by the next year, and since then there has been only a modest recovery. The most substantial overall decline in support occurs among Catholics. Initially very supportive of the Assembly and what it was trying to achieve (as they were all of the power-sharing arrangements), by 2008 only 13 per cent of Catholic respondents thought that the Assembly had achieved 'a lot'. Moreover, by 2010 the large differences that were evident between the two communities in 1998 had mostly disappeared; both communities were generally agreed that the Assembly had not met their expectations.

Another measure of the standing of the devolved institutions in the views of the electorate is how satisfied the respondents were with the

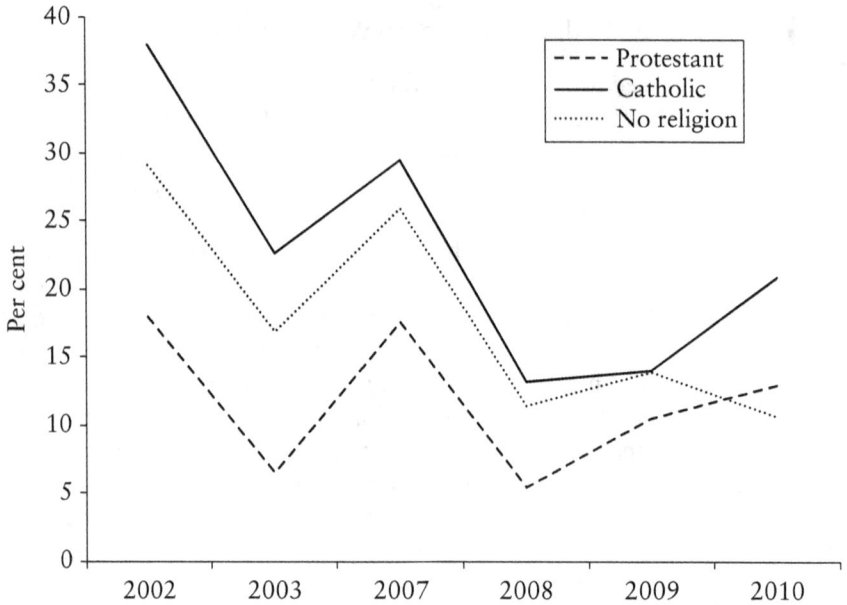

Figure 4.9 Perceptions of the Assembly's achievements, 2002–10
The question was 'Overall, do you think that the Northern Ireland Assembly
has achieved a lot, a little, or, nothing at all?' Figures are for those who said
'a lot'
Source: Northern Ireland Life and Times Surveys, 2002–10

Table 4.8 Satisfaction with MLAs, 2007–10

Per cent satisfied	2007	2008	2009	2010	2007–10 change
Protestants	43	13	21	22	–21
Catholics	54	16	24	27	–27
No religion	35	11	17	19	–16
All	47	14	22	24	–23

The question was 'Are you satisfied or dissatisfied with the way Northern
Ireland MLAs are doing their job?' Figures are for those who said
'very' or 'fairly'
Source: Northern Ireland Life and Times Surveys, 2007–10

performance of their elected representatives (see Table 4.8). The patterns
confirm the findings from the previous analysis, with a collapse in satisfaction after 2007. In 2007, a total of 43 per cent of Protestants and
54 per cent of Catholics were 'very' or 'fairly' satisfied with the way their
Member of Legislative Assemblies (MLAs) were doing their job. This is

a level of satisfaction that is similar to British voters' satisfaction with their MPs in the Westminster parliament.[11] In 2008, this level of satisfaction collapsed by more than two-thirds amid allegations of financial corruption particularly against some DUP members.[12] There has been only a modest recovery in satisfaction since then. By 2010, the level of satisfaction was still only half that found in 2007, no doubt influenced by the Westminster expenses scandal in May 2009, which enveloped 10 of Northern Ireland's MPs (see Clark and Wilford, 2012). In January 2010, these events were followed by allegations of financial impropriety against Iris Robinson and led to the four-week temporary resignation of her husband, Peter Robinson, as first minister.

The system of government that was established in 1998 enshrined a complex set of procedures and principles that were designed to ensure broad cross-community support for legislation. One aspect of this was the designation of members as 'unionist', 'nationalist' or 'other', a process overseen by the Assembly's speaker. While members were free to choose whether or not to participate, the process was important because major legislation requires the support of a majority of both unionist and nationalist members in order to pass.[13] This could occur either through parallel consent (a majority of unionists and nationalists) or by weighted majority (60 per cent of members, including at least 40 per cent each of unionists and nationalists). This system was controversial because it was argued that it devalued the votes of 'other' parties, such as the Alliance Party and the Women's Coalition, since their vote did not count in key decisions. It was also argued that it institutionalized sectarian politics (Taylor, 2009a).

The appointment of an Alliance Party (and undesignated) member, David Ford, as minister of justice in 2010 resolved a dispute between the DUP and Sinn Fein over which party should occupy the position; it is the only ministerial position not allocated by the d'Hondt method. The issue was highly contentious, with the DUP and Sinn Fein disagreeing about the timing of when justice powers should be returned to Northern Ireland. The compromise of appointing the Alliance Party leader as minister satisfied the DUP and Sinn Fein, but angered the SDLP who had regarded the position as theirs, pointing out that, under the d'Hondt method, the Alliance Party would have had insufficient support to gain a ministerial portfolio.

Public support for these aspects of the operation of devolved government shows consistently stronger Catholic than Protestant support (see Table 4.9). There is strongest support for the principles of sharing ministries between unionists and nationalists (supported by 58 per cent of Catholics compared to 36 per cent of Protestants). Protestants are

Table 4.9 Attitudes towards principles of governance, 2010

Per cent who support	Protestant	Catholic	No religion	Total
Shared ministry	36	58	46	46
Designation of MLAs	32	53	32	42
Majority consent legislation	34	53	48	42
Independent justice minister	27	51	38	39
(N)	(516)	(429)	(26)	(971)

The question was 'Can you please tell me how much you agree or disagree with each of the following statements? Ministries should be shared between unionist and nationalist parties. Members of the Assembly should designate as Unionist, Nationalist or Other when elected. Legislation should require the consent of a majority of Unionist and Nationalist Assembly members before it can be passed. The Minister for Justice should not be from the Unionist and Nationalist traditions'. Estimates exclude 'don't know' responses. Numbers of respondents vary due to missing data
Source: Northern Ireland Election Survey, 2010

significantly less supportive of an independent justice minister, reflecting the controversy surrounding the appointment and the delay by the British government in devolving policing and security powers to the Assembly. In general, those with no religion fall between the two communities in their support for the four principles, with the exception of the designation of Assembly members: here, they are no more likely to support it than are Protestants.

Public opinion towards devolved government since 1998 shows that initially high expectations, particularly on the part of Catholics, have generally not been met. Both communities display similar responses to the experience of devolved government, with scepticism about what the Assembly has managed to achieve in its first decade of operation, and high levels of dissatisfaction with the elected representatives themselves after 2007. New political institutions always require a period of consistent achievement in order to gain legitimacy. The dysfunctional operation of devolution since 1998 has made the creation of that legitimacy across the general population hard to achieve.

Attitudes towards constitutional change

British policy towards Northern Ireland has always been based on the principle of consent, namely, that there would be no change in the constitutional position without the consent of the majority (Dixon, 2001).

Support for the principle of consent has been central to every attempt to solve the conflict, starting with the 1973 Sunningdale Agreement and continuing through to the 1985 Anglo-Irish Agreement, the 1993 Downing Street Declaration and most recently the 1998 Belfast Agreement. The exact wording of the principle has varied and has always been delicately composed, because of the Irish government's territorial claim to Northern Ireland, enshrined in articles 2 and 3 of its constitution. The two articles were revised shortly after the Belfast Agreement, and article 3 now states that 'a united Ireland shall be brought about only by peaceful means with the consent of a majority of the people, democratically expressed, in both jurisdictions in the island'. This majority principle is also legislated for explicitly in the 1998 Agreement in that it empowers the Northern Ireland secretary of state to order a referendum on the constitutional position of Northern Ireland 'if it appears likely to him that a majority of those voting would express a wish that Northern Ireland should cease to be part of the United Kingdom and form part of a united Ireland'. The Agreement further stipulates that the referendum may be held only once every seven years.

Nationalists and republicans have traditionally regarded the principle of consent as tantamount to a unionist veto on any future prospect of constitutional change. When it was formed in 1970, the SDLP's constitution was based on the principle of consent (McAllister, 1977), thereby allowing the party to participate in the institutions of the state, something that its predecessor, the Nationalist Party, had refused to do on principle (Murray, 1998). However, the SDLP's nationalist wing, led by John Hume, has always regarded the consent principle as a barrier to political progress. Sinn Fein has had considerably more problems with the consent principle. Sinn Fein and its military counterpart, the Provisional IRA, refused to recognize the legitimacy of Northern Ireland, arguing that the overwhelming support for Sinn Fein across Ireland in the 1918 general election constituted their electoral mandate. After fighting to destroy the state, Sinn Fein finally recognized the existence of Northern Ireland when it signed the Belfast Agreement in 1998 (Murray and Tonge, 2005).

To what extent does the public adhere to the principle of consent, and would they accept any change in the constitutional position of Northern Ireland if the majority voted for it? This question is not simply of academic interest; the results reported earlier in the chapter from the 1978 Northern Ireland Attitude Survey indicated that a majority of the population thought that it was likely there would be some future change in the border. A number of republican leaders, including Sinn Fein president Gerry Adams, have predicted that a united Ireland will come about within a 20-year timeframe (Mac Ginty et al., 2007).

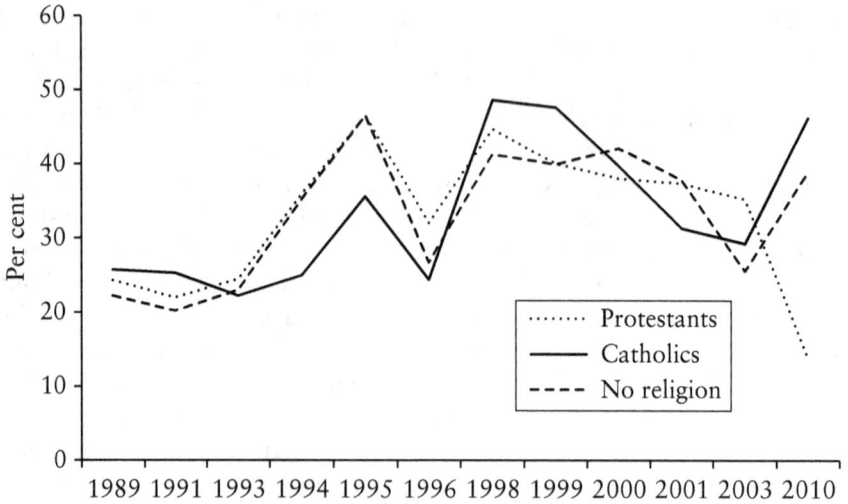

Figure 4.10 Likelihood of Irish unity, 1989–2010
The question was 'At any time in the next 20 years, do you think it is likely
or unlikely that there will be a United Ireland?' Figures are for those who
said 'likely'
Sources: Northern Ireland Social Attitudes Surveys, 1989, 1991, 1993–96;
Northern Ireland Life and Times Surveys, 1998–2003; Northern Ireland
Election Survey, 2010

The Northern Ireland Social Attitudes and Northern Ireland Life and
Times surveys show that upwards of half of the public also believes that
there will be a united Ireland within 20 years. Between 1989 and 2010,
Figure 4.10 shows that support for this view peaked at just under half of
the population in 1998, dropping to just under a third by 2003. The
proportions in each community considering Irish unity likely have also
been remarkably similar. Across most of the 12 surveys, the average
difference between the two communities is only a few percentage points,
an unusually high degree of unanimity on such a contentious issue. For
example, whereas 35 per cent of Protestants thought Irish unity likely
within 20 years in 2003, the equivalent proportion within the Catholic
community was 29 per cent. The only significant exception to this pattern was in 2010, when the Protestant view that Irish unity was likely
declined, while Catholics believed that the likelihood had increased.

There is, then, a widespread belief that Irish unity is becoming more,
and not less, likely, and that these shifts in opinions can be traced to the
changes in institutional arrangements which have given the Irish government a greater say in Northern Ireland affairs. Would Protestants accept

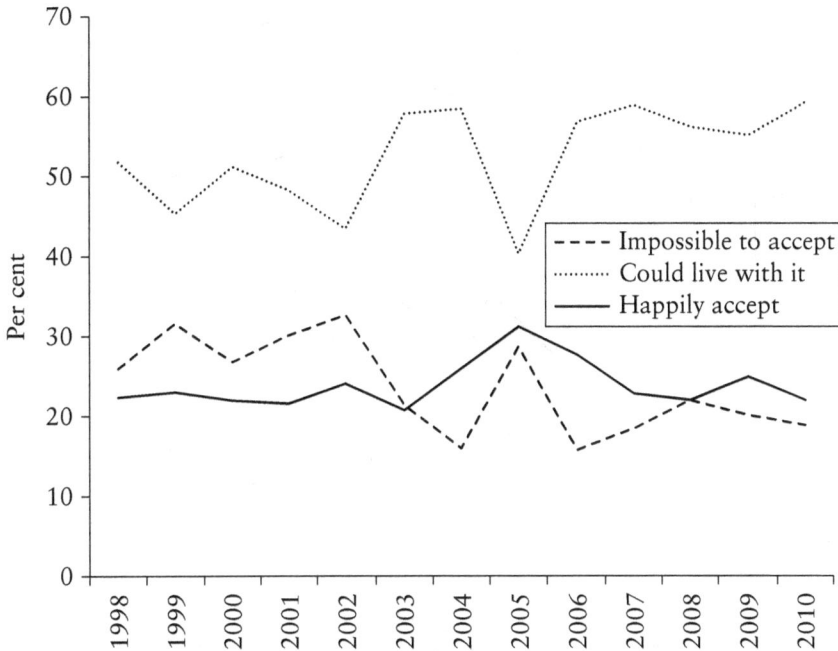

Figure 4.11 Acceptability of majority voting for Irish unity among
Protestants, 1998–2010
The question was 'If the majority of people in Northern Ireland ever voted to
become part of a United Ireland do you think you would find this almost
impossible to accept, would not like it, but could live with it if you had to, or,
would happily accept the wishes of the majority?' Estimates are for Protestants
who favoured continuing union with Britain
Source: Northern Ireland Life and Times Surveys, 1998–2010

Irish unity if a majority voted in favour of it, that is, if it came about
democratically? Figure 4.11 suggests that a majority would accept Irish
unity, though a significant minority would not accept it under any terms.
About half of Protestants opting for continued union with Britain say
that they 'could live with' Irish unity if they had to; the average over the
period of the surveys is 52 per cent. The remaining two groups, those
who would find it 'almost impossible to accept' Irish unity and those
who would 'happily accept the wishes of the majority', both average
24 per cent over the period. These figures suggest, then, grudging acceptance of Irish unity among Protestants but also demonstrate that there is
a significant minority who would simply not accept it, even if it was
democratically expressed.

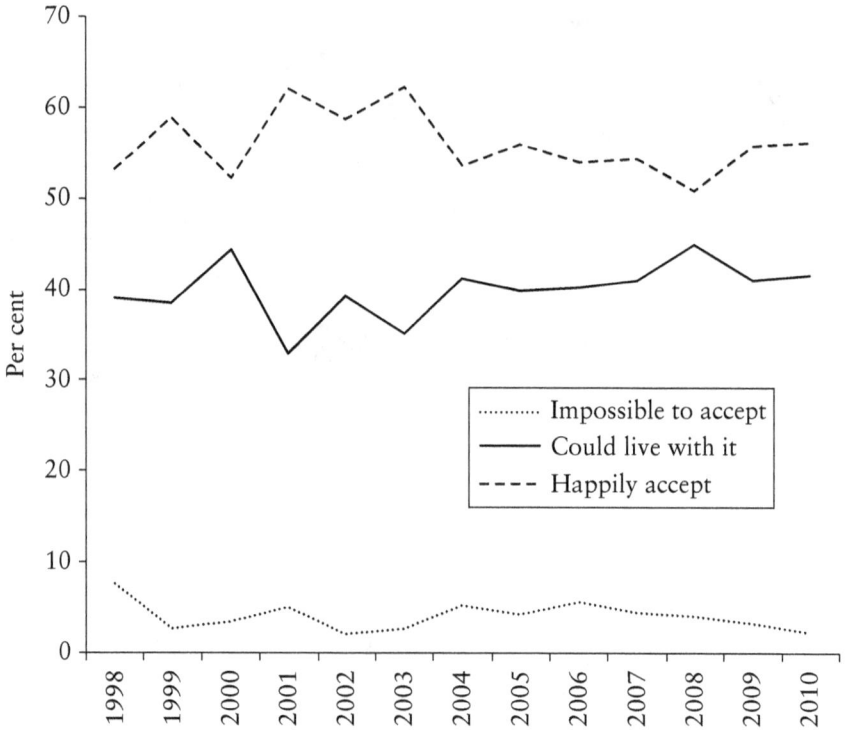

Figure 4.12 Acceptability of majority voting to reject Irish unity among Catholics, 1998–2010

The question was 'If the majority of people in Northern Ireland never voted to become part of a United Ireland do you think you would find this almost impossible to accept, would not like it, but could live with it if you had to, or, would happily accept the wishes of the majority?' Estimates are for Catholics who favoured Irish unity

Source: Northern Ireland Life and Times Surveys, 1998–2010

Catholics, not surprisingly, show less ambiguity about the prospects for Irish unity if it were not to come about through democratic means. When asked about the acceptability of a decision where the majority voted against Irish unity, Figure 4.12 shows that around 6 out of every 10 Catholics would happily accept such a decision, while about two-fifths say that they could live with it; hardly any of the respondents said that they would find such a scenario impossible to accept. Democratic decision-making on the constitutional question would therefore appear to have firmer roots among Catholics than among Protestants, a view that also finds support in earlier research (see Mac Ginty *et al.*, 2007).

If the majority of the Northern Ireland electorate were ever to vote in favour of Irish unity, these results suggest that such a move would encounter significant opposition among Protestants. While most would accept it, either positively or reluctantly, a significant minority remains who would find it difficult to live with. Catholics are much more likely to accept the absence of a majority vote in favour of Irish unity with equanimity. In other words, support for the constitutional status quo is more strongly expressed than is support for constitutional change, whether or not such change is underpinned by the expressed will of the majority. As we noted earlier, the roots of these differences lie in the fact that it is easier to accept the status quo, however imperfect, than it is to embrace a riskier and more uncertain future.

Conclusion

Public opinion in Northern Ireland on the constitution shows a remarkably high level of stability over an extended period. That stability is all the more remarkable when we consider the major changes in political institutions that have taken place during this time, especially with regard to the institutions that were created by the 1998 Belfast Agreement. Among Protestants, for example, 89 per cent supported the continued union with Britain in 1978; more than three decades later, in 2010, that figure is almost unchanged, at 91 per cent. Catholic opinion on the constitution has shown more fluctuation, but even here, 25 per cent supported Irish unity in 1978, and 32 per cent expressed the same view in 2010 – a modest increase. Public opinion on the constitution would therefore seem to be largely impervious to broader political changes. Nor do constitutional opinions appear to be influenced to any significant degree by upward social mobility or general changes across the society as a whole as Richard Breen (1996) has shown.

These findings suggest several implications. First, the hope that institutional design or societal change will remould constitutional preferences in the population has little empirical support. Institutional design may create democratic bodies within which differing constitutional preferences may be accommodated, but there is little or no prospect that these bodies will change public opinion on the constitution. The 1998 Belfast Agreement produced a consociational settlement that accommodated the aspirations of the participants, but did not confront the constitutional preferences or the identity politics that underpin the conflict (Horowitz, 2002). The emphasis of the post-1998 institutions was on executive power-sharing and functional co-operation on socioeconomic policy

(Brown and Mac Ginty, 2003). However, as the surveys show, the erratic operation of devolution has not endeared it to either community.

What the 1998 Agreement did achieve was effectively to remove the constitutional question from everyday politics. With the return of devolved government, particularly during the 2007–11 session, debate has increasingly moved to the social and economic questions of contemporary public policy. It is tempting to speculate what might have been achieved in shifting public opinion away from zero-sum constitutional preferences if the experience of devolution had been more positive. Nevertheless, what is clear is that devolution has produced significantly stronger support for Northern Ireland remaining part of the UK. In the years immediately following the 1998 Agreement, just one in five Catholics supported remaining in the UK; in 2010, that figure was one in two – a remarkable shift in constitutional preferences within a relatively short period of time.

A second implication concerns the prospects for constitutional change in the future. Protestants have traditionally been apprehensive about the possibility of a Catholic majority, given the historically higher levels of Catholic fertility. Extrapolations from census data suggest that there will be a Catholic majority in Northern Ireland sometime in the middle of the twenty-first century (see, e.g., Jardine, 1994). Setting aside the assumptions underlying such a prediction (especially differential fertility and emigration rates between the communities), a Catholic majority will not necessarily result in a majority favouring Irish unity. This is because, as we show in this chapter, just over half of all Catholics now support the union, as do almost all Protestants. Based on current trends in constitutional preferences, it would require a Catholic majority of at least 60 per cent of the population in order to produce a majority in favour of Irish unity.

Many studies have bemoaned the absence of a middle ground in Northern Ireland politics and a base from which inroads could be made into the zero-sum constitutional preferences of the two communities (see, e.g., Ruane and Todd, 1992; Graham and Shirlow, 1998). That the constitutional preferences of the two communities appear to be impervious to either social or political change suggests that the prospects for the creation of a significant middle ground will remain little more than a distant aspiration. Moreover, as we explain in the next chapter, the effective creation of two party systems – one unionist and one nationalist – has further eroded what little support already exists for the political centre. The constitutional preferences of the two communities are at the heart of the Northern Ireland conflict and, despite increasing support for the union among Catholics, look set to remain a key source of division for some considerable time to come.

Notes

1 The *Eire Nua* plan remained Sinn Fein policy until the split in the party and the formation of breakaway Republican Sinn Fein. *Eire Nua* remains the official policy of Republican Sinn Fein.

2 One caveat to this interpretation is the slight variation in question wording between 1968 and 1978, with the 1968 question asking about change in the next 10 years.

3 Much of these first two periods of devolution were marred by the boycotting of meetings by ministers, the abstention (and eventual) rotation of DUP ministers in the executive, multiple attempts to exclude Sinn Fein as well as endless and visceral battles over proxy-sovereign issues, such as policing, flags and decommissioning (see Wilford, 2007; Wilford and Wilson, 2000, 2008).

4 In addition to the electoral dominance of both the DUP and Sinn Fein in the 2007 Northern Ireland Assembly elections, part of the success of the 2007–11 Assembly – the first full term of devolved power in Northern Ireland in a generation – has been attributed to the warm and cordial relationship between Ian Paisley and Martin McGuinness who became collectively known as the 'chuckle brothers' (see Adshead and Tonge, 2009).

5 In a dispute with Margaret Thatcher over the restoration of political status, in all 10 prisoners, including Sands, who was elected an MP to Westminster during the hunger strike, starved themselves to death. The strike radicalized nationalist politics and became the driving force that enabled Sinn Fein to become a mainstream political party (see English, 2003).

6 When the NIO plan was leaked to the DUP, the proposed campaign was abandoned, and the secretary of state was forced to issue an apology (see Elliott, 1999).

7 The actual figures are 50.1 per cent (survey $N=186$) voting yes and 49.9 per cent ($N = 185$) voting no.

8 Indecision among Protestants is also demonstrated by the timing of the respondents' voting decision. Among Protestants, 32 per cent said that they made up their minds either during the last week of the campaign and 12 per cent on polling day itself. Among Protestants who said that they considered changing their vote, no less than 74 per cent said that they only decided on their vote during the last week of the campaign, compared to 48 per cent of Catholics.

9 As Wilford and Wilson (2008) note, the 2006 St Andrews Agreement stands in direct line of descent from the Belfast Agreement.

10 In 1998, the early release of prisoners was a major issue, with 78 per cent of Protestants opposing it, compared to 37 per cent of Catholics. By 2003, the prisoners had been released, and it was no longer a salient part of the Agreement components.

11 A survey of voters in 2005 found that 32 per cent were 'very' or 'fairly' satisfied with how MPs in general were doing their job (Healey *et al.*, 2005: 20).

12 For example, in February 2008, Ian Paisley junior was forced to resign as a DUP minister in the Northern Ireland Executive over a lobbying scandal involving a £50 million government land deal in his North Antrim constituency. His father, Ian Paisley senior, was drawn into the controversy when it emerged that he employed his son as a 'researcher' on a salary that was in addition to his MLA salary.

13 Members could designate themselves in this matter only once in each Assembly session.

5

Political parties

Political parties reflect the societies within which they operate. Competition between parties – in pursuit of resources, power and, occasionally, prestige – is very much based on the competition that occurs between the different social groups that exist within a society. In the new European democracies of the 1920s, the contemporary party systems that emerged were organized around the social cleavages that existed at the time of democratization – the famous 'freezing' hypothesis advanced by Lipset and Rokkan in 1967. In the majority of these societies, class and religion were the principal social divisions that divided the population, and the new parties therefore organized their appeals to voters around these divisions. In practice, religion provided a more cohesive and enduring basis for party support than class (Rose and Urwin, 1969). Class and religion have also provided the principal social divisions around which party competition has emerged in most of the newly democratizing postcommunist societies of central and eastern Europe (McAllister and White, 2007).

The new Northern Ireland party system of the 1920s followed this pattern, with the parties basing themselves exclusively on popular appeals to the two religious communities, reflecting the major social division of the time. In part, this followed the logic of a single social cleavage, sustained by long-term political socialization, acting as an obvious organizing principle for parties. The absence of any cross-cutting cleavages which might have mitigated the polarizing effects of religion also made it an obvious choice for the new parties. In part, too, the nascent party system was shaped by the events that had occurred before partition, starting with conflict over the first Home Rule Bill in 1886 and continuing through to the third Home Rule Bill in 1912. In short, then, the political parties that emerged in the 1920s were essentially sectarian in their appeal, and elections acted simply as religious head counts rather than as opportunities to attract voter support based on policies.

This chapter examines the Northern Ireland party system and the role that it has played in structuring the conflict. The first section examines the relationship between party support and religion since 1968, and the political engineering that the British government has experimented with in order to try and weaken the political salience of religion. The second section covers the social and demographic changes that have taken place since the start of the Troubles and demonstrates their implications for party fortunes. In the third section, the electoral institutions are outlined, with a particular focus on the burden that they place on the parties. The fourth section deals with the patterns of party competition, showing how intra-community party competition is now more important than inter-community party competition. The fifth section analyses the social bases of the parties, while the final section speculates if any of these changes will lead to the development of a pluralist democracy.

Party support and religion

Politics exacerbates the pressures that exist on group loyalty and solidarity and provides a sharp focus for the social divisions that exist within civil society. The ability of parties to manipulate and shape the environment within which they operate has long been recognized (see, e.g., Dalton *et al.*, 2011: chapter 9), and the political parties that dominated the new Northern Ireland state in 1920, the UUP and the Nationalist Party had a major incentive to ensure that religion remained the basis of their support. As we demonstrate later in this chapter, the parties were highly successful in this endeavour, and despite the changes in party labels that have occurred after 1968, religion remains at the heart of party competition today. Table 5.1

Table 5.1 Party identification and religion, pooled sample

	Protestant	Catholic	Other	No religion
Ulster Unionist	50	1	31	20
Democratic Unionist	28	*	32	15
(Total Unionist)	(78)	(1)	(63)	(35)
Alliance	9	6	10	19
SDLP	1	56	5	14
Sinn Fein	*	23	1	6
(Total Nat/Repub)	(1)	(79)	(6)	(19)
Other	12	14	21	27
Total	100	100	100	100
(N)	(10,767)	(8,205)	(1,350)	(1,863)

Estimates exclude those who said they did not have a party identification.
An asterisk denotes less than 0.5 per cent
Source: Northern Ireland Surveys, Pooled Sample, 1989–2010

shows that in the 1989–2010 pooled data set, 78 per cent of Protestants supported a unionist party (either Ulster Unionist or Democratic Unionist), while an almost identical proportion of Catholics similarly supported a party representing their community, either the SDLP or Sinn Fein. These figures are remarkably close to those that Richard Rose found in his 1968 Loyalty Survey, when 79 per cent of Protestants identified themselves as unionist and just 0.5 per cent as nationalist, and 51 per cent of Catholics were nationalist, 27 per cent Northern Ireland Labour Party and 5 per cent unionist (Rose, 1971: 235).

The strong link between party identification and religion has therefore remained stable since 1968, and Figure 5.1 shows little change in the overall patterns between 1968 and 2010, at least for Protestants. In 1978, 74 per cent of Protestants reported identifying with either the

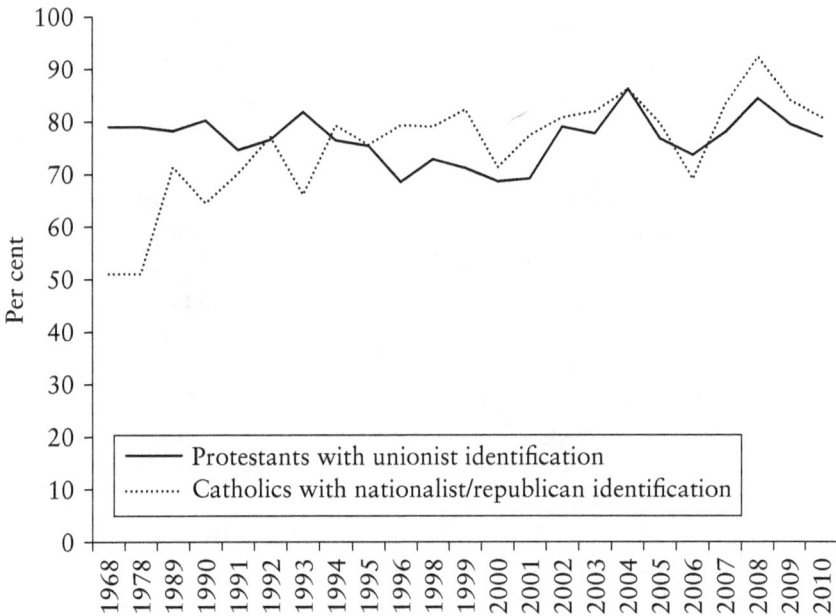

Figure 5.1 Religion and party identification, 1968–2010
Figures are the percentage of Protestants who identified with the Ulster
Unionist or Democratic Unionist parties and the percentage of Catholics who
identified with the SDLP or Sinn Fein. Estimates exclude those who said they
did not have a party identification
Sources: Northern Ireland Loyalty Survey, 1968; Northern Ireland Attitudes
Survey, 1978; Northern Ireland Social Attitudes Surveys, 1989–91, 1993–96;
Northern Ireland Election Survey, 1992; Northern Ireland Life and Times
Surveys, 1998–2010

Ulster Unionist or the DUP; in 1989, the same figure was 78 per cent and in 2010 77 per cent. Among Catholics, political cohesiveness has increased significantly, particularly compared to 1968 or 1978. In 1978, 51 per cent of Catholics identified with either the SDLP or Sinn Fein, rising to 71 per cent in 1989 and 81 per cent in 2010. As we observed in Chapter 4, the changes that have occurred in Catholic political behaviour since the early 1990s appear to have been the result of the perceived success of the Belfast Agreement in 1998 in satisfying Catholic political demands. In the surveys conducted between 1989 and 1996, the mean proportion of Catholics seeing themselves as having a nationalist or republican identification was 73 per cent; in the surveys conducted after the Agreement, the same figure was 81 per cent.

The direct involvement of the British government in Northern Ireland affairs from 1969 onwards began a long series of efforts at political engineering, designed to create cross-pressures on the parties and to reduce polarization around the religious cleavage. These efforts were predicated on the belief that the introduction of new political arrangements and institutions requiring the support of both communities would encourage a greater willingness to compromise on the part of the established parties. It was also hoped that such a change would encourage the emergence of new parties, which would advocate socioeconomic issues that would be less aligned with the dominant religious cleavage. The net effect of such cross-pressures, as pluralist theories of democracy predict, should be a multiparty system competing for voters on a range of socioeconomic interests.

The British government has focused on three areas of political engineering in order to try and create cross-pressures on the main political parties. The first is electoral engineering, perhaps the area most easily manipulated by politicians and the one that is often judged to have the most immediate chance of success. By manipulating the 'rules of the game' that determine which party wins the most seats and forms the government, electoral engineering can have a major impact on which parties run for office and which party (or parties) ultimately forms the government. Historically, the first-past-the-post electoral system that operated between 1929 and 1969 for the Stormont parliament fostered the sectarian two-party system, and the system produced low voter turnout and large numbers of uncontested seats, since there was frequently no incentive for the opposition party to contest a seat when the outcome was assured. The introduction of the single transferable vote (STV) method of proportional representation in 1973 was designed to promote inter-community vote transfers or, at the very least, to encourage vote transfers from one community to the centre ground. The evolution of

Northern Ireland's electoral institutions is examined in detail in the third section of the chapter.

The second engineering approach adopted by the British government was to put in place new political institutions designed to manage the political conflict and to reduce community polarization. This approach assumes that a functioning democracy depends not just on socioeconomic prosperity in order to thrive but on the design of effective political institutions. In turn, it was believed that the new rules enshrined in these institutions could effectively change the nature of the political game itself (Horowitz, 1985). The main institutional principle adopted by the British was that any regional government that was formed had to be based on power-sharing between the two communities, with cross-community support for key decisions. As we outlined in the first chapter, this has remained a core principle of Northern Ireland's institutional design since it was first enshrined in law in 1973.[1]

The third focus of political engineering has been to draw those who have been engaged in violence into electoral politics. Explanations for why the conflict had been so impervious to the many attempts that have been made to resolve it have varied widely, but a common theme has been the commitment of groups in both communities to the use of physical force and how this forms a major barrier to political progress. The IRA's commitment to a prolonged military campaign designed to force a British withdrawal from Northern Ireland is the most obvious example. During the late 1980s and early 1990s, the British government made strenuous efforts to draw the IRA into electoral politics through its political wing, Sinn Fein. This strategy eventually bore fruit with the August 1994 IRA ceasefire, which paved the way for Sinn Fein to contest the 1998 Assembly election, when it won 18 of the 108 seats. And in a move that would have been unthinkable just a few years earlier, two Sinn Fein elected representatives became ministers in the new power-sharing executive, giving *de facto* recognition to the partition of Ireland.

Religion remains the basis of party support in Northern Ireland, and there appears little prospect that this pattern will change, at least in the medium term. Nevertheless, since 1972 successive British governments have made determined efforts to weaken the political salience of religion through a range of political engineering approaches, from changes to the electoral system to the drawing of former paramilitaries into the electoral arena. How successful these attempts have been and what their long-term consequences are likely to be, we examine later in the chapter. Before turning to the long-term consequences of political engineering, we examine the social and demographic changes that have taken place

in Northern Ireland since the 1960s and what implications they have
had for the political parties.

Social and demographic change

Democracy is unthinkable without political parties. The two central
functions of parties within a competitive democracy are to mobilize
voters to turn out to vote and to convert them to their cause. How
parties go about their central tasks of mobilization and conversion is
influenced most crucially by the context within which they have to operate. In the first instance, the context is shaped by the social composition
of the electorate. The diversity of the society will determine which social
groups the parties will try and appeal to, and changes in the relative size
of those groups, or in their composition, will force the parties to adapt
their strategy accordingly, in order to maximize their vote. Second, the
context is determined by the institutional arrangements and by the rules
around which the competition for votes is organized.

The composition of the electorate in Northern Ireland has been
relatively slow to change, although, as we will see, there have been
significant long-term changes which have affected party competition.
The social context of party competition has been dominated, of course,
by the two religious communities. But the size and composition of the
two communities has changed overtime, a process which has had significant implications for the major political parties. Traditionally, Catholics
have had higher rates of fertility than Protestants, thus increasing the
Catholic proportion of the population. In practice, however, two factors
have reduced the Catholic rate of population growth.

The first factor that has affected the size of the Catholic population is
fertility. Since the 1960s, Catholic fertility has been declining to levels
which are similar to Protestants, as family planning has become more
widely accepted by many Catholics (Compton and Coward, 1989). The
patterns are more marked among urban, well-educated Catholics, whose
numbers have been increasing significantly. The second factor is emigration. For most of the last century, the higher rate of Catholic fertility has
been offset by much higher rates of Catholic emigration, sometimes as
high as 60 per cent of all net migration (Compton, 1985). There is also
some evidence to suggest that this higher rate of Catholic emigration
slowed during the late 1980s and 1990s, as Northern Ireland enjoyed
greater economic prosperity and educational and employment opportunities increased.[2]

Second, recent studies have demonstrated that more Catholic than
Protestant school leavers progress to higher education (see McQuaid

and Hollywood, 2008). Moreover, more Protestant than Catholic students, particularly those from middle-class families, tend to go to university in Britain, and as many as two-thirds do not return to Northern Ireland after they graduate (see Osborne, 2004, 2006). This is contrast to Northern Ireland graduates, where 96 per cent remain and are employed in Northern Ireland for at least six months after they graduate; significant numbers still remain even three years later (McQuaid and Hollywood, 2008). One important implication of this change in the relationship between education and migration is, as Robert Osborne (2006: 111) notes in his analysis of the 2001 census data, that the 'graduate labour market in Northern Ireland is becoming majority Catholic'.

There are difficulties in providing longitudinal evidence to support either of these propositions. As we noted in Chapter 2, the census data is complicated by the large proportion who did not answer the religion question – 9.4 per cent in the 1971 census and 18.5 per cent in the 1981 census. This compares to 1.9 per cent who did not answer the question in the 1961 census. Sample surveys do, however, provide an alternative source of longitudinal evidence which, taking into account sampling errors and differences in methodology, provide an indication of the broad trends. We would hypothesize that the Catholic proportion of the population has been increasing, largely because of reduced emigration, and that Catholics in the younger age groups would be increasing at a greater rate than the trend across the total population. Figure 5.2 tests these hypotheses using surveys conducted between 1968 and 2010.

The hypothesis that the Catholic proportion of the population has been increasing is supported by the evidence. The estimates in Figure 5.2 are the Protestant proportion of the total population minus the Catholic proportion of the total population. In 1968, Protestants made up 58 per cent of the total population, and Catholics 41 per cent, thus giving Protestants an advantage of 17 per cent. By 2009 (averaging the results of the 2008, 2009 and 2010 surveys), that advantage had decreased to just 11 per cent, or a 6 percentage-point decrease over the 40-year period covered by the surveys. The bulk of this change appears to have taken place during the 1970s and 1980s. The trends from the survey evidence suggest, then, that Catholics have indeed become more numerous in the population.

The results for the 18–34 age group (in the 1968 survey only aged 21–34, because of the higher voting age at that time) show that between 1968 and 1990, the Catholic proportion of the younger population increased dramatically. In 1968, 57 per cent of the population aged 21–34 were Protestant and 42 per cent Catholic, giving Protestants a 15 percentage-point advantage. By 1990, that advantage had disappeared,

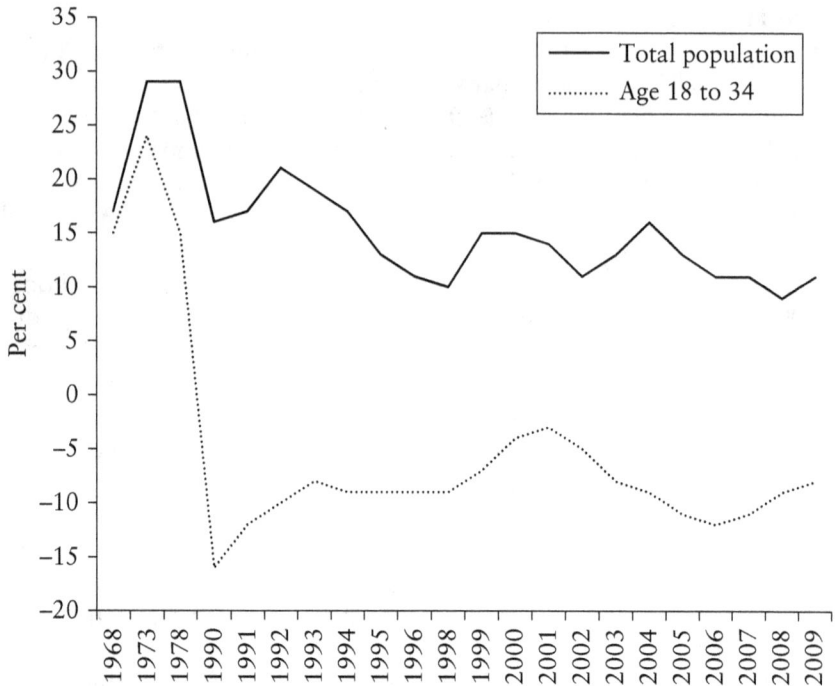

Figure 5.2 Protestant versus Catholic proportion of the population,
1968–2010
Figures are the Protestant proportion of the total population minus the
Catholic proportion of the population, estimated for all respondents and for
those aged 18–34 only. Estimates for 1990 onwards are three-year moving
averages. The 1973 survey was conducted among men only
Sources: Northern Ireland Loyalty Survey, 1968; Irish Social Mobility Survey,
1973; Northern Ireland Attitudes Survey, 1978; Northern Ireland Social
Attitudes Surveys, 1989–91, 1993–96; Northern Ireland Election Survey,
1992; Northern Ireland Life and Times Surveys, 1998–2010

and there were actually 16 per cent more Catholics in the age group
than Protestants. That level of difference has remained relatively stable
since then. Once again, this important demographic change appears to
have taken place during the 1970s and 1980s.

The results therefore provide strong suggestive evidence that not only
were there more Catholics within the Northern Ireland population from
the 1970s onwards – who would be potentially open to mobilization by
the political parties – but that the Catholic proportion of the younger
age groups increased at a disproportionate rate, at least during the 1970s

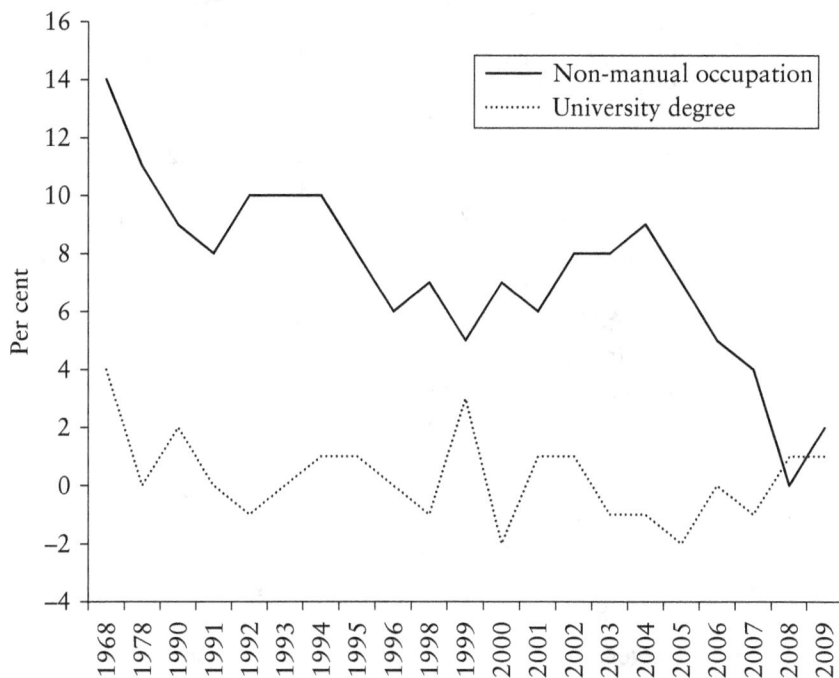

Figure 5.3 Religious differences in education and occupation, 1968–2010
Figures are the Protestant proportion with a non-manual occupation and a
university degree, minus the Catholic proportion. Estimates for 1990 onwards
are three-year moving averages
Sources: Northern Ireland Loyalty Survey, 1968; Northern Ireland Attitudes
Survey, 1978; Northern Ireland Social Attitudes Surveys, 1989–91, 1993–96;
Northern Ireland Election Survey, 1992; Northern Ireland Life and Times
Surveys, 1998–2010

and 1980s. As we will argue later, this important demographic trend has
had significant implications for party support, especially for Sinn Fein.
Moreover, the larger proportion of younger Catholics within the population than in the past also has implications for religious differences in
educational and occupational achievement.

To the extent that there are more younger Catholics in the population,
we would expect this to be reflected in increasing levels of educational
attainments among Catholics and, as a consequence, higher levels of
socioeconomic status. Figure 5.3 tests these hypotheses by using the
surveys conducted since 1968 to examine the trends in the Protestant
versus the Catholic proportion of the population possessing a university

degree and who are employed in a non-manual occupation. Once again, the trends show a clear picture. With respect to university education, 9 per cent of Protestants and 5 per cent of Catholics in 1968 reported possessing a degree, producing a Protestant advantage of 4 percentage points; in 2009 (averaged over the 2008, 2009 and 2010 surveys), 16 per cent of Protestants and 18 per cent of Catholics reported having a degree, a Protestant disadvantage of 2 percentage points. The trends demonstrate a picture of Catholic disadvantage in the 1960s and 1970s, which became a Protestant disadvantage during the 1990s and 2000s. This change, as noted earlier, may be explained by differential educational migration and non-return patterns between the two religious communities. There is a similar pattern with respect to occupation. In the 1960s, significantly more Protestants than Catholics were employed in a white-collar occupation; by the 1990s, that Protestant advantage had declined by about half, though it remained significant. By 2008, the differences were insignificant.

The trends therefore tell a consistent and telling story. Since the early 1990s, there have been more Catholics in the Northern Ireland population than at any time in the recent past, and disproportionately more come from younger age groups. Moreover, there is evidence to suggest that this trend has been caused at least in part by differential education and migration patterns between the two communities, particularly in relation to the probability of subsequently returning to Northern Ireland. Whatever the cause, an important consequence of this change has been the existence of greater proportions of educated and white-collar Catholics in the population. The party political implications of these demographic trends are examined later in the chapter.

The electoral system

The electoral system is the most obvious and direct means of trying to create cross-cutting divisions within a deeply divided society – a 'top-down' initiative. By changing the rules, it is hoped that the political game itself will be altered, away from mutual antagonism and towards co-operation to achieve mutually beneficial goals. As Donald Horowitz (1985: 601) has commented, 'where there is some determination to play by the rules, the rules can restructure the system so the game itself changes'. In deeply divided societies, a major goal of electoral reform is to fragment the party system so that the parties have to make alliances and coalitions in order to win and retain office. Such divided loyalties, it is argued, will help to reduce the cohesiveness of the competing communities. Electoral systems are often regarded as the first item of political

Table 5.2 Northern Ireland electoral systems since 1920

Regional			Westminster		
Elections	System	Members	Elections	System	Members
1921–25	PR STV	52	1920–48	FPTP (two multimember constituencies)	13
1929–69	FPTP	52	1949–82	FPTP	12
1973–82	PR STV	78	1982–95	FPTP	17
1996	Closed party list with party top-up	110	1995–	FPTP	18
1998–	PR STV	108			
	Local			European Union	
1921–69	FPTP		1979–	PR STV	3
1973–81	PR STV	526			
1985–89	PR STV	566			
1993–	PR STV	582			

PR STV, proportional representation single transferable vote; FPTP, first past the post. Post-1970 regional elections were conducted in 1973, 1982, 1996, 1998, 2003, 2007 and 2011
Sources: Elliott (1973); Elliott and Flackes (1999); http://www.ark.ac.uk/elections/

engineering in the conflict manager's toolbox, because of their familiarity to politicians and the quick results that they can sometimes achieve. As Horowitz (1991: 163) puts it, the electoral system is 'the most powerful lever of constitutional engineering for accommodation and harmony in severely divided societies'.

Northern Ireland has experienced a wide range of electoral systems since 1920, at all levels of government. Table 5.2 summarizes the main electoral systems that have operated at the regional, Westminster, local and European Union (EU) levels of government. At the regional level, elections to the Northern Ireland parliament at Stormont were based on the STV method of proportional representation in the 1921 and 1925 elections – the system that the British government had devised for both parts of Ireland and which was intended to ensure that no single party dominated the political system. Proportional representation was replaced by first-past-the-post in 1929, and that system was used for Stormont elections until 1969. Both systems elected 52 members to the lower house, with a further 26 members of the upper house, the Senate, elected by STV from the lower house.[3] When the Stormont system was replaced, it was decided that the number of members would be 78, this figure representing the sum of the lower and upper house members in the Stormont parliament. The system that replaced Stormont was based on STV, the system used in 1921 and 1925, with the exception of the 1996 Forum elections, which were held under a party list system, with a top-up of two seats for the ten parties gaining the highest votes.

Westminster elections have consistently used first-past-the-post, although between 1920 and 1948 there were two multimember constituencies and an additional member elected to represent Queen's University. In 1948, plural and university voting were abolished, and the 12 members were elected from single-member constituencies, increasing to 17 members in 1982 and 18 in 1995. The main contribution of Westminster elections is to provide the constituencies for the regional STV elections conducted since 1973. Since 1998, each of the 18 constituencies has returned 6 members, but in previous elections, because of disparities in population size, the number returned has varied from between 4 and 10.

Local government in Northern Ireland remained unchanged from the late nineteenth century until the late 1960s, organized around 73 local authorities of varying size and administrative capacity. The electoral system, like the unreformed local government system in Britain on which it was based, used plural voting. Many of the boundaries had been manipulated in order to ensure a Protestant majority, most blatantly in Londonderry (Whyte, 1990). As a result of a report commissioned by the Stormont government (Macrory Report, 1970), the system was reformed into 26 district councils encompassing 526 councillors elected by STV. As a consequence of several boundary changes, the number of councillors had increased to 582 by 1993.

Since 1979, local, provincial and Westminster elections have been complemented by elections to the EU parliament. EU elections have all used STV to return three members, with Northern Ireland forming one constituency. EU elections have been held every five years since 1979. Also worthy of note are the three referendums that have been held. The first, in 1973, was on Northern Ireland's constitutional future and was a key part of the Sunningdale Agreement. The second, held in 1975, was a UK-wide referendum on entry into the Common Market. The third referendum in 1998 was on the ratification of the Belfast Agreement, which was conducted simultaneously in Northern Ireland and in the Irish Republic; that referendum was analysed in detail in Chapter 4.

The plethora of electoral systems at different levels of government has particular implications for the political parties in Northern Ireland. Contesting these many and varied elections has considerable resource implications for the parties, since they must maintain local party organizations which have the capacity to mobilize the vote. Since 1970, if we count regional, Westminster, EU and district council elections, plus the three referendums, Northern Ireland has averaged nearly one election per year. For each of these elections, the parties must develop an election strategy and a set of policies and mount a campaign, all of which are complicated by the different electoral systems that are used. This electoral complexity has placed a considerable burden on the parties, particularly the smaller parties which often lack a full-time organizational base. The diversity of the systems and the considerable resources required to compete in them creates a significant entry barrier for new political parties.

The burden of contesting elections has limited the parties' ability to mobilize the vote. Traditionally, differential turnout between the two communities has been a distinctive feature of electoral competition in Northern Ireland. Prior to 1969, abstention among Catholics was widespread.[4] In part, this was a practical consequence of the large proportion of uncontested seats in Stormont elections. Between 1918 and 1970, no less than 37.5 per cent of all constituencies returned their members unopposed: since a Protestant majority was assured in many seats, nationalists had little incentive to nominate a candidate and contest the seat.[5] Even when seats were contested, Catholics often had little incentive to vote for a Nationalist candidate since the Nationalist Party's permanent minority status in parliament meant that they had no influence on public policy. One consequence of this situation was a high level of spoiled ballots, which was partly a protest against the lack of electoral choice, but also a means of ensuring that a person's vote was not impersonated.

The survey evidence suggests that up until the 1990s, Catholic rates of abstention were significantly higher than the same rates for Protestants (see Figure 5.4). In the 1968 Loyalty Survey, which asked about turnout in the 1965 Stormont election, 30 per cent of Catholics said that they had not voted, compared to 16 per cent of Protestants. In 1973, the gap between Protestant and Catholic abstention was similar, at 13 percentage points. Although we have no surveys from which to trace the trends between 1973 and 1992, the evidence in Figure 5.4 suggests that the differential rate of abstention between the two communities gradually decreased through the 1980s, dropping to just 6 percentage points in 1992. More dramatically, the trend actually reversed in the 1998 Assembly election, when 1 per cent more Catholics reported turning out to vote than Protestants.[6] Similar conclusions about greater Catholic electoral participation can be drawn from comparing turnout in nationalist-held constituencies compared to unionist-held ones (Evans and Tonge, 2009: 1026).

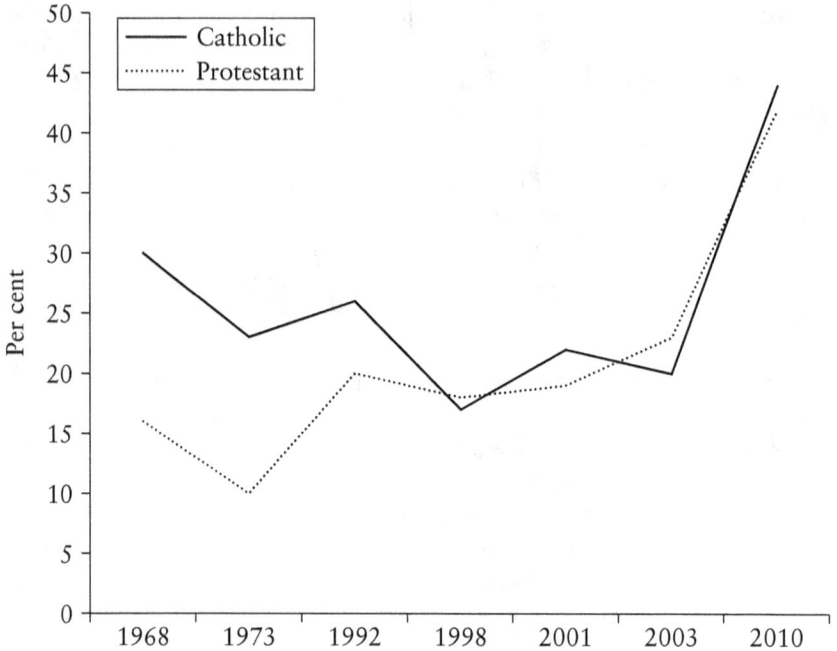

Figure 5.4 Non-voting by religion, 1968–2010
Questions relate to turnout at the election immediately prior to the survey
in question, except in the case of 1973, which relates to whether or not the
respondent 'usually' voted. The 1973 survey was conducted among men only
Sources: Northern Ireland Loyalty Survey, 1968; Irish Social Mobility Survey,
1973; Northern Ireland Election Surveys, 1992, 2001, 2003, 2010; Northern
Ireland Referendum and Election Survey, 1998

    While we cannot directly attribute this major change in Catholic vot-
ing behaviour to the electoral intervention of Sinn Fein, it is reasonable
to assume that Sinn Fein's entrance onto the electoral stage has played a
major role in mobilizing many Catholics to vote who would otherwise
have abstained. This is particularly the case for younger, less educated
Catholics who are disproportionately more likely to abstain from voting
and for whom Sinn Fein emerged as an attractive alternative to the SDLP.
At the same time, with the loss of self-government and the imposition of
power-sharing, Protestants have had less incentive to vote: in 2003, for
example, twice as many Protestants reported abstaining when compared
to 1973.
    For a population little more than the size of an average British or U.S.
city, Northern Ireland has had a wide diversity of electoral systems at

four levels of government. It has also sustained an electoral cycle that in recent years has averaged almost one election per year. This is a level of electoral complexity and activity that has few parallels in the advanced democracies. The changes in the election rules that have occurred since 1970 have also coincided (or been the cause of) a significant change in electoral participation, as we have shown here. Catholics are now as likely to vote as Protestants, following half a century when the level of Catholic abstention was higher than that for Protestants. All of these structural and behavioural changes have had profound implications for the party system, and these are examined in the next section in the context of post-1969 changes in party competition.

Patterns of party competition

Since the establishment of Northern Ireland in 1920, party competition has been organized around the dominant religious cleavage, reflecting the differing constitutional goals of the two communities. From 1920 up until the late 1960s, Northern Ireland had an essentially two-party system, with one unionist party and one nationalist party. In line with the British government's political engineering which started in 1972, the party system began to fragment, first on the unionist side and then later, in the 1980s, on the nationalist side. Since then, Northern Ireland has effectively maintained two-party systems, one unionist and one nationalist, and competition takes place within each (Evans and Duffy, 1996). More recently, it has been argued that intra-community party competition has evolved into 'ethnic outbidding', with the main groups competing to take on the role of each community's representative (Mitchell *et al.*, 2009).

From 1920 until 1969, the UUP was the embodiment of mainstream unionism. The UUP has its origins in Protestant opposition to home rule in the late nineteenth century, and with the partition of Ireland in 1920, it became the unchallenged representative of the Protestant community, employing a hegemonic rule that effectively stifled political opposition from other parts of the Protestant community. The only minor threat to the UUP prior to the outbreak of the Troubles came during the 1960s, when the nascent Northern Ireland Labour Party began to make some inroads into UUP support among the Protestant working class in Belfast. More a movement than an organized, disciplined political party, the UUP was characterized by a federal structure and links to the Orange Order.[7] The two major attempts at reform of the UUP – when Terence O'Neil was Prime Minister in the 1960s and under the leadership of Brian Faulkner in the early 1970s – both ended in failure (Walker, 2004).

The UUP's main competitor for the unionist vote has been the DUP. The DUP was formed in 1971 mainly from activists in the Protestant Unionist Party, who were opposed to the reforming efforts of Terence O'Neill. Largely associated with the charismatic figure of Ian Paisley, the DUP has had strong links to the Free Presbyterian Church, which Paisley had founded in 1951 (see Bruce, 1986). The DUP's strong emphasis on social issues attracted the support of Protestant working-class voters, particularly in Belfast, while Paisley's religious fundamentalism proved particularly appealing to many rural Protestants. Throughout the 1980s and 1990s, the DUP remained intractably opposed to any compromise on the constitutional issue and was able to capitalize on Protestant disaffection with 1998 Belfast Agreement, using the highly emotional slogan 'the Union is under threat'. The DUP was particularly effective in mobilizing Protestant support around the IRA's reluctance to decommission arms and the British government's commitment to the early release of paramilitary prisoners.

The shifting electoral fortunes of the UUP and the DUP from the 1969 Stormont election to the 2011 Assembly election are shown in Figure 5.5. Two observations are worthy of note. The first is that the total unionist and loyalist vote over the period has declined consistently. In the 1969 Stormont election, the total unionist vote was 67.4 per cent; in the 2011 Assembly election, that vote declined to 42.4 per cent, an overall decline of 25 percentage points. This decline has several explanations, which have been touched upon earlier in the chapter. One is the decreasing proportion of Protestants within the general population, so that there are simply fewer potential Protestant voters available to support the parties. The other explanation is the patterns of differential turnout between Catholic and Protestant voters. More Protestant voters have decided to abstain from voting, particularly after the 1998 Belfast Agreement, thereby further reducing the overall unionist vote.

The second observation from Figure 5.5 is the steady decline in the UUP vote over the period and the equally steady rise in the DUP vote. The DUP first exceeded the UUP vote in the 2003 Assembly elections,[8] when the DUP won 25.6 per cent of the first preference vote and the UUP 22.7 per cent. However, in both the subsequent 2005 Westminster election and in the 2007 and 2011 Assembly elections, the DUP's vote was about double that of the UUP. Indeed, in the 2005 election, the UUP won only one seat, with the party leader, David Trimble, ignominiously losing in his Upper Bann constituency, while the DUP won nine out of a total of 18 seats. The 2005 and 2007 election outcomes represented a significant reordering of politics in Northern Ireland, with the DUP becoming the preferred choice of the unionist community. As a result,

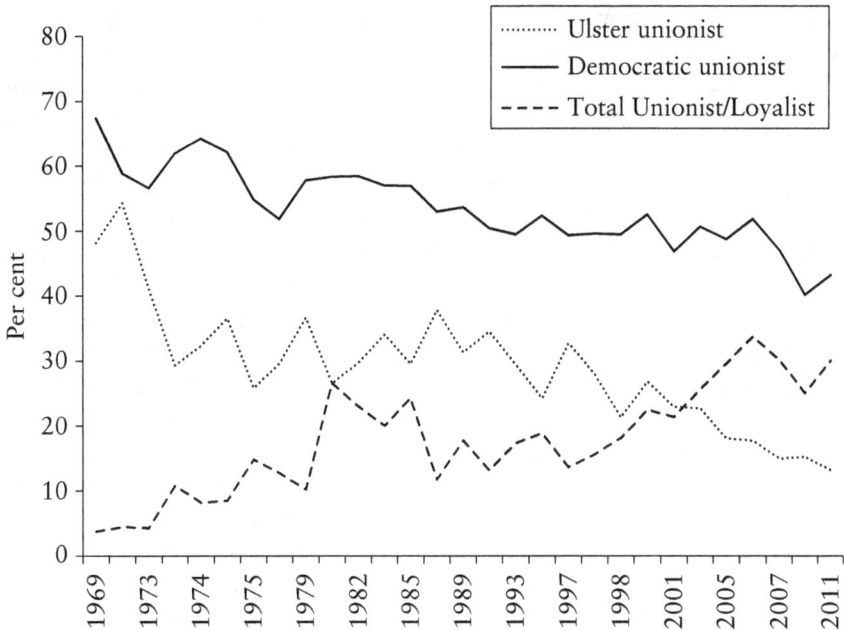

Figure 5.5 Unionist and loyalist support in Northern Ireland elections, 1969–2011

The elections are as follows: 1969, Stormont; 1970, February and October 1974, 1979, 1983, 1987, 1992, 1997, 2001, 2005, 2010, Westminster; 1973, 1975, 1982, 1996, 1998, 2003, 2007, 2011, Assembly (in 1975 Convention, in 1996 Forum); and 1973, 1977, 1981, 1985, 1989, 1993, 1997, 2001, 2005, District Council. In 1969 and 1970, the DUP results are for Protestant Unionist and in June 1973 Democratic Unionist Loyalist Coalition
Sources: Elliott and Flackes, 1999; http://www.ark.ac.uk/elections/

the party became the lead negotiator in the talks with Sinn Fein that led to the St Andrews Agreement in 2006, and in May 2007 Paisley became first minister in the power-sharing executive with Sinn Fein's Martin McGuinness as his deputy.[9]

The party system within the Catholic community is equally bifurcated, with again one party in decline and one party displaying an incremental increase. Between 1920 and 1969, the main representative of the Catholic community was the Nationalist Party, the Northern Ireland remnant of the Irish Parliamentary Party that had dominated nationalist politics from the 1880s to the First World War. In Northern Ireland, the Nationalist Party was characterized by periodic abstention from parliament, a concern with local, clientelist politics, and ambiguity towards the use of violence by the IRA. The rise of the civil rights movement effectively sidelined the Nationalist Party and made the creation of a new party, capable of effectively representing the nationalist community, more pressing (Purdie, 1990). In August 1970, the SDLP was formed, bringing together civil rights leaders and members of the National Democratic Party, the Northern Ireland Labour Party and the Republican Labour Party (McAllister, 1977; Murray, 1998; Murray and Tonge, 2005).

From the outset, the SDLP represented an uneasy balance between traditional nationalist goals and socialist ideology. Although the party recognized that the constitutional position of Northern Ireland could only be changed by the consent of the majority, several of the original founders, notably John Hume (who was party leader from 1979 to 2001), clearly viewed the SDLP as a means of advancing nationalist goals without resorting to political violence. The party's socialist credentials are reflected in its membership of the Socialist International and its links to the British and Irish labour parties, as well as to other European centre-left parties. The party's first leader, Gerry Fitt, was a committed socialist, and he resigned from the party in 1979 over the party's desire to include the Irish government in any future political settlement in Northern Ireland, a key principle for the nationalist wing of the party.

During the 1970s and 1980s, the SDLP experienced little competition for the nationalist vote. That began to change in the late 1980s, with the increasing interest of Sinn Fein, the political wing of the IRA, in electoral politics. For most of the twentieth century, Irish republicanism had existed primarily as a military organization, eschewing politics and suspicious of those who espoused it. Excursions into electoral politics were few and often bitter; most republicans refused to recognize the legitimacy of the Northern Irish state and therefore regarded elections as illegitimate. During the 1970s and 1980s, the Provisional IRA embarked on an intense military campaign, and although it maintained Sinn Fein as its political mouthpiece, it was entirely subservient to the movement's military strategy. In practice, the SDLP became the political representative of the Catholic community and reaped whatever political gains flowed from the IRA's military campaign (McAllister, 1977; Murray, 1998).

In the 1970s, many Irish republicans believed that the IRA's military campaign could on its own achieve the goal of removing the British from Northern Ireland, but by the early 1980s, the prospect of a quick military victory had receded. A series of IRA ceasefires in the mid-1970s had not delivered any tangible political progress, and the election of Margaret Thatcher's Conservative government in 1979 brought major reversals. The British government prepared for a long-term military commitment to Northern Ireland. The failure of the 1981 hunger strikes to gain significant concessions from the British convinced a new generation of IRA leaders that Britain would not withdraw from Northern Ireland in response solely to a military campaign (O'Brien, 1999: 124). The key to integrating a political strategy with a military one to force a British withdrawal was taken in 1986 when the long-standing abstentionist policy was reversed. The IRA had now decided on a dual approach to achieving its goals: electoral activity combined with a military campaign – 'a ballot paper in one hand and an Armalite in the other' (McAllister, 2004).

By 1988, Gerry Adams, the Sinn Fein leader, and John Hume had commenced talks to try and identify any common ground in their respective approaches to solving the Northern Ireland problem; these rapidly became more formal discussions between the two parties. Although the talks ended in September 1988 without agreement, they paved the way for the IRA to declare an indefinite ceasefire in 1994 and, after a return to military activity between 1995 and 1997, a permanent ceasefire in 1997, followed by the decommissioning of IRA weapons in 2005. Since the 1980s, Sinn Fein has deftly shaped its appeal in order to converge with majority nationalist opinion and to portray itself as the main representative of the nationalist community, displacing the SDLP. It has emphasized the rhetoric of equality between the communities, which dovetails into the consociational nature of the Belfast Agreement through the principle of 'parity of esteem'. Several studies have observed how the rhetoric of equality has come to dominate Sinn Fein thinking, moving nationalists away from an identity based on their traditional role as a victim (McGovern, 2004).

The patterns of electoral support for nationalism and republicanism in Northern Ireland since 1969 show a steady increase in overall support, starting at 18.8 per cent in 1969 and rising consistently, reaching 42.0 per cent in the 2010 Westminster election (see Figure 5.6). The SDLP has attracted around about one in five of all of the votes cast, although that declined to 14.2 per cent in the 2011 Assembly election, its lowest vote share since 1973. By contrast, Sinn Fein, starting at 10.1 per cent in the 1982 Assembly election, increased its vote consistently immediately after the hunger strikes, gaining its highest ever vote – 26.9 per cent – in the 2011 Assembly election. Indeed, Sinn Fein has consistently exceeded the SDLP vote since 2001. Until the late 1990s, the entry of Sinn Fein into competitive elections had not harmed the SDLP's vote; this resulted from Sinn Fein's mobilization of a disproportionate number of previous Catholic non-voters, notably younger, less educated men (McAllister, 2004). However, since 2001 the continued growth in the Sinn Fein vote does appear to have been at the expense of the SDLP, with the total nationalist and republican vote remaining stable.

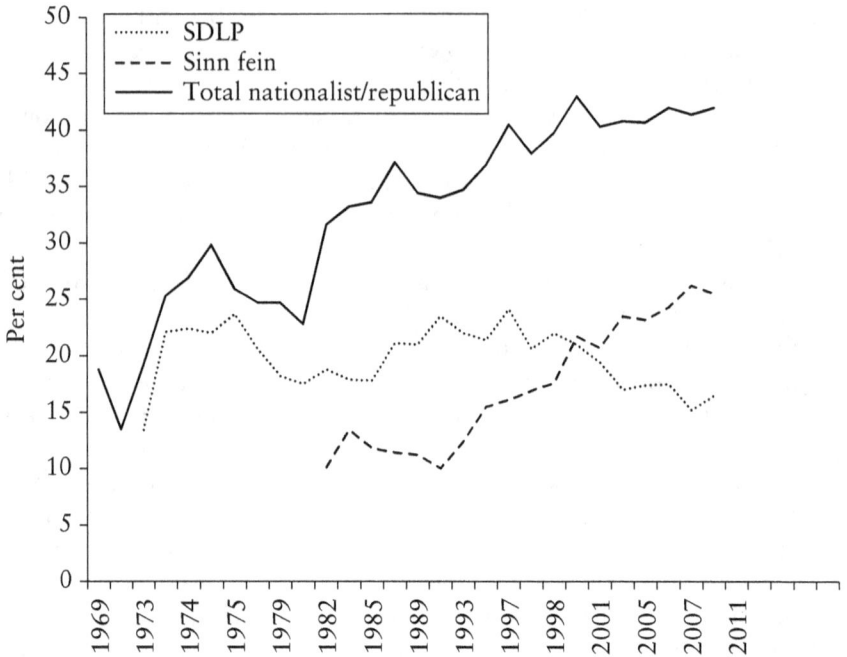

Figure 5.6 Nationalist and Republican support in Northern
Ireland elections, 1969–2011
See notes to Figure 5.5 for election dates
Sources: Elliott and Flackes, 1999; http://www.ark.ac.uk/elections/

The nature of the Northern Ireland party system – with parties competing for support solely from their respective communities – has meant
that the centre ground has inevitably been small; indeed, so illusive has
the centre ground been that Paul Arthur and Keith Jeffery (1996: 51)
refer to it as 'mythical'. Nevertheless, at various times around 10 per cent
of the vote has been cast for parties that can be regarded as biconfessional, in the sense that they reject the confessional politics of the unionist
and nationalist communities. In the 1950s and 1960s, the Northern
Ireland Labour Party attempted to occupy this middle ground by bringing
Protestants and Catholics together on socioeconomic issues while avoiding
sectarian ones; as Richard Rose (1971: 231) notes, this approach meant
that the party was better described as inter-confessional rather than
biconfessional. By the early 1970s, the party had been swept away by
the twin effects of the Troubles and the formation of the Alliance Party
as a more effective vehicle for mobilizing the biconfessional centre
ground (Evans and Tonge, 2001).

The Alliance Party was formed in 1970 from moderate unionists who had supported Terence O'Neill's attempts to reform the UUP and moderate nationalists who wished to see an accommodation between the two religious communities. Until the 1990s, the party attracted around 1 in every 10 votes cast, although it has generally performed better when sectarian tensions were low. Since the late 1990s, the consociational nature of the Belfast Agreement and its explicit recognition of the need to accommodate unionism and nationalism have challenged Alliance's basic assumption that 'unionism and nationalism ... [are] ... ideologies to be overcome, rather than accommodated' (Evans and Tonge 2003: 27). In effect, the recognition of the sectarian nature of the conflict and its institutionalization in the political system has marginalized the centre ground.[10]

The changes that have taken place in party competition in Northern Ireland since 1969 have been relatively small, but their consequences are nonetheless profound. First, where two parties once dominated party competition across a religious cleavage, there are now four parties, and within each community, there are two parties which compete for the support of voters. Second, while overall support for unionism has declined, support for nationalism and republicanism has increased. We have already speculated on the reasons for this, such as an increase in the proportion of Catholics within the population and changes in the rates of differential election turnout between Catholics and Protestants. Third, it is the newer 'radical' parties that are now electorally dominant within their respective communities. Most of these changes have come about as a result of the British government's efforts at electoral engineering, demonstrating the potential of changes to the 'rules of the game'. But while these efforts have produced a multiparty system, they have not carved out a centre ground from which a pluralist democracy could emerge. Electoral engineering clearly has its limits.

The social bases of the parties

Theories of political socialization predict that voters inherit the partisanship of their parents. Given the changes that have taken place in the Northern Ireland party system over the past 40 years, it would appear that voters inherit less a specific party political attachment than a broad unionist or nationalist attachment. Within each broad attachment, individual parties may compete for the loyalties of Protestant or Catholic voters, and the voters themselves are not wedded to any specific party label. This means that the parties may therefore appeal to particular social groups within their respective communities, based on what they calculate will be most likely to maximize their vote (Evans and Duffy, 1996). There is already some evidence that this has taken place within the two communities, with the DUP and Sinn Fein making a distinctive appeal to voters based on their socioeconomic interests, above and beyond their stances on the constitutional issue.

While the two communities are divided on religion, there have been historically important divisions among the Protestant denominations in terms of party support. The most obvious is between the Free Presbyterians and the other Protestant denominations, caused by Ian Paisley's dual role as founder of both the Free Presbyterian Church and the DUP (Bruce, 1986). However, we might also expect religiosity to influence party support, insofar as more fundamentalist Protestants would tend towards the more religiously aligned DUP, while more liberal Protestants might tend to support the UUP, or perhaps the Alliance Party. The large sample size in the pooled surveys enables us to address these and other issues with some certainty and to overcome the small sample size problem that has hindered firm conclusions in other studies (see, e.g., Evans and Duffy, 1996: footnote 36).

There are significant differences between the Protestant denominations in their party support. Table 5.3 shows that the DUP, as expected, attracts more Free Presbyterian support than the UUP, while the UUP garners more support from Church of Ireland and Presbyterian members. Although Free Presbyterians constitute only 1.2 per cent of our pooled sample, no less than 77 per cent of them report identifying with the DUP, and just 9 per cent support the UUP. The DUP also attracts more support from the small Protestant denominations, which are disproportionately fundamentalist in their religious outlooks. Support for the biconfessional Alliance Party is also notable for its denominational base, with the Alliance Party gaining support from Methodists.

The evidence for religiosity in the second part of Table 5.3 is more ambiguous, at least for the two main Protestant parties. The DUP has fewer devout supporters than the UUP and almost twice as many supporters who are nonattenders. This suggests that DUP support represents a coalition of the devout and the secular, united by a common opposition to compromise on the constitutional issue, as Bruce (1994) and others (see, e.g., McAuley, 2004) have argued. There are also important variations in religiosity between SDLP and Sinn Fein supporters; while both parties draw over 9 out of every 10 of their supporters from the Catholic community, Sinn Fein supporters are significantly less likely to be frequent church attenders than their SDLP counterparts. For example, while 69 per cent of SDLP supporters attend church once a week or more, the same figure for Sinn Fein supporters is 51 per cent. We explore below

Table 5.3 Religious affiliation, church attendance and party identification, pooled sample

	UUP	DUP	SDLP	SF	Alliance
Church affiliation					
Protestant					
Anglican	33	25	2	1	20
Presbyterian	43	39	1	*	22
Methodist	7	6	*	*	6
Free Presbyterian	1	7	*	0	*
Other	2	4	*	0	2
(Total Protestant)	(86)	(81)	(3)	(1)	(50)
Catholic	1	1	91	93	25
Other	7	11	1	1	7
No religion	6	7	5	5	18
Total	100	100	100	100	100
(N)	(6,211)	(3,815)	(5,033)	(2,044)	(1,877)
Church attendance					
Once a week or more	40	33	69	51	45
Two or three times a month	12	9	9	11	12
Once a month	10	8	5	7	8
Several times a year	13	13	6	10	11
Less often	12	17	6	12	11
Never	13	20	5	9	13
Total	100	100	100	100	100
(N)	(5,801)	(3,500)	(4,750)	(1,921)	(1,513)

An asterisk denotes less than 0.5 per cent support
Source: Northern Ireland Surveys, Pooled Sample, 1989–2010

whether this is an artefact of the parties' social support or a distinct difference in its own right.

Predictions about gender and age differences in party support are more difficult to make than those based on religion. We might expect men to be more supportive of Sinn Fein than women, since the party's origins are as the political mouthpiece of a physical force movement and women are traditionally less supportive than men of physical force. We might also expect the newer parties – the DUP and Sinn Fein – to gain more support from younger people than the established parties since they might be seen as more active and dynamic. These predictions are partially born out in the results in Table 5.4. Men are more likely to support Sinn Fein than any of the other parties, but in general the

Table 5.4 Gender, age and party identification, pooled sample

	UUP	DUP	SDLP	SF	Alliance
Gender					
Male	46	47	43	49	42
Female	54	53	57	51	58
Total	100	100	100	100	100
(N)	(6,266)	(3,853)	(5,053)	(2,050)	(1,891)
Age					
18–24	4	11	7	16	4
25–34	11	20	17	23	14
35–44	16	20	20	22	19
45–54	17	14	18	15	20
55–64	19	14	15	12	20
65–74	18	13	14	7	14
75+	15	8	9	5	9
Total	100	100	100	100	100
(N)	(6,246)	(3,844)	(5,035)	(2,048)	(1,888)

Source: Northern Ireland Surveys, Pooled Sample, 1989–2010

differences are not large. The young are more likely to support the DUP than the UUP and to support Sinn Fein rather than the SDLP. Here, the differences are more substantial: while 61 per cent of Sinn Fein's support comes from those aged under 45, the same figure for the SDLP is 44 per cent. The differences are even bigger for the two unionist parties: 61 per cent of the DUP's supporters are aged under 45, compared to 31 per cent for the UUP.

In theory, intra-community political differences should be more strongly based on attained characteristics, such as education and occupation, rather than on ascribed characteristics such as age or gender. Both the DUP and Sinn Fein have projected their appeals, particularly in their formative years, to working-class voters, by adopting a centre-left stance on many social issues. In the early years of intra-unionist competition, for example, the DUP's position on social issues was brought into sharp relief by the UUP's traditional alliance with the British Conservative Party. Although this link was finally severed in 1985 in protest against the Anglo-Irish Agreement, the UUP is still popularly regarded as ideologically close to the Conservatives (Walker, 2004). Sinn Fein, too, has been able to cast itself as a centre-left party. Although the SDLP has formally socialist goals, its leadership has always been middle class, and Sinn Fein have been able to exploit this by portraying themselves as the

Table 5.5 Education, occupation and party identification, pooled sample

	UUP	DUP	SDLP	SF	Alliance
Education					
Degree	11	7	16	10	27
Postsecondary	18	16	19	18	26
Secondary	26	27	22	26	25
No qualifications	45	50	43	46	22
Total	100	100	100	100	100
(N)	(6,266)	(3,853)	(5,053)	(2,050)	(1,891)
Occupation					
Professional	4	2	4	2	8
Managerial	27	18	28	21	36
Skilled non-manual	27	25	21	17	26
(Total non-manual)	(58)	(45)	(53)	(40)	(70)
Skilled manual	17	20	18	23	12
Partly skilled	17	22	19	25	14
Unskilled	8	13	10	12	4
(Total manual)	(42)	(55)	(47)	(60)	(30)
Total	100	100	100	100	100
(N)	(3,616)	(2,442)	(3,136)	(1,320)	(996)

Source: Northern Ireland Surveys, Pooled Sample, 1989–2010

legitimate representative of the Catholic working class and by being more active on community issues (Murray and Tonge, 2005).

There are substantial attained differences between the two competing parties in each community. Table 5.5 shows that UUP and SDLP supporters have generally higher social status than their intra-community competitors, the DUP and Sinn Fein, respectively. For example, 11 per cent of UUP supporters possess a degree compared to 7 per cent of DUP supporters. SDLP supporters are even more likely to have a degree, with 16 per cent saying that they possess a university education. In terms of occupation, 53 per cent of SDLP supporters are employed in non-manual occupations, compared to 40 per cent of Sinn Fein supporters; the pattern is similar for the two unionist parties. The party attracting the largest proportion of supporters with higher socio-economic status is the Alliance Party: 27 per cent of Alliance supporters have a university education, and 70 per cent work in a non-manual occupation.

Many of the effects reported in the bivariate results in Tables 5.3–5.5 are strongly inter-correlated so that, for example, differences in church

Table 5.6 Explaining intra-community party competition, pooled sample

	UUP vs. DUP		SDLP vs. SF	
	Est	(SE)	Est	(SE)
Protestant denomination (Anglican)				
Presbyterian	−0.24**	(0.05)	na	
Methodist	−0.09	(0.10)	na	
Free Presbyterian	−3.19**	(0.21)	na	
Other Protestant	−0.92**	(0.08)	na	
Church attendance	0.56**	(0.06)	0.70**	(0.09)
Gender (male)	0.01	(0.04)	−0.28**	(0.06)
Age	0.04**	(0.00)	0.04**	(0.00)
Education (tertiary)				
Secondary	−0.48**	(0.08)	−0.62**	(0.09)
No qualifications	−1.19**	(0.08)	−1.19**	(0.10)
Political period (pre-Agreement)				
Agreement/immediate aftermath	−0.22**	(0.07)	−0.74**	(0.10)
Direct rule	−1.06**	(0.07)	−1.40**	(0.10)
Restoration of the Assembly	−1.44**	(0.08)	−1.78**	(0.11)
Constant	0.03		0.62**	
Pseudo R-squared	0.14		0.11	
(N)	(9,244)		(6,470)	

Significant at $**p < 0.01$; $*p < 0.05$
Logistic regression results showing parameter estimates and (in parentheses) robust standard errors predicting UUP (scored 1) versus DUP (scored 0) and SDLP (scored 1) versus Sinn Fein (scored 0) support, for Protestants and Catholics, respectively. All variables are binary except for age which is scored in single years and church attendance which is scored on a scale from 0 (never attends) to 1 (attends once a week or more). Anglican is the omitted category for religious denomination among Protestants, tertiary education is the omitted category for education, and surveys undertaken in the pre-Agreement period (1989–96) are the omitted category for political events.
Source: Northern Ireland Surveys, Pooled Sample, 1989–2010

attendance may be an artefact of socioeconomic status. In order to control for these various confounding factors, Table 5.6 reports the results of a logistic regression analysis which predicts UUP versus DUP support among Protestants and SDLP versus Sinn Fein support among Catholics.[11] Because occupation is relevant only to those who are labour force participants, it is excluded. Since our sample is based on pooled surveys conducted between 1989 and 2010 and support for the various parties has fluctuated significantly over this time period, we also include a series of dummy variables to capture the influence of these changes. These variables represent four key transitional periods: before the signing of the Belfast Agreement (1989–96), immediately after the Agreement was signed (1998–2002), during the last sustained period of the suspension of the Assembly (2003–06) and when devolution was restored (2007–10).

Within both communities, social support for the newer of the two parties – the DUP among Protestants and Sinn Fein among Catholics – is very similar. In both communities, age is important, with younger supporters preferring the newer of the two. The political period in which the survey was conducted is also important, with the newer party attracting consistently more support with the passage of time. The other social factors also work in similar ways. UUP supporters are more likely to be better educated, as are SDLP supporters, and more frequent church attendance also leads to support for the established party in each community. The only social factor of little importance is gender, although men are more likely to support Sinn Fein as we demonstrated in the bivariate results. Finally, the importance of denomination in shaping party support among Protestants is largely confirmed.

These findings confirm the patterns of social support that we observed in Tables 5.3–5.5, but they also clarify them in important ways. First, age and particularly the passage of time explain much of the increasing support for the DUP and Sinn Fein. Both parties have managed to appeal to younger supporters in their communities, and the attractiveness of that appeal has clearly resonated more strongly with the passage of time. Second, there are clearly emerging socioeconomic divisions in party support within each community which have the potential to provide some cross-cutting cleavages. While these cleavages are not inter-communal, and therefore will not have the consequences for democratic stability that pluralist theories imply, they may represent emerging sources of division if and when the dominant constitutional issue was to become less relevant.

Party support and the Belfast Agreement

Of all the issues that have emerged in Northern Ireland over the past half a century, the 1974 Sunningdale Agreement and the 1998 Belfast Agreement have perhaps been the most contentious for the political parties. The Sunningdale Agreement brought representatives of the Ulster Unionists, SDLP and Alliance into a power-sharing government for the first time. However, sustained opposition from the DUP and other loyalists resulted in a general strike in May 1974 which brought the collapse of the power-sharing experiment. As we discussed in chapter 1, the 1998 Belfast Agreement was equally divisive, with the DUP being again the party that was most vociferously opposed, particularly to the provisions governing the early release of paramilitary prisoners and the decommissioning of paramilitary weapons.

To what extent did party supporters change their views about the 1998 Agreement as the experience of devolution progressed? Table 5.7 examines how far Democratic Unionist, Ulster Unionist and Alliance identifiers support seven of the core principles enshrined in the Agreement.[12] The experience of having their party and leaders in government proved appealing to Democratic Unionists, and support for power-sharing among this group doubled between 1998 and 2011. Similarly, albeit starting from a much lower base, support for north–south bodies increased from 18 per cent in 1998 to 52 per cent in 2011. The changes in views among Ulster Unionists are more modest, at least partly because in 1998 support for the core principles of the Agreement was already high. There are more substantial changes among Alliance supporters, most notably in their support for the Northern Ireland Assembly, which declined from 100 per cent in 1998 to 76 per cent in 2011.

These are substantial changes, and the extent to which they vary between the three groups of party supporters indicates how well the identifiers believed their party was faring under the new arrangements. Overall, DUP supporters show a net increase in support for the Agreement principles of 11 percentage points between 1998 and 2011. However, Ulster Unionists show a net decline of 3 points and Alliance supporters a net decline of 10 points. DUP supporters in particular clearly felt that the decommissioning of paramilitary weapons and the eventual appointment of their leaders as successive first ministers in the power-sharing executive in 2007 was testament to their party's key role. By contrast, the UUP's failure to maintain their original significant representation in the government under the d'Hondt formula obviously resonated with its supporters.

We might expect a similar pattern to emerge among the nationalist parties, with the supporters of the parties gaining most from the Agreement showing increases in support, and those gaining less from the Agreement decreases. This expectation is not supported by the evidence in Table 5.8, which shows that there is a consistent decrease in support for both Sinn Fein and SDLP identifiers across all of the Agreement principles. The net change over the period among Sinn Fein supporters is −12 percentage points, while for the SDLP it is a more substantial −17 points. The higher levels of SDLP disaffection with the Agreement probably reflects the perception that the SDLP had not gained much from it; this may be the cause of the very substantial drop in support for the removal

Table 5.7 Support for Agreement principles, DUP, UUP and Alliance supporters, 1998–2011

Per cent who support	1998	2000	2003	2011	1998–2011 change
(Democratic Unionists)					
Northern Ireland remain part of UK	99	96	96	95	−4
North–south bodies	18	19	37	52	+34
Northern Ireland Assembly	60	38	71	71	+11
Removal of claim to Northern Ireland	85	87	87	73	−12
Decommissioning	92	95	98	—	—
Early release of prisoners	9	5	—	11	+2
Power-sharing executive	35	21	68	72	+37
(N)	(119)	(221)	(220)	(243)	
(Ulster Unionists)					
Northern Ireland remain part of UK	99	97	99	96	−3
North–south bodies	60	40	65	52	−8
Northern Ireland Assembly	89	77	91	79	−10
Removal of claim to Northern Ireland	86	82	78	74	−12
Decommissioning	96	99	99	—	—
Early release of prisoners	5	3	—	10	+5
Power-sharing executive	76	50	89	85	+9
(N)	(251)	(453)	(179)	(185)	
(Alliance)					
Northern Ireland remain part of UK	97	85	78	87	−10
North–south bodies	88	82	89	76	−12
Northern Ireland Assembly	100	90	85	76	−24
Removal of claim to Northern Ireland	68	61	54	55	−13
Decommissioning	97	99	100	—	—
Early release of prisoners	10	8	—	18	+8
Power-sharing executive	97	77	98	88	−9
(N)	(60)	(82)	(46)	(170)	

See Table 4.7 for question wording. Numbers of respondents vary due to missing data

Sources: Northern Ireland Referendum and Election Study, 1998; Northern Ireland Life and Times Survey, 2000; Northern Ireland Election Survey, 2003; Northern Ireland Social and Political Attitudes Survey, 2011

Table 5.8 Support for Agreement principles, Sinn Fein and
SDLP supporters, 1998–2011

Per cent who support	1998	2000	2003	2011	1998–2011 Change
		(Sinn Fein)			
Northern Ireland remain part of UK	57	34	68	52	–5
North–south bodies	88	85	95	85	–3
Northern Ireland Assembly	83	82	97	69	–14
Removal of claim to Northern Ireland	31	13	15	16	–15
Decommissioning	70	58	86	—	—
Early release of prisoners	66	66	—	45	–21
Power-sharing executive	92	81	99	79	–13
(N)	(71)	(85)	(99)	(224)	
		(SDLP)			
Northern Ireland remain part of UK	80	56	80	63	–17
North–south bodies	93	84	92	85	–8
Northern Ireland Assembly	97	89	90	79	–18
Removal of claim to Northern Ireland	52	28	32	16	–36
Decommissioning	94	85	99	—	—
Early release of prisoners	34	30	—	17	–17
Power-sharing executive	95	85	97	90	–5
(N)	(212)	(318)	(156)	(185)	

See Table 4.7 for question wording. Numbers of respondents vary due to
missing data
Sources: Northern Ireland Referendum and Election Study, 1998; Northern
Ireland Life and Times Survey, 2000; Northern Ireland Election Survey, 2003;
Northern Ireland Social and Political Attitudes Survey, 2011

of the Irish government's territorial claim to Northern Ireland, from
52 per cent in 1998 to 16 per cent in 2011.

By advocating specific policies, parties structure the views of their
supporters on particular issues. How the supporters of the major parties
have changed their views on the Agreement reflects, to some degree,
their party's policies on it. The results suggest that, with the progress of
time, DUP supporters have become more enamoured of the Agreement,
while Sinn Fein supporters much less so, particularly since 2003. The

three parties that have arguably benefited least – the UUP, Alliance and SDLP – all show declines in support for the Agreement principles; this is especially the case for the SDLP, which is also the party that has gained least from the new institutional arrangements.

In summary, the results suggest a notable change in opinion among party supporters, particularly since 2003. In all but one case, attitudes among DUP partisans in support of the Agreement have weakened. And, while the decline in support among the UUP, Alliance and SDLP supporters can be explained by their absence from key decision-making bodies, the recent reversal in Sinn Fein support is more difficult to explain. Part of explanation may be a growing Catholic disillusionment with Sinn Fein's failure to implement the promised equality agenda (see Bean, 2007). As Gerry Adams put it in the Sinn Fein 2003 Assembly election manifesto: 'At the core of our agenda for government is one simple word – equality ... as republicans we are totally committed to ending inequality and bringing about a society where all are treated equally'. However, despite Sinn Fein's dramatic political success, Northern Ireland remains a divided and unequal society, with Catholic unemployment rates still significantly outstripping that of their Protestant counterparts.[13] A second explanation may be a growing dissatisfaction among traditional Sinn Fein supporters with this overriding quest for equality of opportunity rather than the pursuit of Irish unity, a view widely endorsed by Republican dissidents (Tonge, 2003).

Conclusion

At one level, the Northern Ireland party system has remained remarkably stable since its foundation in the 1920s and more particularly since the start of the Troubles in 1969. Religion is still the dominant social cleavage and the basis for party competition: almost 8 out of every 10 Protestants and Catholics identify with a party from their respective religious community. The political parties that appeal for voter support are the recognizable descendants, with some changes in labels, of the parties that were active half a century or more earlier. Superficially at least, this is the sort of enduring stability that Lipset and Rokkan (1967: 50) had in mind when they talked about the 'freezing' of party systems around the cleavage structures that existed in the 1920s.

Just as studies have questioned the applicability of the Lipset and Rokkan model to modern party systems (for reviews, see Mair, 1997), the findings presented here have shown considerable evidence of change within the Northern Ireland party system. First, there has been substantial social and demographic change in the population, with a larger proportion of younger Catholics in the population, most probably as a result of a change in emigration patterns between the two communities, particularly among the young. At the same time, there is a larger proportion of Catholics with higher socioeconomic status. Second, the high rates of Catholic abstention from voting that characterized Stormont elections from 1921 to 1969 have been reversed, and now more Protestants than Catholics abstain from voting. Third and not least, the change in the electoral system from a plurality to a proportional representation system has fragmented the party system, achieving the purpose for which it was designed.

The net effect of these changes, each small when considered individually but collectively substantial, has been to produce a party system that is based less on *inter*-community than on *intra*-community party competition. The emergence of the DUP as the main unionist party and Sinn Fein as the main nationalist party have both been made possible by these underlying changes in the society as a whole and in the design of the electoral and political institutions that shape the competition for political office. Ironically, these changes, notably the consociational nature of the Belfast Agreement which assumes an agreement between the religious communities, have also seriously weakened the centre ground of Northern Ireland politics. Starting in the 1960s, the centre ground – represented variously by the Northern Ireland Labour Party, the Alliance Party and the Women's Coalition – was often seen as the long-term solution to the conflict. But the consociational agreement has also helped the DUP and Sinn Fein to eclipse their respective rivals, the UUP and the SDLP; in effect, these parties have been the victims of their own success by bringing the Belfast Agreement to fruition (Tonge, 2003).

These changes have not created the type of pluralist democracy that would render the religious cleavage irrelevant, with many parties competing across multiple cleavages and forcing the parties to adapt and compromise in their search for votes. Rather, what has occurred is ethnic outbidding, with new ethnic parties tackling 'established parties on their own terms, presenting themselves as more committed and authentic alternatives to the tired parties of the past' (Coakley, 2008: 788). Nor is this process of ethnic outbidding something new: the almost complete replacement of the Irish Parliamentary Party by Sinn Fein in 1918, and the Nationalist Party by the SDLP in 1970, shows both the cyclical nature of the process and how rapid the turnover can be. The more recent examples of the process have been facilitated by electoral reform and by changes in the political incentive structure, so that the new parties can portray themselves as more effective representatives of their communities – so-called tribune parties (Mitchell *et al.*, 2009).

The emergence of intra-community party competition has made it easier for the British government to establish devolved institutions in Northern Ireland and to sidestep the blocking tactics of any single party. It has also ensured that the salience of the religious cleavage remains high since intra-community competition depends on competition within and not between the ethnic blocs. Moreover, ethnic outbidding results in a switch in electoral support from moderate parties to their more extreme counterparts, who appear to attract stronger community representation. As such, the sort of pluralist democracy envisaged as a solution to ethnically divided societies by Donald Horowitz (1985, 1990, 2000) and others remains as distant as ever. The hope must be that as these more extreme parties engage in government and are forced to confront the routine resource allocation of day-to-day politics, they will be forced to make alliances with groups across the religious divide.

Notes

1 More radical solutions have been proposed, such as integrating the Northern Ireland party system with that of Britain, but these have generally been discounted in favour of electoral engineering and power-sharing between the parties (Roberts, 1990).

2 See Osborne and Shuttleworth (2004) for a comprehensive account of these changes, particularly as they relate to educational and employment opportunities.

3 In total, 24 members were elected by STV, with the two remaining members (the mayors of Belfast and Londonderry) being ex officio.

4 Although it was also the case that there was a greater level of disenfranchisement among Catholics than Protestants.

5 This usually worked to the benefit of unionists: for example, the safe Protestant constituency of South Londonderry was contested just twice in the 10 Stormont elections conducted between 1929 and 1969. Occasionally, nationalists benefited as well; the constituency of Mid-Tyrone, for example, returned a Nationalist MP unopposed at every election between 1929 and 1949.

6 Among the youngest respondents (those aged 18–29) 53 per cent of Protestants abstained in 1998, compared to 46 per cent of Catholics.

7 So intense was Protestant opposition to the Belfast Agreement that the Orange Order ended its close relationship with the UUP in 2005.

8 In the 1981 district council elections, the DUP narrowly exceeded the UUP vote by 0.1 per cent of the first preference vote.

9 There have also been a variety of fringe unionist parties, often linked to paramilitary organizations. These groups have generally exhibited a distrust of mainstream unionism and taken a leftwing perspective on many social issues, such as women's rights, abortion, the environment, and energy (McAuley, 2004).

10 From 1996 to its disbandment in 2006, the Northern Ireland Women's Coalition also occupied the centre ground of policies, advocating an end to sectarian violence and the introduction of integrated education.

11 Small numbers of those of the opposite religion support these parties, but in order not to further complicate the analyses, these respondents were excluded.

12 The results in Table 5.7 (and later in Table 5.8) differ slightly from those reported by Mitchell and Evans (2009) due to the exclusion of those who reported 'don't know' from our analysis. Moreover, their investigation was much more restrictive in focus, being limited to just two periods of study, 1998 and 2003.

13 See Chapter 6 for the more detailed discussion of this issue.

6

Community relations

While institutional design is viewed as the most effective means of resolving divisions in post-conflict societies, there has also been an emphasis on peace building at the grass-roots level. It is often argued that successful conflict resolution is as much about the reconstruction of communities and societies as it is about the design of political institutions and states. This is particularly acute when the experiences of ordinary citizens in coming to terms with previous injustices are considered. As Timothy Donais (2005: 142) argues in his study of post-conflict Bosnia, 'since intra-state conflicts are inevitably social as well as political crises, re-establishing the social foundations of a post-conflict political community is an essential element of moving from conflict to sustainable peace'. In short, institutional design can facilitate political change, but meaningful social change depends on the reconstruction of civil society.

The Northern Ireland peace process, culminating in the 1998 Belfast Agreement, has attracted similar responses about the disjuncture between institutional design and community initiatives.[1] A common criticism of the peace process has been that while the Agreement has helped political elites to reach a compromise, it has had a detrimental effect on relations between ordinary citizens. In this view, the top-down politics introduced by the consociational power-sharing arrangements has entrenched sectarian political divisions and stifled local-level initiatives aimed at mutual understanding. As Anthony Oberschall and Kendall Palmer (2005: 87–88) put it, 'in the absence of an institutional underpinning at the political level, greater social integration is not likely to occur. Instead, people view separation...as the guarantor of security in daily life, and they view cross-community transacting as burdened with uncertainty and trouble one should avoid'.

In order to examine the social dimension of peace building as experienced by the mass public, this chapter focuses on the views of ordinary citizens towards community relations. Using a wide range of survey data, we examine the nature and extent of communal divisions and address the question of whether or not public perceptions of relations between the two main religious communities have changed since the introduction of the Belfast Agreement in 1998. The first section outlines government policy in relation to community relations in Northern Ireland, with particular emphasis on the obligations of public bodies as specified in the 1998 Agreement. The second and third sections focus on the nature and extent of communal division as well as public attitudes towards greater integration. The fourth focuses on perceptions of community relations both now and in the future, while the final section examines the implications for post-conflict reconciliation.

Community relations policy

The conflict in Northern Ireland has long been defined as a problem of poor community relations between Protestants and Catholics, a view that has been particularly prevalent among the British establishment (Nagle and Clancy, 2010). Since the outbreak of the conflict in 1969, the British government has introduced a range of community relations initiatives aimed at containing the violence (see Knox and Hughes, 1996). Based on theories of intergroup and interpersonal behaviour originally emanating from the work of Gordon Allport in his famous 1954 book, *The Nature of Prejudice*, the underlying rationale for these initiatives – the contact hypothesis – was that conflict arises from a lack of information about the other group and from the absence of opportunities to gain such information. Provided certain core conditions are met during the process of intergroup contact – equal status among groups, common goals, protection against competition and the provision of institutional support – conflict resolution could be achieved by promoting contact between the two main religious communities and, thus, creating more tolerant attitudes.[2] This approach to conflict resolution was advocated by policymakers as well as members of the academic community (Hayes *et al.*, 2007). However, it was not until the establishment of the Central Community Relations Unit in 1987 and the Northern Ireland Community Relations Council in 1990 that community relations became a policy priority for the British government.

Since the late 1980s, the British government has adopted a twin-track approach to resolving the Northern Ireland conflict (see Hughes and Donnelly, 2004). Through a range of political initiatives, such as the 1985 Anglo-Irish Agreement and the 1993 Downing Street Declaration, the government's emphasis was to find a constitutional settlement that would prove acceptable to both unionist and nationalists. At the same time, improving community relations in combination with a commitment to tackling problems of disadvantage, discrimination and inequality also became policy priorities. A range of measures was adopted to promote equity of treatment focused on targeting areas of special economic and social need. These included the 1989 Fair Employment Act, to tackle discrimination in the workplace; the introduction in 1991 of the Targeting Social Need programme as a spending priority; and the establishment in 1994 of Policy Appraisal and Fair Treatment guidelines, to secure equitable policymaking and implementation in all areas of public-sector provision. The earlier and much criticized 'symptom-driven' approach to community relations policy, with its emphasis on segregation and division, was replaced by a twin-track approach which aimed at addressing the underlying causes of the conflict, namely, structural inequality and discrimination.

This holistic approach to resolving the conflict was reflected in the Belfast Agreement. As Joanne Hughes (2007) notes, central to the Agreement is the principle of equality as well as a commitment to promote a 'culture of tolerance'. In light of this factor, the Agreement outlined a range of measures that were designed to create a more inclusive and just society which would protect equally the interests and cultural traditions of the two main communities. In other words, the proposed top-down power-sharing structures were meant to be institutionalized at the local level, via public bodies such as the Equality Commission and the Northern Ireland Human Rights Commission, with statutory obligations to improve community relations and advance social justice. Moreover, the interdependence of equality and good relations was recognized and enshrined in section 75 of the 1998 Northern Ireland Act, which places a statutory obligation on all public authorities to not only promote equality of opportunity but also to 'have regard to the desirability of promoting good relations between persons of different religious belief, political opinion or racial group'.

The effectiveness of these bodies in bringing about reconciliation has been a matter of much contention.[3] Critics have pointed not only to the absence of support for these commissions within both communities but also to their lack of public accountability, complicated decision-making rules and overlapping responsibilities. Research undertaken by Anthony Oberschall and Kendall Palmer (2005) found that while both unionists and nationalists pointed to their lack of public accountability, unionists were also more likely to stress their preoccupation with achieving ethnic quotas rather than meeting social need. Even the newly created Equality Commission, the main body charged with overseeing section 75 of the Northern Ireland Act, is not without its detractors.[4] For example, an independent review of the working of the Commission identified

20 weaknesses, as compared to just three strengths, the most damaging of which was its excessive emphasis on process rather than outcome. As Eithne McLaughlin and Neil Faris (2004a: 31), in a critical review of the workings of the Commission, concluded, 'its operations permit those who wish to do so to engage in slavish following of "procedures" and "a tick box approach" to equality'. The net effect, it has been suggested, is that in a substantial number of cases, such as public housing provision, public bodies are failing to meet their section 75 obligations, namely, the delivery of equality of opportunity (see Taylor, 2009a).[5]

There has also been public concern about government initiatives to deal with the vexed question of community relations. Despite pledges by the Executive to strive for 'a shared and better future for all', government policy in this area to date has been ineffectual (Northern Ireland Executive, 2008: 6). The first policy document to focus on the question of community relations, *A Shared Future* (OFMDFM, 2005), pointed to overwhelming public support for a shared society and stressed its vital role in promoting reconciliation. Arguing for a culture of tolerance at every level of society including initiatives to encourage integrated education and mixed housing, it stated that 'separate but equal is not an option' (see OFMDFM, 2005: 15).[6]

In 2007, the policy outlined by *A Shared Future* was abandoned by the devolved DUP–Sinn Fein Executive and replaced with a more benign view of community relations, as outlined in a *Programme for Cohesion, Sharing and Integration* (OFMDFM, 2010).[7] The new policy was a compromise between the DUP's position, which was to maintain the status quo, and that of Sinn Fein, who argued that the problem of poor community relations was not a result of a lack of tolerance but derived from structural inequalities and social disadvantage. The compromise policy sought to manage, rather than eradicate, sectarianism via the promotion of greater understanding between the two communities. By replacing the Executive's prior strategic goal of reconciliation in favour of encouraging mutual accommodation, the new policy advocated a return to the 'separate but equal' approach, an option rejected previously in the *Shared Future* document as impractical (see Knox, 2011).[8] Nevertheless, some recent public pronouncements, particularly from within the DUP, have stressed the need to revisit government policy in relation to the complex question of community relations.[9]

Whatever the disagreements within the Executive about community relations policy, the Belfast Agreement has resulted in significant change. The Agreement brought about the disarmament of paramilitary groups, most notably the IRA in 2005. This led not only to a cessation in direct levels of political violence but also to the re-establishment of the

Assembly with a power-sharing executive in 2007. The end of political violence has also made Northern Ireland the recipient of funds for major economic regeneration (see Irvin and Byrne, 2004). Prior to the global financial crisis, this major investment had been accompanied by increasing levels of employment opportunity and economic prosperity. This rise in employment opportunities, particularly within the public sector, has led to an increasingly prosperous middle class, particularly within the Catholic community (Shirlow and Murtagh, 2006; Smyth and Cebulla, 2008).

Nevertheless, despite this economic progress, major disparities in economic prosperity remain.[10] Even prior to the financial crisis, Northern Ireland remained a deeply unequal society. Paddy Hillyard and his colleagues (2003), in one of the most comprehensive investigations of this issue, found that the number of households living in poverty was 4 percentage points greater in Northern Ireland than in Britain – 30 per cent versus 26 per cent. Among the group living in poverty, individuals from working-class communities were particularly disadvantaged, irrespective of religion. Moreover, while poverty levels were higher among Catholics than Protestants, the main distinction was less religious than economic – between the poorly educated living in economically deprived households versus the well-educated and prosperous middle class.[11] Nevertheless, economic disparities between the two communities remain, with the lack of educational achievement and feelings of marginalization, particularly among the young, being increasingly more marked among Protestants than Catholics (see Kenway et al., 2006; Purvis, 2010).[12]

Despite the Belfast Agreement and the major political changes that it has initiated, Northern Ireland therefore remains a deeply divided society. Contrary to the aims of its designers to create a more inclusive society, the post-Agreement period has been marked by increasing rates of segregation and growing levels of mistrust between the two communities. While the extent to which residential segregation has increased in the post-Agreement period is disputed,[13] there is now a general consensus that not only have levels of residential segregation increased since the late 1960s, but they have done so in terms of a 'ratchet effect', with large increases after outbreaks of violent conflict, but with little or no decrease when the violence declines.[14] Furthermore, the perceived recent rise in territorial division has been accompanied by an increase in 'chill factors', such as the demarcation of sectarian boundaries with graffiti, flags, kerb paintings and other manifestations of paramilitary association and cultural political identity.[15] This is a phenomenon that is particularly marked during the Northern Ireland 'marching season'.[16] There have also been low but consistent levels of intercommunal violence, again most evident in deprived working-class interface areas, resulting in greater levels of fear and mistrust between the two communities.[17]

To what extent are these changes evident in terms of levels of social contact and public perceptions concerning community relations? In other words, has the erosion in levels of trust between the two communities led to what has recently been referred to as a 'benign form of apartheid' as well as more a pessimistic view of community relations among the public? To what degree is this phenomenon most marked among the young? It is to an empirical investigation of these various questions that we now turn.

Levels of social contact

Segregation is a long and established feature of social life in Northern Ireland. For the most part, Protestants and Catholics lead largely separate lives in a situation of 'benign apartheid'. As noted earlier, nowhere is the segregation more prevalent than in residential location. These widespread levels of segregation have been identified as one of the most obvious and pervasive manifestations of the conflict. As Brendan Murtagh (2003: 209) comments, 'residential segregation has been one of the most enduring and brutal images of the Northern Ireland conflict'. As a consequence, it has been possible for a substantial number of people, particularly those within working-class urban or rural areas, to study, live, work and socialize almost exclusively for most of their lives with members of their own community and not develop any close or sustained relationships with someone from the other community.[18] Moreover, as we pointed out in Chapter 2, on the occasions when contact happens, it is characterized by politeness and avoidance of any acknowledgement of difference than any attempt to engage in a meaningful and genuine interaction. Or as Seamus Heaney (1975), in referring to this long-established Northern Ireland maxim in his eponymous poem first published in *North*, put it, 'Whatever you say, say nothing'.

These high levels of segregation across all aspects of people's lives are reflected in Table 6.1 in the extent of social contact between the two religious communities via kinship, friendship and residence patterns in 2010. A majority of individuals confine their living arrangements and social interaction networks exclusively to their own community. This is particularly the case with regard to kinship patterns, where 8 out of 10 say that 'most' or 'all' of their relatives are from their own religion. A similar pattern emerges with regard to friendship networks and residential location. In both cases, around three-fifths of individuals reported that 'most' or 'all' of either their friends or neighbours were from their

Table 6.1 Levels of social contact, 2010

| | *(Per cent of the same religion)* | | | |
	Protestant	*Catholic*	*No religion*	*Total*
Friends				
All/most	66	64	45	63
Half	25	28	39	28
Less than half/none	9	8	16	9
(N)	(573)	(439)	(143)	(1,155)
Relatives				
All/most	81	83	72	81
Half	12	12	18	13
Less than half/none	7	5	10	6
(N)	(579)	(439)	(147)	(1,165)
Neighbours				
All/most	63	61	57	61
Half	27	25	27	26
Less than half/none	11	14	17	13
(N)	(524)	(411)	(120)	(1,055)

The questions were 'And how many of your friends would you say are the same religion as you?', 'What about your relatives, including relatives by marriage? About how many are the same religious as you?' and 'What about your neighbours? About how many are the same religion as you?'
Source: Northern Ireland Life and Times Survey, 2010

own religion. By any standards, these results point to a significant absence of social contact across the religious divide.

These high levels of segregation hold for both communities and, to a lesser extent, for those with no religious affiliation. Around three-fifths of both Protestants and Catholics report that 'most' or 'all' of their friends are from their own religion, while the equivalent proportion among the religiously non-affiliated is lower at 45 per cent. Similar results emerge for residential location. Perhaps the most striking finding in Table 6.1 is again the lack of contact in terms of kinship patterns, a phenomenon that also occurs even among the religiously non-affiliated. While just over 80 per cent of both Protestant and Catholic respondents say that 'most' or 'all' of their relatives are from their own religion, the equivalent proportion among those who claim no religion is 72 per cent.

There are also high levels of segregation in rates of marital homogamy. As the data in Figure 6.1 demonstrates, although the number of marriages between people of the same religion has declined by 9 per cent

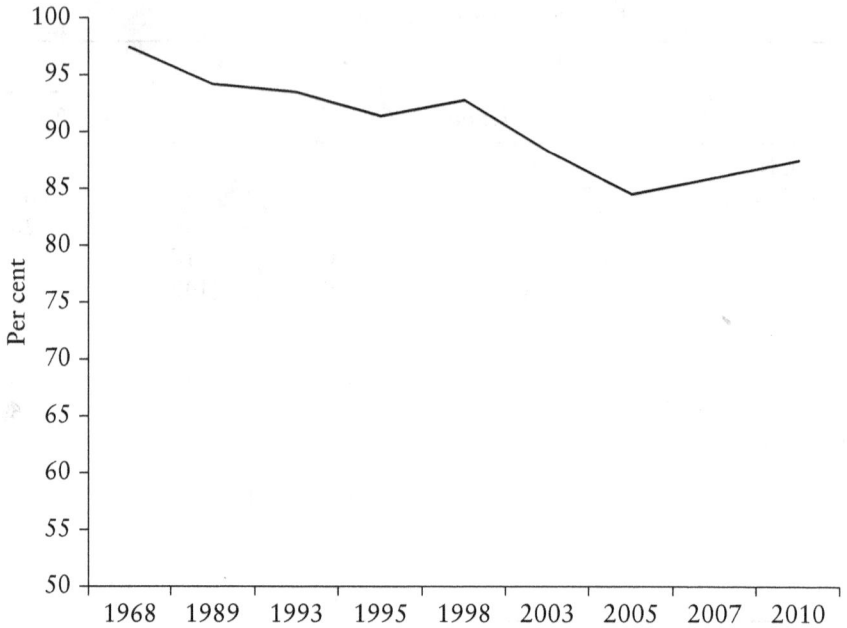

Figure 6.1 Levels of marital endogamy, 1968–2010
The questions were (1968–2005) 'Is your (husband/wife/partner) the same
religion as you?' and (2007, 2010) 'Does your (husband/wife/partner) regard
themselves as belonging to any particular religion? If yes, which?'
Sources: Northern Ireland Loyalty Survey, 1968; Northern Ireland Social
Attitudes Surveys, 1989, 1993, 1995; Northern Ireland Election and
Referendum Study, 1998; Northern Ireland Life and Times Surveys, 2003,
2005, 2007, 2010

since 1968, single-faith marriages still remain, by far, the dominant
feature of marital life in Northern Ireland. A staggering 97 per cent of
individuals reported that their marital partner was of the same religion
in 1968; by 1995, this had fallen to 91 per cent, or an annual decline of
just 0.2 per cent. By the following decade, the rate of intra-community
marriages declined by a further 6 percentage points to reach its lowest
level of 85 per cent in 2005. Since then, rates of marital homogamy have
increased slightly so that, by 2010, nearly nine out of all adults in
Northern Ireland currently have a husband, wife or partner of the same
religion as their own.

There have also been some fluctuations in intra-community contact
via social networks and residential patterns, particularly since the 1980s.
Figure 6.2 shows that although rates of exclusivity in contact within

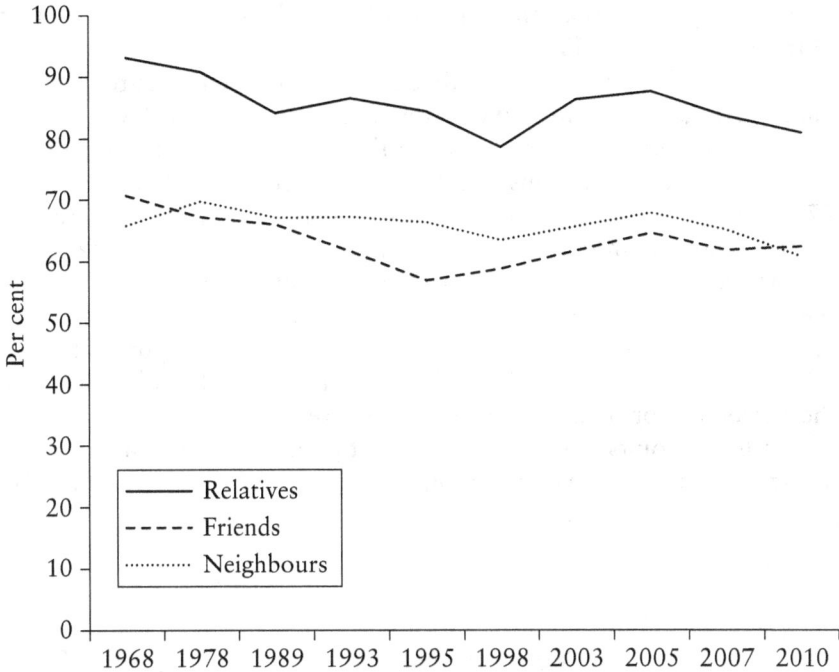

Figure 6.2 Levels of social contact, 1968–2010
Estimates are the per cent who said 'most' or 'all' were of the same religion.
There were no estimates for friends or neighbours in the 2003 survey
Sources: Northern Ireland Loyalty Survey, 1968; Northern Ireland Attitude
Survey, 1978; Northern Ireland Social Attitudes Surveys, 1989, 1993, 1995;
Northern Ireland Election and Referendum Survey, 1998; Northern Ireland
Life and Times Surveys, 2003, 2005, 2007, 2010

one's own religious community declined consistently in the period
running up to the 1998 Agreement, by 2005 this trend had been reversed.
Across all three contact indicators, levels of segregation increased and
this was particularly the case for kinship patterns. Between 1998 and
2005, the proportion of respondents who claimed that 'all' or 'most' of
their relatives were from the same religion rose from 79 per cent to
88 per cent, representing an increase of 1.3 per cent per year over the
seven-year period. The equivalent annual rise in terms of friendship
patterns and residential location was lower at 0.8 per cent and
0.7 per cent, respectively. Since then, levels of intra-community contact
have fallen back consistently, more so in terms of kinship patterns and
residential location than friendship networks, although they still remain

considerably lower than those reported immediately prior to the onset of the Troubles in 1968.

Since friendship networks established in youth often endure throughout a lifetime, the extent to which these patterns hold for the young has long-term implications. The trends in Figure 6.3 show that the patterns for the younger age groups – in this case those aged 18–26 years and 27–35 years – are very similar to the general population. There was greater cross-community social contact among the young after the paramilitary ceasefires in 1994 and, to a lesser extent, after the ratification of the Agreement in 1998. In 2010, however, this downward trend was reversed. Between 2007 and 2010, the proportion of respondents aged 18–26 years who claimed that 'all' or 'most' of their friends were from the same religion increased from 63 per cent to 70 per cent, or just 4 percentage points lower than its highest point – 74 per cent – in 1968. These results are repeated among those aged 27–35 years although,

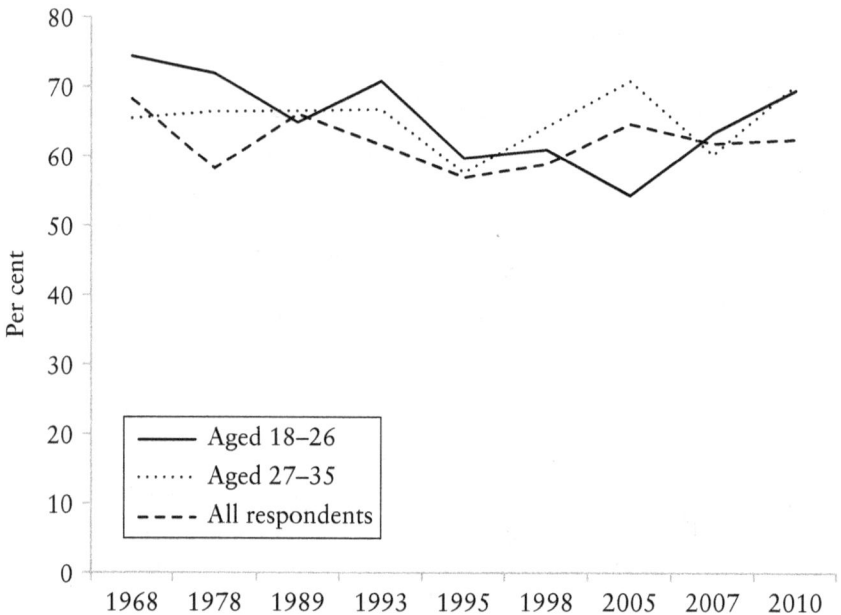

Figure 6.3 Friendship networks among the young, 1968–2010
Estimates are the per cent who said 'most' or 'all' of their friends were from the same religion
Sources: Northern Ireland Loyalty Survey, 1968; Northern Ireland Attitude Survey, 1978; Northern Ireland Social Attitudes Surveys, 1989, 1993, 1995; Northern Ireland Election and Referendum Survey, 1998; Northern Ireland Life and Times Surveys, 2005, 2007, 2010

at 70 per cent, current levels of intra-community social contact are just 1 percentage point below the high point reached in 2005.

The results reported in the graphs show that a large majority of individuals in Northern Ireland confine their living arrangements and social interaction networks exclusively to their own community. This is particularly the case when marriage and kinship patterns are considered, reflecting the high level of selection of marriage partners from within a person's own community. Contrary to what we might have expected, the younger members of the population demonstrate increasing segregation, and not integration, suggesting that these patterns will persist for a long time in the future. The next section considers whether these patterns remain when attitudes towards social contact are examined.

Attitudes towards social contact

A key plank in the British government's policy efforts to improve community relations is better intercommunity contact. As noted earlier, both government policy and academic research has long endorsed social contact as a mechanism for alleviating communal division. More so than any other factor, the lack of inter-group contact between the two main religious communities is considered both a consequence of and a catalyst for the conflict, whose diminution could only be achieved via increased interaction between them. From the onset of the conflict in the late 1960s, all government initiatives, sometimes referred to as 'the good relations industry', were based on this assumption (see Nagle and Clancy, 2010: 107).

There is considerable public support for this view, as Table 6.2 demonstrates. The overwhelming majority of respondents from both

Table 6.2 Preferred solution to community relations, 2010

| | (Percentages) | | | |
	Protestant	Catholic	No religion	Total
More mixing	87	89	83	87
Don't know	9	8	15	10
More separation	4	2	2	3
(N)	(573)	(439)	(143)	(1,155)

The question was 'Some people think that better relations between Protestants and Catholics in Northern Ireland will only come about through more mixing of the two communities. Others think that better relations will only come through more separation. Which comes closest to your views?'
Source: Northern Ireland Life and Times Survey, 2010

Table 6.3 Support for much greater religious integration, 2010

| | (Per cent who favour 'much more' mixing) | | | |
	Protestant	Catholic	No religion	Total
Primary schools	56	51	78	57
Secondary/grammar	53	52	74	55
Where people live	43	49	63	48
Work	49	60	67	55
Leisure or sport activities	53	61	68	58
Marriages	30	37	58	36

The question was 'Are you in favour of more mixing or more separation in: primary schools; secondary and grammar schools; where people live; where people work; people's leisure or sports activities; people's marriages.'
Source: Northern Ireland Life and Times Survey, 2010

communities support more mixing as a mechanism to improve community relations. By contrast, only 3 per cent advocate increasing separation and just 1 in 10 are undecided on the issue. While there is slightly more equivocation among those with no religion, more than 8 out of every 10 still support more mixing. Thus, in confirmation of a range of earlier opinion poll data,[19] the results suggest that as far as mixing between the two religious communities is concerned, the vast majority of people in Northern Ireland continue 'to want to live together than apart' (Hadden *et al.*, 1996: 48). This is in marked contrast to 1968, when a majority of individuals in both religious communities endorsed the view that 'people with the same religion ought to stick together' (Rose, 1971: 495).

While the vast majority of the public favour more mixing, a more nuanced pattern emerges when the respondents are asked to specify the areas of their everyday lives in which they would like to see greater cross-community contact. The results in Table 6.3 reveal that only a minority of respondents favour 'much more' mixing across a majority of social settings. Whereas just 29 per cent support mixing across all six settings, when the two items with least support – marriage and where people live – are excluded from the calculation, this proportion rises to 42 per cent. There is most support for mixing in the area of sport or leisure activities, followed by schools, work and residence. Support for greater integration in marriage, however, is markedly lower; only around one in three respondents in both communities endorse this view. Thus, in further confirmation of our earlier analysis, choice of marital partner continues to remain one of the most entrenched and divisive markers of communal relations.

Across all six areas, it is the non-affiliated who stand out as the most supportive of integration. Around three-quarters of those with no religion advocate more mixing in schools, declining to two-thirds in residence, work and leisure. The two religious communities are broadly similar in their views, although Protestants are slightly more supportive of mixing in education than Catholics, and Catholics are more supportive than Protestants in the non-education areas. Among both Protestants and Catholics, however, support for much greater integration in terms of cross-community marriages is much lower, although Catholics are more positive than Protestants in their views.

To what extent are attitudes towards mixing influenced by levels of social contact? In other words, as stipulated by the social contact hypothesis, has increasing contact between the two religious communities led to a greater willingness to adopt a more integrationist stance in relation to community relations? The results in Table 6.4 address this question by focusing on the impact of levels of contact between the two main communities on attitudes towards support for greater integration in education, residence, work, leisure and marriage. For the purposes of this analysis, cross-community contact is operationalized by the degree of contact via friendship, kinship and residential patterns as well as the impact of cross-community or mixed-faith marriages.

The results in Table 6.4 support the view that cross-community contact, particularly in both a friendship and marriage setting, leads to more support for integration in community relations. Even when a range of background control variables such as gender, age and education are included in the models, levels of cross-community contact both in terms of friendship networks and marriage partners emerge as consistently strong and positive predictors of attitudes towards greater religious integration. Individuals who either had friends from outside their own religious community or were in a mixed-faith marriage are significantly more likely to advocate increasing contact between the two communities than those who were not. Moreover, this result holds for all five settings – education, residence, work, leisure and marriage. By contrast, neither cross-community contact in residence nor, to a lesser extent, kinship patterns are a significant determinant of attitudes. Other important predictors include education and age. In confirmation of our earlier analysis, it is again older individuals who stand out as consistently more likely to endorse more integration in community relations. This view is also more prevalent among the better educated.

Although the overwhelming majority of the population in Northern Ireland support more mixing as a mechanism to resolve community relations, they are less enthusiastic when they consider the processes involved

Table 6.4 Support for religious integration and levels of social contact, 2010

	Schools		Neighbourhood		Work		Leisure		Marriage	
	b	Beta	b	Beta	b	Beta	b	Beta	b	Beta
Religion (Protestant)										
Catholic	0.01	0.01	0.04*	0.10	0.05**	0.12	0.03	0.07	0.07**	0.14
No religion	0.01	0.02	-0.01	-0.01	-0.03	-0.06	-0.01	-0.02	0.04	0.06
Gender (male)	-0.01	-0.01	-0.01	-0.01	0.01	0.01	0.02	0.05	0.02	0.04
Age (years)	0.01**	0.14	0.01**	0.17	0.01**	0.14	0.01**	0.13	0.01	0.01
Education (tertiary)										
Secondary	-0.05**	-0.13	-0.05**	-0.12	-0.06**	-0.14	-0.04*	-0.10	-0.02	-0.04
No qualification	-0.07**	-0.16	-0.04*	-0.09	-0.05*	-0.11	-0.02	-0.06	-0.03	-0.05
Cross-community contact										
Relatives (high)	0.06	0.07	0.07	0.08	0.08	0.08	0.07	0.08	0.20**	0.18
Friends (high)	0.13**	0.13	0.14**	0.14	0.16**	0.15	0.11**	0.11	0.17**	0.14
Neighbours (high)	-0.02	-0.03	0.05	0.06	0.01	0.01	-0.01	-0.01	0.01	0.01
Religious exogamy										
Mixed-marriage	0.09**	0.21	0.09**	0.20	0.09**	0.20	0.08**	0.19	0.10**	0.19
Constant	0.73**		0.64**		0.68**		0.71**		0.56**	
Adj R-squared	0.09		0.11		0.11		0.07		0.15	
(N)	(648)		(648)		(647)		(647)		(647)	

Significant at **p < 0.01; *p < 0.05

Ordinary least squares regression analysis showing partial (b) and standardized (beta) coefficients predicting the probability of support for more mixing in (both primary and secondary) schools, where people live, work, leisure or sports activities and marriages. Support for more mixing in schools is a 10-point scale coded from 0 (much more separation) to 1 (much more mixing), and support in terms of where people live, work, leisure or sports activities and marriages is a five-point scale coded from 0 (much more separation) to 1 (much more mixing). Protestant is the omitted category for religious affiliation, and tertiary education is the omitted category for education. See Table 6.3 for question wording

Source: Northern Ireland Life and Times Survey, 2010

and the areas of their lives that it may be applied to. This is particularly the case with respect to cross-community marriage, where there is least support for more integration. As a group, it is those who experience more instances of cross-community contact, in terms of either friendship patterns or mixed-faith marriages, and the well-educated and older individuals who stand out as most supportive of integration. The next section examines if these patterns also apply to public perceptions of community relations.

Perceptions of community relations

A key aspect of the Belfast Agreement is the statutory responsibility of public bodies to not only promote equality of opportunity between the two religious communities but to also have due regard to the desirability of promoting good relations between them. To what extent have they been successful in this latter aim? The two indicators that have been used to monitor this issue are, first, people's perceptions of relations between the two main communities over the previous five years and, second, their perception of relations in the next five years. For both indicators, respondents were asked whether relations between Protestants and Catholics were better, worse or about the same.

The trends in the public perceptions of community relations suggest that opinions have fluctuated in line with the level of communal conflict in three distinct phases (see Figure 6.4). In the first phase, there was a marked decline in community relations in the first two decades of the conflict. In 1989 (the first year after 1968 for which we have data), just under a quarter of respondents believed that relations between the two communities had improved, while almost half believed that they had stayed the same, and 29 per cent stated that they had become worse. This is in marked contrast to public opinion in 1968, when only 6 per cent of the population thought that community relations had become worse and just over three-fifths thought they had improved. Thus, the onset of the current phrase of the conflict led to considerable pessimism about community relations.

In the second phase, between 1994 and 1999 and covering the signing of the Belfast Agreement, public perceptions concerning relations between Protestants and Catholics became more optimistic. The percentage of respondents who claimed that relations between the two communities had improved nearly doubled, from 27 per cent to 51 per cent. Perhaps more importantly, this increase was accompanied by a significant decline in the proportion – from 28 per cent in 1994 to just 7 per cent in 1999 – who believed that community relations had in fact worsened. This radical change in public opinion particularly in the space of only

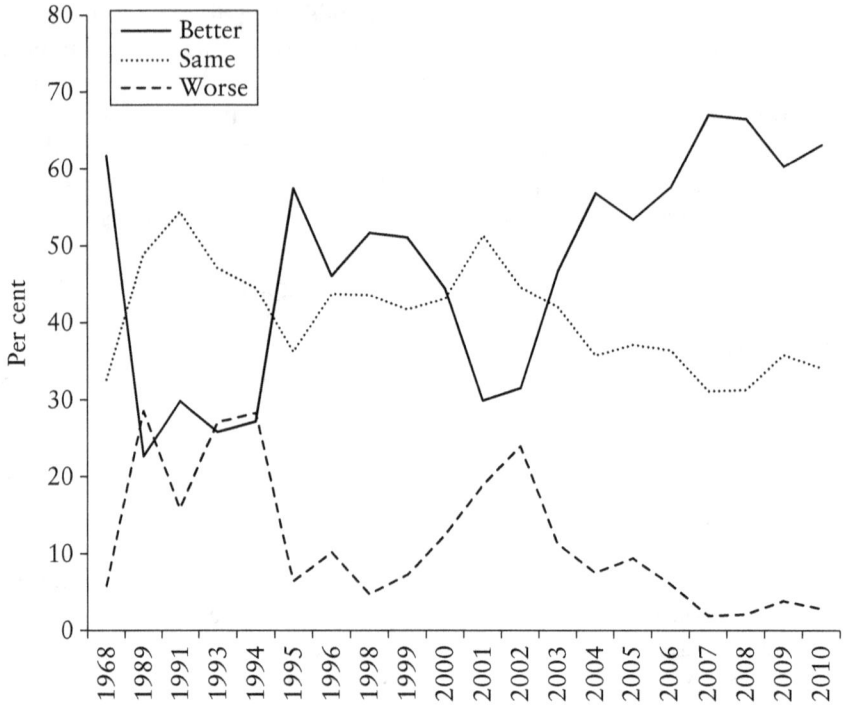

Figure 6.4 Perceptions of current community relations, 1968–2010
The question was 'What about relations between Protestants and Catholics?
Would you say they are better than they were 5 years ago, worse, or about the
same as then?'
Sources: Northern Ireland Loyalty Survey, 1968; Northern Ireland Social
Attitudes Surveys, 1989, 1991, 1993–96; Northern Ireland Life and Times
Surveys, 1998–2010

a year reflects the effects of the IRA ceasefire in 1994 which, after being
suspended in 1996–97, was then made permanent.

In 2000, this positive trend in popular views of community relations was
reversed, marking the beginning of a third phase. This decline was not unex-
pected given the heightened intercommunal tension surrounding the three-
month blockade of Holy Cross Primary School which began in September
2001.[20] Between 1999 and 2002, the proportion who believed that relations between the two communities had improved dropped from a narrow
majority to just under one-third. From 2003 onwards, the period which
included the formal end of the IRA military campaign as well as the restoration of the Assembly, opinion gradually became more positive. Since 2007,
around two-thirds have said that community relations have improved.

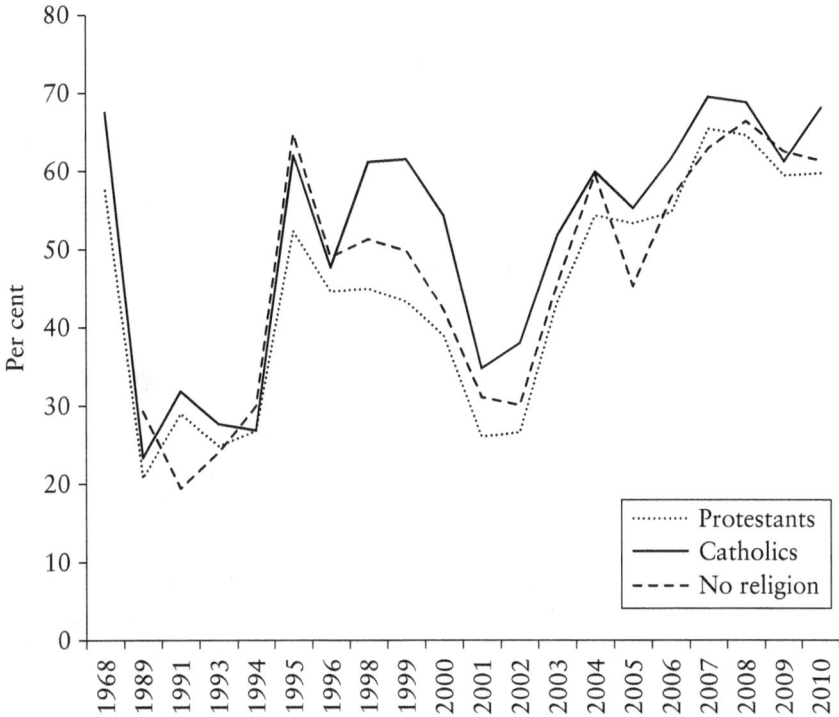

Figure 6.5 Current community relations by religion, 1968–2010
See Figure 6.4 for question wording. Estimates are the per cent who see
current community relations as better
Sources: Northern Ireland Loyalty Survey, 1968; Northern Ireland Social
Attitudes Surveys, 1989, 1991, 1993–96; Northern Ireland Life and Times
Surveys, 1998–2010

A more diverse pattern emerges when Protestants, Catholics and those
claiming no religious affiliation are considered separately (see Figure 6.5).
Across all of the surveys for which data are available, Catholics are consistently more optimistic about community relations than Protestants.
However, prior to the 1998 Agreement, the religious differences were
relatively modest – on average around 4 percentage points separated the
communities. That changed with the 1998 Agreement which, as we saw
in Chapter 4, was highly popular with Catholics but much less so
among Protestants. In the three surveys immediately after the Agreement,
the religious difference was on average 17 percentage points, and for the
1998–2010 period, although somewhat lower, the average difference
still remained a substantial 8 percentage points.

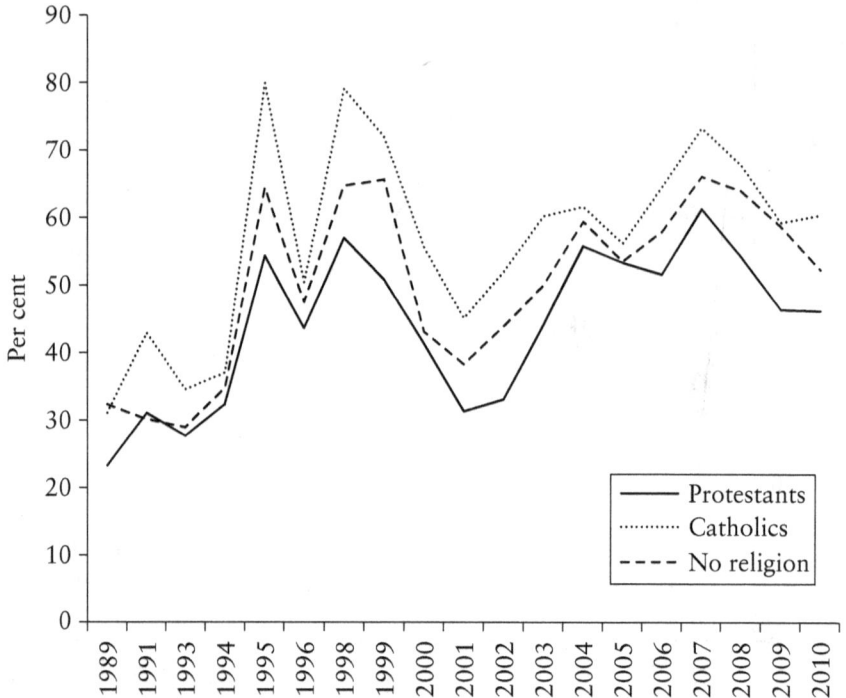

Figure 6.6 Perceptions of future community relations by religion, 1989–2010
The question was 'And what about in 5 years time? Do you think relations
between Protestants and Catholics will be better than now, worse than now, or
about the same as now?' Estimates are the per cent who see future community
relations as better
Sources: Northern Ireland Social Attitudes Surveys, 1989, 1991, 1993–96;
Northern Ireland Life and Times Surveys, 1998–2010

An even greater level of diversity appears when future community
relations are considered or the degree to which respondent believed that
relations between Protestants and Catholics would be better in five years
time than they are now. Here, significant differences emerge and persist
between the three religious groupings. The results in Figure 6.6 suggest a
growing disparity in attitudes throughout the post-Agreement period,
with Catholics being consistently more positive in their opinions than
either Protestants or those who claim no religious affiliation. In 1995, for
example, 80 per cent of Catholics believed that relations between the two
communities would improve in the next five years, while the equivalent
figure for Protestants was just 54 per cent. As with perceptions of current
community relations, this differential was particularly marked after the

Table 6.5 Determinants of attitudes towards community relations, 2010

	Current		Future	
	Est	(SE)	Est	(SE)
Religion (Protestant)				
Catholic	0.68**	(0.19)	0.85**	(0.18)
No religion	−0.03	(0.35)	−0.07	(0.33)
Gender (male)	0.06	(0.17)	0.03	(0.16)
Age (years)	0.01*	(0.01)	0.01*	(0.01)
Education (tertiary)				
Secondary	0.08	(0.19)	0.31	(0.18)
No qualification	−0.58**	(0.22)	−0.30	(0.21)
Cross-community contact				
Relatives (high)	−0.47	(0.44)	−0.24	(0.43)
Friends (high)	−0.25	(0.47)	−0.12	(0.46)
Neighbours (high)	0.58	(0.35)	0.39	(0.34)
Religious exogamy				
Mixed-marriage	0.24	(0.31)	0.29	(0.29)
Constant	−0.29		−0.70	
Nagelkerke R-squared	0.05		0.06	
(N)	(613)		(614)	

Significant at **$p < 0.01$; *$p < 0.05$

Logistic regression analyses showing parameter estimates and (in parentheses) robust standard errors predicting the probability that community relations are/ will be better (coded 1) versus are/will be the same/worse (coded 0). Protestant is the omitted category for religious affiliation and tertiary education is the omitted category for education. See Figures 6.4 and 6.6 for question wordings.
Source: Northern Ireland Life and Times Survey, 2010

1998 Agreement, but has declined somewhat since then. However, in 2010, 60 per cent of Catholics were optimistic compared to just 46 per cent of Protestants, a still substantial difference of 14 percentage points.

To what extent does the religious difference in attitudes towards community relations remain after a range of potentially confounding background characteristics are taken into account? Table 6.5 addresses this question by focusing on the impact of a range of socio-demographic variables, including age, cross-community contact levels and religious exogamy, on attitudes towards current and future relations in 2010. The results show that the effect of religion remains important. Judged against the excluded category, Catholics remain significantly more optimistic than Protestants, and, indeed, religion is the most important predictor in the equation. Those with no religion are not significantly different in their views, once other factors have been taken into account. It is again older individuals who emerge as the most optimistic in their views, as are those with higher educational attainment.

By contrast, neither levels of cross-community contact nor rates of religious exogamy emerge as a predictor of attitudes towards community relations. In comparison with our previous analysis on attitudes towards more mixing, these results suggest that while cross-community contact, particularly via a friendship and marriage, may lead to more support for integration, it does not translate into a more optimistic view of community relations. Moreover, this lack of a relationship holds for both current and future perceptions of community relations. These results suggest that while government policies to promote greater contact between the two religious communities may break down divisions at the individual level, they do not lead to a hoped for 'feel good factor' at the societal level.

Our overview of public opinion towards community relations demonstrates that a majority of the public believe that relations between the two religious communities are better now than they were five years ago. However, opinions are more pessimistic about future community relations, where only a bare majority endorse this view. There are, of course, important religious differences in these patterns, and throughout the period of study, Catholics have been consistently much more positive in their views than either Protestants or those with no religion. There is no evidence that this pattern will change in the short to medium term. The trends also suggest that the public's optimism has probably peaked and that the most likely future pattern – in the absence of any major political crises – will be for around two-thirds of the population to express optimism and the remainder to feel that relations have stayed the same. After four decades of intense conflict and little more than a decade of devolved government, this represents a modest achievement.

Conclusion

One feature of the post-cold war era is the settlement of several protracted ethnic conflicts through the adoption of consociational models of government. Power-sharing arrangements among political elites have now moved centre stage as the key mechanism for conflict resolution in post-conflict societies (Rothchild and Roeder, 2005). By contrast, the social and economic dimensions of peace building as experienced by ordinary citizens remain under-researched and neglected. Yet, this preoccupation with systems of governance in resolving ethnic division in post-conflict societies may well be premature. Some analysts suggest that such arrangements further encourage sectarian division at the political level and fail to address the social and economic dimensions of peace building, thus doing little to resolve community divisions (McCartney, 2003; Donais, 2005). Or, to use Johan Galtung's (1996) pioneering distinction, they are more likely to lead to a 'negative' rather than a 'positive' peace, one based simply on the absence of violence rather than on the achievement of justice and communal integration.

There is also disagreement about the impact of the consociational institutions that emerged from the 1998 Agreement. While there are obvious potential benefits, such as the restoration of devolved government to Northern Ireland, the contribution of consociational institutions to reducing community divisions is debatable. The danger of reinforcing sectarian political divisions has already been mentioned. Another frequent criticism is that such institutions inevitably focus public attention on the role of systems of governance at the expense of the public bodies that have to deal with the social and economic aspects of the conflict. Such a focus carries the risk that it will exacerbate community division and undermine the efforts of ordinary citizens to bring about reconciliation (Oberschall and Palmer, 2005).

The results of this investigation lend support to this latter view. Contrary to the optimistic expectations of supporters of the Agreement, this chapter has demonstrated that despite considerable gains over the whole period, community relations have not improved significantly in the past decade. Our evidence in support of this proposition is threefold. First, irrespective of religious background, a majority of individuals still confine their living arrangements and social interaction exclusively to their own community. This is particularly the case among the young, for whom increasing segregation, and not integration, is the norm. Second, although the overwhelming majority of adults say that they are in favour of more mixing as a mechanism to improve community relations, when the details of ways in which this might occur are examined, support remains tepid at best – a finding that is again particularly marked among the young. Third, levels of optimism about community relations have either remained stable or declined in recent years. At present, only a bare majority of respondents believe that community relations will be better in five years time. If consociational institutions are functioning as they are supposed to, we might have expected optimism to increase.

One consistent finding is the higher level of Catholic optimism about community relations compared to that of Protestants. The explanation for this rests in who is seen to have most benefitted from the Agreement. A key aspect of the Agreement was what British Prime Minister Tony Blair referred to as 'mutually assured benefit'.[21] Yet, as noted in Chapter 4, no sooner was the Agreement signed than Protestants, particularly from the working class, felt that the so-called peace dividends had disproportionately benefitted Catholics at their expense. The extent of Protestant disillusionment with the Agreement led the Secretary of State, John Reid, to warn in 2001 that Northern Ireland must not become a 'cold place for Protestants'.[22] It is this widespread sense of Protestant disillusionment with the Agreement and its promised benefits that explains their more negative attitudes towards integration and community relations.

The results presented here have a number of implications for post-conflict peace-building agendas based on consociational models of governance. First, an exclusive concentration on a resolution to the political aspects of the conflict is not enough; the social and economic dimensions of the conflict as experienced by ordinary citizens also need to be addressed. In other words, top-down peace accords also need to connect with local-level aspirations (Mac Ginty *et al.*, 2007: 2). Mechanisms to facilitate these local-level aspirations, such as the economic and social regeneration of communities, must also be considered a vital component in the reconstruction of post-conflict societies. Without such mechanisms there is a risk that the perpetuators of the conflict – the most marginalized and younger members within a society – will return to violence, thus negating the peace-building efforts of the political elite.

Notes

1 See, for example, Oberschall and Palmer (2005) and Oberschall (2007: 157–84).

2 See Pettigrew (1997) for a comprehensive discussion of this issue.

3 See particularly the comments in Oberschall and Palmer (2005), Oberschall (2007) and Taylor (2009a).

4 See, for example, McLaughlin and Faris (2004a, 2004b), Wilson (2007), Taylor, (2009a).

5 Current estimates suggest that over 90 per cent of public housing in Northern Ireland is segregated on religious grounds, with 91 per cent of the most polarized estates having more than 80 per cent of one community. While there is evidence that estates became significantly more segregated between 1971 and 1991, this does not seem to be the case between 1991 and 2001 when little change occurred (see Independent Commission on the Future for Housing in Northern Ireland, 2010).

6 The next chapter presents a comprehensive discussion of integrated education, including its relationship to community relations.

7 Whereas *A Shared Future* was devised by British ministers during the direct rule era, the *Programme for Cohesion, Sharing and Integration* was the result

of protracted negotiations between the DUP and Sinn Fein who squabbled publicly about its content.

8 To date, responses to the programme have been overwhelmingly negative. See Todd and Ruane (2010) for a critical discussion of this issue.

9 For example, as recently as 26 November 2011, Peter Robinson, in a speech at the annual DUP conference at Castlereagh, called for Catholics and Protestants to unite in creating a shared society and end sectarian division. Rejecting explicitly the view that he advocated a separate but equal policy towards community relations, he stated that 'I don't want a society that people live close together, but live separate lives. If we want a better society it can't be "them and us". It can only be "all of us"'.

10 See Hillyard *et al.* (2003), Shirlow and Murtagh (2006) and Smyth and Cebulla (2008).

11 Based on two surveys carried out between 2002 and 2003, this investigation found that whereas the gap between the number of poor Protestants and poor Catholics had narrowed, the gap between the rich and the poor within the Protestant community and within the Catholic community had, in fact, widened.

12 Estimates from the 2010 Northern Ireland School Leavers Survey suggest that, among those from the most disadvantaged areas, more Catholic school leavers than Protestant school leavers attend institutions of higher education. Current estimates suggest that whereas a socially disadvantaged pupil in a Catholic (maintained) school now has a one in five chance of going to university, the equivalent odds for a similar pupil in a Protestant (controlled) school is just 1 in 10 (see Purvis, 2010). The future importance of this differential should not be underestimated. Northern Ireland has the youngest population of any part of the UK and is also its poorest region (see Horgan and Monteith, 2009).

13 While a number of analysts point to an increase in segregation rates, particularly in urban areas such as Belfast (see Shirlow and Murtagh 2006; Hughes *et al.*, 2007) others, while accepting that segregation levels markedly increased between 1971 and 1991, point to little or no increase between 1991 and 2001 (see Shuttleworth and Lloyd, 2009).

14 See Boal (1995) for a detailed discussion and explanation of this issue.

15 See OFMDFM (2002), Shirlow and Murtagh (2006) and Hughes *et al.* (2007) for a detailed discussion and evaluation of this issue.

16 Between Easter and the end of August, nearly 3,000 parades take place in Northern Ireland each year. The overwhelming majority of the marches are undertaken by the Protestant Orange Order, a few of which pass through areas populated by Catholic nationalists. And, while the vast majority pass off peacefully, some, the most notable being the standoff in Drumcree in the latter half of the 1990s, have resulted in serious civil disorder and rioting. In an effort to resolve the issue, the Labour government established a Parades Commission in 1998, responsible for either banning or placing restrictions on any parades deemed contentious or offensive. The Orange Order has a policy of nonengagement with the Commission (see McAuley *et al.*, 2011).

17 In some interface areas, the level of intercommunal violence has resulted in many existing 'peace walls' being heighted and reinforced, and a feature of the violence is the prominent involvement of young people in what has become known as 'recreational rioting', a social activity caused by boredom and bravado rather than politics (see Jarman and O'Halloran, 2001).

18 Recent survey research in some of the most intensively segregated parts of Belfast support these findings. Shirlow and Murtagh (2006), in a survey of 4,800 households at interface areas, found growing levels of fear, segregation and enmity between the two religious communities. This pattern was most marked among the young. Nearly one in seven young persons aged 18–25 years old claimed to 'have never had a meaningful conversation' with people belonging to another religion.

19 See Hughes and Donnelly (2002) for a review of the opinion poll data.

20 Holy Cross School is a Catholic primary school which caters for female pupils between the ages of 4 and 11 and is located in a small Protestant enclave in a predominantly Catholic area of North Belfast. During a three-month period beginning in September 2001, young children and their parents were forced to fight their way through a loyalist mob hurling sectarian abuse and missiles (see Rowan, 2003: 216).

21 Speech by Tony Blair at Castle Buildings Stormont, Belfast, 10 April 1998 following the conclusion of the multiparty talks.

22 Speech by John Reid at the Institute of Irish Studies, University of Liverpool, 21 November 2001.

7

Education

How educational systems operate in divided societies is an increasingly important question for conflict resolution. Traditionally seen as an institution which reflects social differences, more recent views of education are that it has the capacity to generate significant social change, by identifying sources of conflict and by developing strategies to ameliorate them. As a result, the education system has now moved to centre stage as a core component in the reconstruction of post-conflict societies. Educational reconstruction is also viewed as crucial for creating the economic stability that underpins successful reconciliation. As a recent study by the World Bank (2005: 27) commented, 'education has a critical role to play in the wider reconstruction of the society, from building peace and social cohesion to facilitating economic recovery and getting the country onto an accelerated development track'.

The role of education in promoting social cohesion in post-conflict societies is often controversial. Although it is assumed that better education decreases the likelihood that individuals will engage in conflict, recent research questions this assumption.[1] For example, Lynn Davies (2004: 2003) suggests that education often contributes more to the underlying cause of a conflict than it does to peace, through its magnification of 'ethnic and religious segregation or intolerance'. A recent cross-national study of the role of education in perpetuating conflict across a range of ethnically divided countries lends further support to this view. Rejecting the widely held belief that education promoted peace and tolerance, Matthew Lange (2012) found that education commonly contributes to aggression, especially in environments with ethnic divisions, limited resources and ineffective political institutions. Research commissioned by the UK Department for International Development stresses that while education is an essential tool for human development, unless properly managed it may also perpetuate conflict, especially within segregated educational systems based on religion (Smith and Vaux, 2003: 30–1).

Although the role of the educational system in perpetuating the Northern Ireland conflict has a long and controversial history (for a review, see Smith, 2001), most research on its impact has been confined to the school-age population and has generally been inconclusive.[2] While several studies have stressed the positive benefits of formally integrated schools in promoting cross-community friendships, other studies suggest that it has little or no impact. Some commentators have even suggested that rather than weakening divisions, integrated education may in fact reinforce them. Recent research focusing on the long-term impact of integrated education on the adult population questions these pessimistic findings. Using pooled data from the Northern Ireland Life and Times Surveys, Bernadette Hayes *et al.* (2007) found that individuals who had attended either a formally or informally integrated school were significantly more likely than their religiously segregated counterparts to occupy the centre ground in identity politics and to disavow bipartisan territorial allegiances.

Differing findings have also emerged with respect to the impact of segregated schooling on communal divisions. While many observers have long pointed to its potential harmful effects on community relations (Darby *et al.*, 1977; Murray, 1985), religious authorities, most notably the Catholic Church, remain unconvinced. Since the foundation of the Northern Ireland state in 1921, the Catholic hierarchy has strongly supported segregated schooling and considered it to be a crucial mechanism in maintaining religious identity. They have also argued that because Catholic schools contain a commitment to the promotion of tolerance and pluralism, they are just as well placed as integrated schools to promote reconciliation (Catholic Bishops of Ireland, 2001). As Cardinal Cathal Daly put it in 1993, 'if ... integrated education were the best way to ferment good relations then I would be bound to favour it. I am not thus convinced' (quoted in Moffat, 1993: 145).

This chapter explores these competing interpretations by examining the nature of the educational system in Northern Ireland and evaluating its consequences for community contact. Using our extensive collection of public opinion surveys, we address the key question of whether or not integrated education has a significant long-term effect on the outlooks and behaviour of the adult population. The first section briefly outlines the evolution of the educational system in Northern Ireland, while the second section focuses on the nature and growth of integrated education. The third section examines public support for integrated education and its party political dimensions, while the fourth section deals with previous patterns of schooling among the adult population. The fifth section focuses on the consequences of type of education system – integrated or segregated – on cross-community contact within the adult population. The sixth and final section evaluates the role of integrated education on community relations.

The evolution of the educational system

Since its foundation as a state in 1921, Northern Ireland has had two separate, religiously based educational systems at both the primary and secondary level. The state ('controlled') system is attended by Protestants with a number of voluntary grammar schools also attended predominantly by Protestants. Catholics attend schools which are all voluntary (as opposed to state controlled) and, although also state financed, are operated by the Catholic Church and commonly known as the maintained sector. This bipartite system long predates the present constitutional arrangements in Northern Ireland. Prior to partition, most schools were owned by the church authorities. The first legislation passed by the new Northern Ireland parliament in 1923, Lord Londonderry's Education Act, attempted to replace church schools with a single unified system in which there would be no denominational bias in organization, administration, staffing or curriculum. The legislation, however, was vehemently rejected by all churches, Protestant and Catholic. So widespread was the church opposition that the government was forced to accede to their demands and establish a *de facto* segregated education system.[3] This situation continues largely to this day, despite some ill-fated government initiatives to develop a more integrated approach to education (Gallagher, 2004: 119–24).[4]

In addition to their religious composition and management structure, the most obvious difference between the two educational systems was the curriculum. For the most part, the pupils took different subjects, learnt different religions, read different books and, most importantly of all, learnt different histories.[5] Tony Gallagher (1995) studied the GCSE subjects taken by a sample of school students attending different grammar schools. He found that the largest differences were in culturally specific subjects; for example, while 82 per cent of the Catholic pupils took religious education, the same figure for Protestants was just 21 per cent. Similarly, while 23 per cent of Catholics studied the Irish language, no Protestants took the subject. Protestant students were more numerous than Catholics across a majority of the science subjects, especially biology and mathematics. More importantly, even when religious education was conducted at either the primary or secondary level, there was little attempt to deal with 'the problems of comparative religion which lies at the root of so many problems in Northern Ireland, the Protestant-Catholic division' (Greer quoted in Gallagher, 1995: 26).

More than religious education, however, is the differences encountered in the teaching of history in Protestant and Catholic schools (Gallagher, 2003: 65–66). For decades, Catholic children were taught Irish history, often with overtly political overtones. In many history books, there was an obsession with the Anglo-Irish conflict, and Sean Farren (1976: 29) found in some a 'justification for the nationalist cause in terms that could often be accused of bias and of a lack of proper historical perspective'. By contrast, Protestant children were rarely taught about Irish history, except when it intersected with British history. Many of these biases began to be addressed from the 1970s onwards, notably through the common curriculum introduced in 1990. However, it still remains the case that a Catholic school student is likely to study more Irish history than a Protestant school student, and a Protestant will study more British history than a Catholic.

In summary, the present-day segregation of education can be traced back to the failed 1923 Education Act, which sought to educate Catholic and Protestant children together, without religious instruction. While the main opposition to the Act came from both the Protestant and Catholic churches, a key contributory factor in its replacement by the 1930 Education Act was the willingness of the government to capitulate to church demands. Since then, there have been occasional divisions between church leaders and politicians, notably over the proposed McIvor shared-schools plan in 1974.[6] This initiative was supported by some Protestant religious leaders, but it was vehemently opposed by the Catholic hierarchy. Such initiatives, however, have been few; as the next section on the growth of integrated education demonstrates, the initial demand for integrated education came from parents, not from local politicians.[7]

The growth of integrated education

While Northern Ireland has a long history of religiously segregated education, in recent years this dual denominational system has become increasingly fractured with the establishment of an integrated school sector.[8] The impetus behind the push for integrated education came from a parent-led initiative, known as All Children Together (ACT), who believed that the traditional school system had reinforced divisions between Protestants and Catholics.[9] As Bettie Benton, one of the founders of the ACT, put it in 1974: '… how can we become one community, one people, when our children continue to grow up separately?' (quoted in Bardon, 2009: 37). What was required was religiously mixed schooling in order to overcome sectarian division and mutual suspicion. However, it was not until 1981 and against vitriolic objections from both Protestant

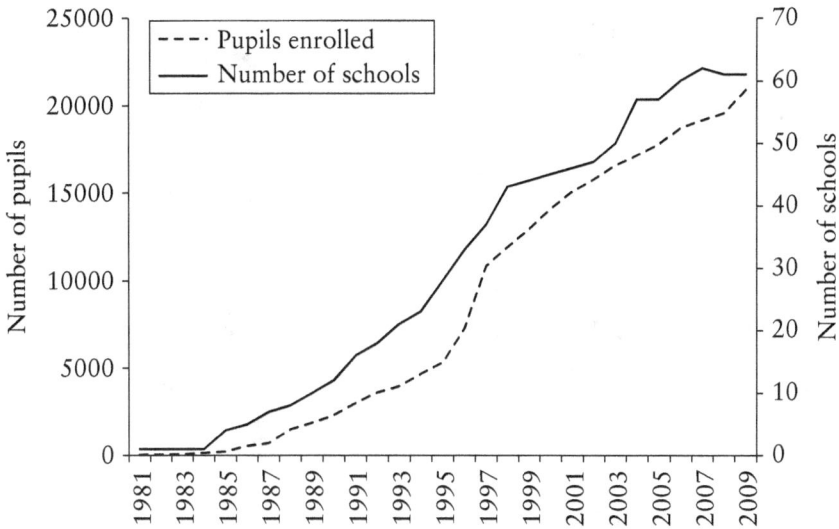

Figure 7.1 The growth of integrated schools, 1981–2009
Figures include all children being educated in integrated schools, including
pre-school provision and those with statements of special needs
Sources: NICIE, Annual Reports, 2006–07: 36–37; 2007–08: 47; Integrated
Education Fund, Chair's Report, 2011: 2

and Catholic church leaders that the first integrated school, Lagan
College, was established.[10] So great was the opposition to its establishment that is was originally funded from private sources, notably the
Joseph Rowntree Charitable Trust and the Nuffield Foundation, although
in 1984 it achieved government funding and became a grant-maintained
college, with a student enrolment of 140 students.

Since then, between two and three new integrated schools a year have
been opened by the government (see Figure 7.1). For example, by 1991,
or just one decade after the establishment of Lagan College, there were a
total of 16 schools with a student enrolment of just over 3,000 students.
In the following two decades, the number of schools nearly quadrupled
so that, by 2011, there were a total of 62 schools, all government funded,
with an enrolment of just under 20,000 pupils (see Northern Ireland
Assembly, 2011). Of these 62 schools, 42 are primary schools and just 20
are secondary schools; there are no formally integrated grammar schools.
As a consequence of this increase in government support, the integrated
education sector has flourished since 1989. For example, government figures shows that in 2001–02, 3.2 per cent of primary school children were
in integrated schools as compared to 2.4 per cent in 1998–99, and a total

Table 7.1 Religion of pupils in Northern Ireland schools, 2010–11

	Protestant	Catholic	Non-Christian	No religion/not stated	All
Protestant controlled	90.3	5.0	62.3	84.0	46.0
(Primary)	(46.0)	(2.5)	(37.0)	(49.7)	(24.0)
(Secondary)	(22.3)	(0.4)	(7.9)	(14.7)	(10.4)
(Grammar)	(22.0)	(2.1)	(17.4)	(19.6)	(11.6)
Catholic maintained	1.5	90.1	24.9	4.8	47.2
(Primary)	(0.9)	(46.0)	(17.1)	(3.3)	(24.3)
(Secondary)	(0.3)	(26.9)	(4.0)	(1.1)	(14.0)
(Grammar)	(0.3)	(17.2)	(3.8)	(0.3)	(8.9)
Integrated	8.2	4.9	12.8	11.2	6.8
(Primary)	(3.1)	(2.0)	(6.2)	(5.9)	(2.8)
(Secondary)	(5.1)	(2.9)	(6.6)	(5.3)	(4.0)
Total	100.0	100.0	100.0	100.0	100.0
(N)	(121,556)	(154,573)	(1,582)	(24,643)	(302,354)

Protestant schools include 'controlled' or state schools at the primary and secondary level, which are *de facto* Protestant schools, as well as voluntary grammar schools and preparatory schools at the primary level which are fee-paying but state-subsidized departments attached to Protestant grammar schools. Catholic schools include Catholic-maintained schools at the primary and secondary level as well as voluntary Catholic grammar schools. Integrated schools include grant-maintained and controlled integrated schools
Source: DENI, 2011

of 10.0 per cent of secondary school children attended integrated schools in 2001–02, compared to 5.7 per cent in 1998–99.[11]

The most recent government statistics, based on the religious composition of pupils in Northern Ireland schools in 2010–11, further confirms this growth in integrated education (DENI, 2011). Although a bipartite system based on religious segregation still remains the norm – 90 per cent of both Protestant and Catholic children attend a school which is effectively controlled by their own community – there is evidence to suggest religious mixing occurs particularly within the secondary school sector (see Table 7.1). For example, whereas 7 per cent of all children attend an integrated school, a slightly greater proportion is located in the secondary rather than the primary sector. When these figures are recalculated in terms of our earlier government statistics – the proportion of children in integrated education within the primary and secondary sector – 5.2 per cent of all primary school children and 14 per cent of all secondary children are currently in integrated schools.

A similar pattern emerges when each of the religious groupings is considered separately. Only 3 per cent of all Protestant primary school children attend an integrated school, compared to 5 per cent of secondary school children. This preference for integrated education is disproportionately concentrated among both the non-Christian and the no religion/not stated religious category. In contrast to their Protestant counterparts, the proportion of children attending an integrated secondary school within the non-Christian category accounts for 7 per cent of all children within this religious grouping. Although the proportion of children attending an integrated primary school is slightly lower by comparison – accounting for just 6 per cent of all primary school children in the non-Christian category – it is still double the equivalent proportion of children from within the Protestant community and three times that of children from a Catholic background. Similar differences emerge when the number of children attending integrated schools in the no religion/not stated religious category and those from either the Protestant or Catholic community is compared.

There is also a small minority of Protestant and Catholic students (3.2 per cent, or 9,612 pupils in 2010–11) who cross the religious divide and attend a segregated school different to their own religion, which may be considered a 'religiously mixed' or informally integrated school. This crossover in attendance is more common among Catholics (2.6 per cent) than Protestants (0.6 per cent). While the crossover is relatively small in both primary and secondary schools, it is more marked in grammar schools: 1.3 per cent of students in Catholic grammar schools are Protestant, but 11 per cent of pupils in Protestant-controlled schools are Catholic. These schools are essentially Protestant schools with a minority of Catholic pupils in attendance.

In addition to their religious composition, integrated schools also differ radically from religiously segregated schools both in terms of their ethos as well as their overall management structure. The overarching goal of integrated education is to foster an understanding of both the dominant traditions and to overcome negative stereotypes (NICIE, 2004a; 2004b). Attended in roughly equal numbers by Protestant and Catholic children and based on a Christian ethos, integrated schools are defined by government as schools which have a 30 per cent minimum enrolment from whatever side of the community forms a minority within that school. By educating children from both religious communities together and encouraging them to understand their historical and religious differences, it is hoped that they will feel less threatened by the traditions of the other community and form enduring cross-community relations. In the most contentious area, religious education, integrated schools provide any interdenominational religious education that is requested by the parents. In the other area of contention, the teaching of history, the integrated curriculum emphasizes local history in order to create a common heritage.

Importantly, no single model of integration unites Northern Ireland's integrated schools, and they vary considerably with regard to how actively they promote integration (Montgomery *et al.*, 2003). Furthermore, not all staff in integrated schools have been equally proactive in achieving an integrationist ethos. Caitlin Donnelly (2004) found considerable disparity among teachers with regard to how an ethos of tolerance and respect could be created and maintained in the school. Donnelly and Hughes (2006) support these findings and demonstrated that not only is there considerable disparity among parents, teachers and principals as to what constitutes an integrated ethos, but discussions with pupils concerning politically contentious issues are deliberately avoided. However, more so than any other factor, the key difference between integrated and segregated schools is their commitment to constitutional and structural safeguards to encourage joint ownership by the two traditions. To demonstrate joint ownership, all integrated schools have adopted the principle that both students and staff should be drawn from both cultural traditions and it is not unusual for parents from both religious communities to constitute roughly half of the governing body in integrated schools (Smith, 2001).

The growth of integrated schooling in Northern Ireland is a remarkable achievement, although it has not been without tension and conflict (Morgan and Fraser, 1999). This is particularly the case since the mid-1990s, when government restrictions on educational expenditure has discouraged the further establishment of these schools and instead sought to promote the conversion of existing controlled or maintained schools to integrated status – the establishment of 'transformed' schools. Although the transformation of existing schools to integrated status was legally conceded as far back as the late 1970s,[12] it was not until the late-1990s that a growing number of schools began to embark on this route (Smith 2001: 571). Currently, around two dozen schools have achieved transformed status, all of which have been pre-existing state-controlled schools traditionally associated with the Protestant community. While some have welcomed the establishment of such schools, notably small Protestant schools threatened with closure, supporters of integration have expressed concerns about many aspects of the process, such as the proportion of cross-community enrolment deemed necessary or the recruitment of a balanced staff (Morgan and Fraser, 1999).

Recent government estimates of the religious composition of pupils in integrated schools lend support to these concerns about the granting of integrated status (see Northern Ireland Assembly, 2011). Based on the statistics for the 2010–11 school year, around 44 per cent of integrated schools – 19 primary and 8 post-primary – do not have a 30 per cent or more intake of pupils from a minority community. Moreover, some integrated schools attract less than 5 per cent of their intake from the minority community, fewer than some state-controlled schools. As expected, these schools are associated with the Protestant community or schools that transformed to integrated status from within the controlled sector. Overall, 35 of the 62 schools are predominantly attended by Catholic children. There is also a minority of schools – 14 of the 62 – that have an even balance of Protestant and Catholic pupils. The trend towards the transformation of existing schools to an integrated status will be a matter of much debate in the future.[13]

In summary, by any standards, the emergence and growth of integrated education in Northern Ireland must be considered an extraordinary accomplishment. Initiated by parents during one of the most troubled periods in the history of the most recent phase of the conflict, and despite considerable opposition by both the Catholic hierarchy and a number of local politicians, the integrated sector has expanded and flourished in Northern Ireland since the first and privately funded integrated school was established in a scout's hut in Belfast in 1981. Currently, there are 62 integrated primary or post-primary schools, the vast majority of which are new schools founded by groups of parents committed to educating Protestant and Catholic children together. In fact, more so than any other issue, it was this factor – a determination by parents to educate Protestant and Catholic children together in the hope of breaking down communal divisions – which lies at the heart of the growth of integrated education.

Although opposition to integrated education is now more muted than in the past, some significant detractors still remain, most notably the continuing hostility of the Catholic Church. As recently as 2010, Cardinal Brady, the Primate of Ireland, explicitly rejected a plea by Peter Robinson, the first minister, for a single unified educational school system.[14] As Cardinal Brady, in arguing instead for the primacy of parental choice, put it, 'Recent suggestions that schools in Northern Ireland should be forced into a single state system are stark warnings to all those who respect diversity and the rights of parents. It seems strange that people in Northern Ireland are being told that they should accept a lower standard of rights and freedoms that they would have if they lived in Britain, Scotland or the south of Ireland'. This position has also found sympathy among several nationalist politicians, including the SDLP. As Dominic Bradley put it, 'The SDLP believes strongly in parental choice in education, be it Catholic, maintained, integrated or Irish medium education'.[15] Despite this continuing opposition to integrated education, to what extent has the growth in integrated education also been accompanied by its increasing acceptability among the general public? The next section examines public support for religiously mixed schools.

Public support for integrated schools

The public overwhelmingly supports some form of integrated education. A public opinion poll conducted in 2011 found that the vast majority of the population supported schools sharing facilities, as well as partnering or collaborating on specific tasks, if they were from different religious traditions. These included sharing facilities for one-off projects, sharing capital facilities, sharing teachers and facilities between schools at both the primary and secondary level, and support for integrated schools in general. Although the highest level of support was for sharing at a minimal level – one-off projects (95 per cent) or the sharing of capital facilities (94 per cent) – 88 per cent of the respondents favoured formally integrated schools (see Ipsos, 2011: 40). By any standards, this is a high level of public support for integrated education.

The opinion poll evidence suggests that this high level of support for integrated education has existed since at least the 1980s. Despite our previous analysis in Chapter 6, demonstrating limited support for greater school integration, the results in Figure 7.2 show that when their own children are concerned, around 7 out of every 10 adults report that they

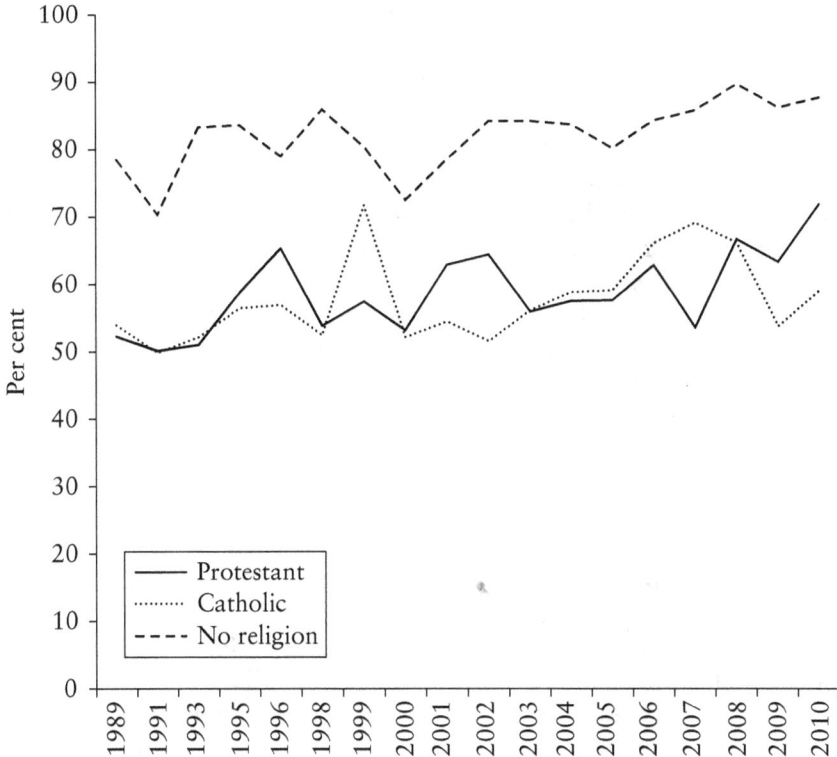

Figure 7.2 Public support for religiously mixed schools, 1989–2010
The question was 'And, if you were deciding to send your children to school,
would you prefer a school with children of only your own religion or a mixed-
religion school?'
Sources: Northern Ireland Social Attitudes Survey, 1989–96; Northern Ireland
Life and Times Surveys, 1998–2010

would prefer to send their child to a religiously mixed school rather than
to a religiously segregated one. Moreover, public support for religiously
mixed schools has increased significantly over the last decade. In 1991,
just over half the adult population stated that they would prefer to send
their children to a religiously mixed school; by 2010, the proportion had
increased to 69 per cent.

There are also important differences between the two religious communities in relation to this issue. While Protestant and Catholic preferences in terms of their support for religiously mixed schools were
broadly similar throughout most of the period of study, since 2008

Catholic support for religiously mixed schools has declined. Currently, 72 per cent of Protestants say that they would prefer to send their child to a religiously mixed school compared to 59 per cent of Catholics. Preferences for religiously mixed schools are highest among those with no religion, a pattern that has been consistent throughout the last two decades. Thus, despite our previous analysis in indicating only limited public approval for the principle of integrated education, there is much greater support for integration when the question related to the respondent's own children.

Although high levels of public support for mixed schooling have been present since the late 1980s, the attitudes of local politicians have traditionally lagged behind that of the general public. As noted earlier, with the exception of the Alliance Party, throughout much of the history of integrated education, local politicians have been either hostile or largely indifferent in their views (see O'Connor, 2002; Bardon, 2009). Moreover, this disjuncture in attitudes between the politicians and the public seems to have been particularly marked among the DUP and Sinn Fein, albeit for different reasons.[16] However, as noted earlier, there is some evidence to suggest a significant shift in the views of the DUP. To what extent are these changing attitudes among politicians towards integrated education also reflected in the views of their supporters?

Figure 7.3 addresses this question by focusing on attitudes towards integrated schooling broken down in terms of support for the five main political parties – the DUP, the UUP, Alliance, SDLP and Sinn Fein. The results suggest that with one exception – Sinn Fein – the proportion in favour of sending their children to a religiously mixed school has increased dramatically since 1989. For example, whereas just under half of UUP and SDLP supporters indicated a preference for a religiously mixed school in 1989, by 2010, around 7 in 10 held this view. A similar pattern emerges when DUP supporters are considered. While 37 per cent of DUP supporters indicated a preference for a religiously mixed school in 1989, by 2010 the same figure was 65 per cent.

The results also suggest some marked differences in patterns of support for integrated education. The most important difference is between SDLP and Sinn Fein supporters; over two-thirds of SDLP identifiers support religiously mixed schools, compared to less than half of Sinn Fein identifiers. This difference is consistent with the policies of the two parties and has remained relatively constant over time. There are also significant differences in opinion between supporters of the DUP and UUP. While general unionist support for sending their children to a religiously mixed school has increased substantially over the last two decades, support among DUP supporters continues to lag behind that of their UUP counterparts.[17]

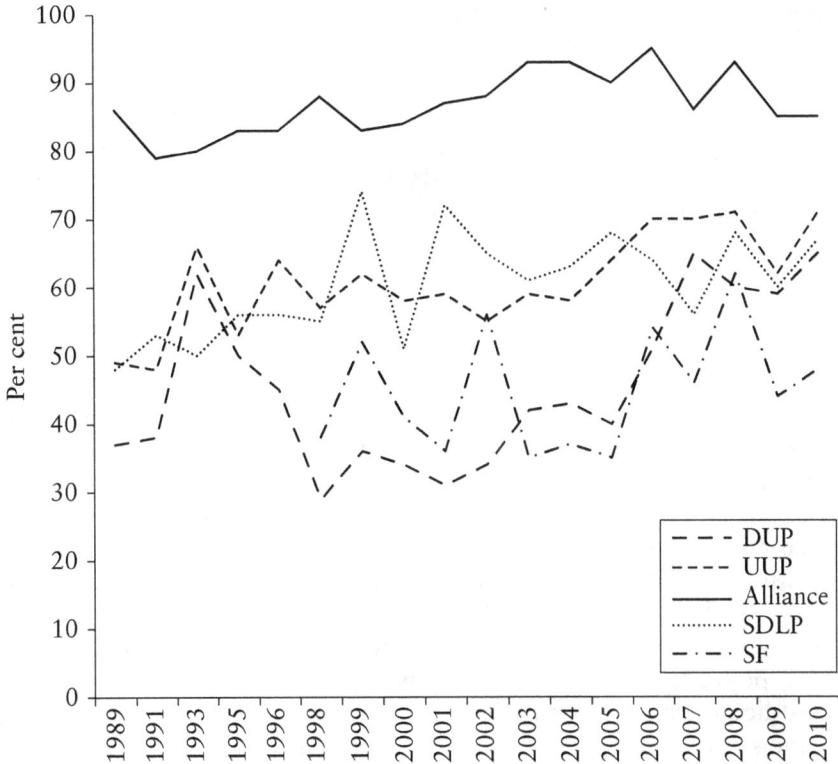

Figure 7.3 Party support for religiously mixed schools, 1989–2010
See Figure 7.2 for question wording. Estimates before 1998 for Sinn Fein are
based on too few respondents for reliability and are excluded
Sources: Northern Ireland Social Attitudes Survey, 1989–96; Northern Ireland
Life and Times Surveys, 1998–2010

Indeed, it was not until 2006 that a majority of DUP supporters indicated
their preference for integration. Since then, support for integration has
increased dramatically among DUP supporters, rising to 65 per cent in
2007. Finally, as expected, Alliance supporters are consistently and overwhelmingly in favour of religiously mixed schools.

Thus, contrary to religious background, attitudes towards religiously
mixed schools are now divided within, rather than along, traditional
party political lines. The changes in attitudes among unionist supporters
are particularly important, with increasing support for religiously mixed
schools, even among DUP supporters. However, integration continues to
be rejected by the Catholic Church, and it has also been criticized by

several Sinn Fein representatives, including Martin McGuinness, a recent convert to the advantages of integrated education (see O'Connor, 2002: 46).[18] Nevertheless, the overwhelming majority of the public supports some form of integrated education. Furthermore, this high level of support has existed since at least the late 1980s, less than a decade after the first integrated school was established in 1981. Politicians, by contrast, have traditionally been much more reticent and divided in their views.

Educational integration and segregation

While much has been written on the nature and extent of religious division within the school population, the educational experiences of the adult population remain largely unexplored, whether in a formal or informal school setting. While one explanation is the relative newness of these schools, another explanation is the preoccupation of educationalists with the consequences of religious division on the school population. Even among those who have experienced integrated schooling, follow-up studies investigating their adult experiences remain rare (McGlynn et al., 2004). This section outlines the previous educational experiences of the adult population, using nationally representative samples of the adult population from 1989 onwards.

Although government statistics indicate low levels of religious mixing at the school level, the survey evidence suggests a much less segregated picture in terms of informal integration within the adult population. Between 1989 and 2010, 14 per cent of the respondents said that they attended a mixed school. This is, of course, a very considerable overestimate of those attending a formally integrated school, based on the official figures. Most of the respondents who said that they had attended an integrated school are interpreting the question as whether or not there were any pupils of the opposite religion at their school, rather than whether or not it was a formally constituted integrated school. While it has limited utility, the measure of the religious composition of the school does have value in showing the proportion of the population who have had some experience of meeting children of the opposite religion in the education system. The measure is also useful in comparing the overtime trend in informal integration between the two communities.

The trend in Figure 7.4 suggests that such informal mixing in the school environment has declined since 1989, when 21 per cent reported attending a mixed school, the highest annual figure over the period. The lowest estimate is in 2006, when just 10 per cent said that they attended such a school. The trends for the two main religious groupings show few differences, and all display a consistent decrease, although as in the early

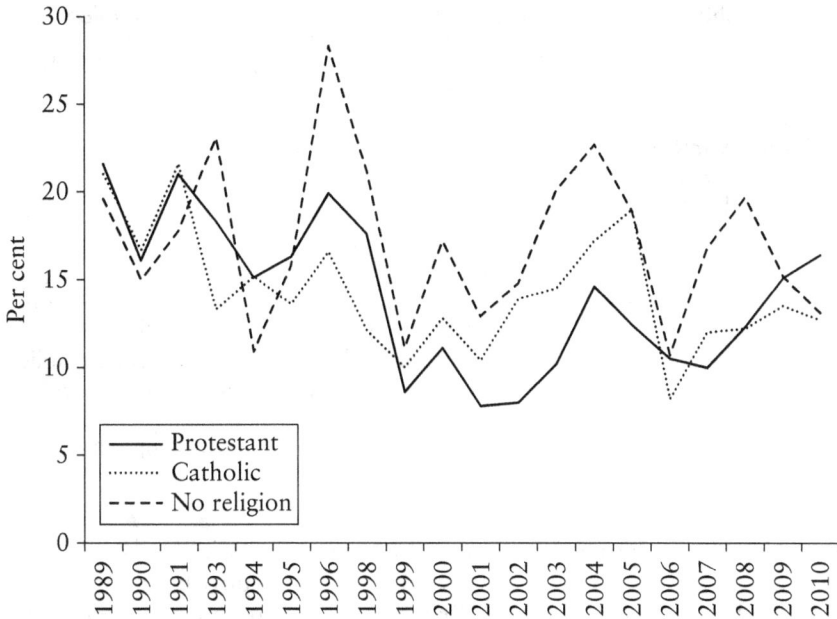

Figure 7.4 Attendance at an integrated school, 1989–2010
The question was 'Did you ever attend a mixed or integrated school in
Northern Ireland, that is, a school with fairly large numbers of *both*
Catholic *and* Protestant children?'
Sources: Northern Ireland Social Attitudes Survey, 1989–96; Northern Ireland
Life and Times Surveys, 1998–2010

1990s Protestants are currently more likely to report higher levels of
attendance than Catholics. A reverse pattern emerges when the non-
affiliated are considered. With few exceptions, the level of attendance at
a mixed school among individuals reporting no religious affiliation
remained relatively stable over time – averaging around 17 per cent across
the survey years. In the vast majority of cases, this figure is significantly
higher than that of either their Protestant or Catholic counterparts.

In order to estimate the proportion attending a formally integrated
school, rather than simply a school that had some pupils of the opposite religion, from 1998 onwards a supplementary question was asked
of those making a positive response to the question about integrated
education, inquiring if the school was 'formally integrated' as opposed
to 'just fairly mixed'. This leads to a much lower estimate of 2 per cent
for those attending an integrated school (see Table 7.2). By contrast,
10 per cent who reported attending a mixed school said that it was

Table 7.2 Type of education by religion, limited pooled sample

	Protestant	Catholic	No religion	All
Integrated				
Formally integrated	2	2	3	2
Fairly mixed	11	9	12	10
Segregated	87	89	85	88
Total	100	100	100	100
(N)	(11,305)	(8,048)	(2,319)	(21,672)

The questions were 'Did you ever attend a mixed or integrated school in Northern Ireland, that is, a school with fairly large numbers of *both* Catholic *and* Protestant children?' and 'Was this a formally integrated school or was it a school that was just fairly mixed?'
Source: Northern Ireland Surveys, Restricted Pooled Sample, 1998–2010

not a formally integrated school, just one that was 'fairly mixed'.[19] A higher proportion of those with no religion report having attended a formally integrated school – 3 per cent as compared to 2 per cent for the two religious communities. This suggests that there may be a pattern whereby parents with no religion are more likely to send their children to an integrated school compared to parents who identify with a religion.

This hypothesis can be tested by predicting the probability of experiencing integrated education (either in a formally integrated school or through one that is 'fairly mixed') from the religion of the respondent's parents. Because attendance at a formally integrated school is more prevalent among the young, we need to control for age. We also test the hypothesis that there may be gender differences in patterns of integration and segregation, given previous evidence as to the traditionally larger uptake of integrated education among male pupils than female pupils, particularly in the primary school sector (see Montgomery *et al.*, 2003).

The results in Table 7.3 suggest relatively little effect for parental religion. Compared to Protestant parents (the excluded category), respondents with Catholic parents were significantly less likely to have attended a fairly mixed school, but there are no significant differences between the two main religious groupings with respect to formally integrated schools. This preponderance of adults from a Protestant background who attended informally integrated schools may simply be explained by the Protestant nature of these schools. Respondents who reported that their parents claimed no religious affiliation were more

Table 7.3 Parental religion and type of education, limited pooled sample

	Formally integrated		Just fairly mixed	
	Est	(SE)	Est	(SE)
Background characteristics				
Gender (male)	−0.24*	(0.10)	−0.07	(0.04)
Age (years)	−0.04**	(0.01)	−0.01**	(0.01)
Parental religion (Protestant)				
Catholic	0.11	(0.10)	−0.32**	(0.04)
No religion	0.53*	(0.25)	−0.11	(0.10)
Constant	−2.01**		−1.53**	
Pseudo R-squared	0.06		0.01	
(N)	(19,710)		(21,614)	

Significant at **$p < 0.01$; *$p < 0.05$
Logistic regression equations showing parameter estimates and (in parentheses) robust standard errors predicting the probability of formally integrated school or schooling in a fairly mixed school, as against segregated schooling. Both models include year dummy variables for unobserved heterogeneity. Protestant is the omitted category for parental religious affiliation
Source: Northern Ireland Surveys, Restricted Pooled Sample, 1998–2010

likely to attend a formally integrated school, but the estimate for fairly mixed schools fails to reach statistical significance. Other consistent differences include the negative effect of age, with older individuals being significantly less likely to have attended either a formally integrated or fairly mixed school than their younger counterparts.

For the vast majority of adults in Northern Ireland, religious affiliation and school experience remain coterminous. As the results from the analysis reported above demonstrate, the vast majority of the adult Protestant population have attended Protestant-controlled schools, and Catholics have been disproportionately concentrated in Catholic-maintained schools. There remains a small but growing proportion from both religious communities who have experienced a formally integrated education, particularly among the young. The evolution of this third element in the educational system – integrated schools – is based on the assumption that contact between polarized groups within an educational setting can improve intergroup relations. The next section investigates the long-term impact of the educational system on intercommunity contact within the adult population.

Education and intercommunity contact

As we noted in the previous chapter, one of the most frequently applied approaches to conflict resolution is the contact hypothesis. Since it was originally advanced in the 1950s, the contact hypothesis has been extensively tested, particularly with respect to education. Research on the effects of desegregation on the U.S. student population points to its positive effects on racial attitudes (Pettigrew, 1998). There is also evidence that interracial school contact is a more effective mechanism in countering racial and ethnic stereotypes than contact in the community or workplace (Dixon and Rosenbaum, 2004). The only comprehensive study of the long-term impact of school desegregation on the adult population has reached similar conclusions. As Holme et al. (2005: 23), in assessing the impact of desegregated education on the U.S. population, conclude, 'the experience of attending racially diverse schools may break down the cycle of segregation by giving them increased comfort in racially mixed settings, and decreased fear of racially mixed environments'. Finally, the few available studies focusing on the long-term impact of integrated education on the adult population in Northern Ireland point to the importance of religiously mixed schools in breaking down communal division (see Hayes et al., 2007; Hayes and McAllister, 2009b).

Using the contact hypothesis as our guiding theoretical framework, this section examines the impact of integrated education on cross-community contact within the adult population. The key question to be investigated is the degree to which adults who had experienced an integrated education are different in their attitudes and behavioural patterns compared to those who had attended religiously segregated schools. One caveat concerning our results is the inability to determine causality. Since our results are aggregated cross-sectional surveys, we do not know the outlooks of the respondents or their parents before they entered an integrated school. For example, it could be argued that more liberally minded parents are more likely to send their children to integrated schools and that the effects we attribute to schooling may in fact be due to parental choice. Our response to this is fourfold.

First, recent research suggests that it is the school environment and not parental influence which promotes greater religious tolerance (see McGlynn, 2003: 11–28). Second, earlier research on the motives of parents whose children attended an integrated school indicates a variety of reasons for their choice, ranging from the quality of the education, dissatisfaction with an existing school, or simply convenience (Morgan et al., 1992). Third, there is survey evidence to suggest that not only do young people who attend integrated schools hold a more favourable opinion of people from the other religious community than those who do not, but they are less likely than their religiously segregated counterparts to claim that their parent was the most influential factor in determining their views (see Schubotz and Robinson, 2006). Finally, there is a growing body of research – longitudinal, experimental and meta-analytic – both in Northern Ireland and elsewhere which suggests that intergroup contact can lead to a reduction in prejudice (Pettigrew and Tropp, 2006; Hewstone *et al.*, 2008; Wells *et al.*, 2009). This is an issue, however, that can only be definitely resolved by extensive, long-term panel studies which are currently unavailable.

Across the total population, the results in Table 7.4 support the positive long-term effects of integrated schooling on community relations. Significant differences between the two communities emerge in terms of support for greater cross-community contact between those who had attended a segregated school and those who had not. For example, over 7 out of every 10 adults who had attended either a formally integrated or 'fairly mixed' school indicated that they would prefer to send their children to a religiously mixed school, compared to just 59 per cent among those who had experienced a segregated education. A similar pattern emerges with respect to preferences towards religiously mixed or more integrated neighbourhoods and workplaces; in both cases, it is again individuals who have experienced a non-segregated education who stand out as being the most inclusive in their views.

The findings are repeated when Protestants, Catholics and those with no religious affiliation are examined separately. As the subsequent panels of Table 7.4 show, irrespective of religious background, individuals who had attended a non-segregated school were more likely to support integration in schooling, residential practices and work environment than their religiously segregated counterparts. For example, 8 out of every 10 Protestant adults who had attended a formally integrated school and around 7 out of every 10 who had attended a religiously mixed school supported a religiously mixed school for their children, compared to just 55 per cent of those who had attended a segregated school. The patterns are similar for those with no religion; around 9 out of every 10 individuals who had attended either a formally integrated or fairly mixed school supported an integrated education for their children. Among Catholics, it is those who attended a fairly mixed school who stand out as most in favour of integration.

These findings about the importance of integrated education on attitudes towards community contact are also supported in terms of workplaces and neighbourhoods. Although the differences are not as clearly

Table 7.4 Schooling and attitudes towards religious integration, limited pooled sample

| | (Per cent who prefer mixed) | | |
	Integrated	Fairly mixed	Segregated
All			
School	79	75	59
Neighbourhood	84	84	73
Workplace	93	92	85
(N)	(427)	(2,331)	(19,283)
Protestant			
School	82	74	55
Neighbourhood	87	80	69
Workplace	91	90	82
(N)	(179)	(1,305)	(9,821)
Catholic			
School	68	71	58
Neighbourhood	80	89	76
Workplace	93	96	88
(N)	(170)	(691)	(7,187)
No religion			
School	94	90	79
Neighbourhood	87	90	82
Workplace	99	94	90
(N)	(71)	(276)	(1,972)

The questions were 'Now I would like to ask you some questions about relations between people of different religions living in Northern Ireland. These particular questions are about relations between Protestants and Catholics. If you had a choice, would you prefer to live in a neighbourhood with people of only your own religion or a mixed-religion neighbourhood?', 'And if you were working and had to change your job, would you prefer a workplace with people of only your own religion or a mixed-religion workplace?' and 'And if you were deciding to send your children to school, would you prefer a school with children of only your own religion or a mixed-religion school?' Ns for individual items vary due to missing data
Source: Northern Ireland Surveys, Restricted Pooled Sample, 1998–2010

differentiated as they are for schools, once again it is individuals who experienced a non-segregated education who emerge as being the most supportive of integration. These less decisive results may be because individuals have less control over the religious composition of their neighbourhoods or, especially, their workplaces. By contrast, the nature of the school that a parent chooses for one's child represents a clear choice and one which reflects his/her preferences and outlooks.

The results are unequivocal and show the important moderating influence of integrated education. Individuals who had experienced a non-segregated education are more likely to endorse a religiously mixed environment than those who had not; this is particularly the case with regard to attitudes towards the education of their children. Furthermore, whereas attendance at a formally integrated school is the key distinguishing factor among Protestants and those with no religious affiliation, for Catholics it is individuals who had attended a fairly mixed school who stand out as being the most integrationist in their views. To what extent are these differences in attitudes reflected in actual behavioural patterns in addition to outlooks? Are individuals who had attended non-segregated schools also likely to exhibit different patterns of social behaviour?

Table 7.5 addresses this question by focusing on the relationship between schooling and the extent of religious exclusivity in social contact between the two communities; this is measured by kinship and friendship patterns and by residential location. The results provide support for the role of integrated schools in weakening social divisions and demonstrate the long-term effects of integrated schooling in promoting a more moderate stance in social behaviour. In two of the social contact networks – friendship and residential location – clear differences emerge in terms of the level of contact between the two communities in relation to those who had attended a segregated school versus those who had not; this is particularly marked in friendship patterns.

The results in Table 7.5 show that around 7 out of every 10 adults who experienced a segregated education reported that 'most' or 'all' of their friends were from their own religion. This compares with much lower proportions among those educated in a mixed school, especially those educated in formally integrated schools. While just over half of those educated in a fairly mixed school claimed that 'most' or 'all' of their friends were from their own religion, the equivalent proportion among the formally integrated was lower at just 43 per cent. There is a similar pattern in actual levels of contact between the two religious communities; just 7 per cent of those who had experienced a segregated education claimed to have 'less than half' or 'no' friends of the same religion, compared to 8 per cent and 15 per cent among those educated in an integrated school, respectively.

The residential locations of individuals who had experienced a formally integrated education are the least religiously exclusive. Around 7 out of every 10 adults who experienced a segregated education reported

Table 7.5 Schooling and social relations, limited pooled sample

	(Per cent who are of the same religion)		
	Integrated	*Fairly mixed*	*Segregated*
Friends			
All/most	43	52	65
Half	42	40	28
Less than half/none	15	8	7
(N)	(226)	(995)	(8,318)
Relatives			
All/most	77	82	84
Half	16	13	11
Less than half/none	7	6	6
(N)	(217)	(966)	(7,816)
Neighbours			
All/most	52	57	68
Half	34	31	22
Less than half/none	15	12	10
(N)	(184)	(765)	(6,370)

The questions were 'And how many of your friends would you say are the same religion as you?', 'What about your relatives, including relatives by marriage? About how many are the same religious as you?' and 'What about your neighbours? About how many are the same religion as you?'
Source: Northern Ireland Surveys, Restricted Pooled Sample, 1998–2010

that 'most' or 'all' of their neighbours were from their own religion, while the equivalent proportions among those who had experienced a fairly mixed or formally integrated educational background were just 57 per cent and 52 per cent, respectively. As far as friendship patterns and geographical location are concerned, the results are clear. Individuals who had attended a non-segregated school are much less religiously exclusive in terms of both their friendship and residential patterns than those who have attended a segregated one.

Patterns of intermarriage display different results. The most striking finding in Table 7.5 is again the lack of contact between the two communities in terms of their choice of marriage partners, irrespective of school background. Although there is some impact for the type of school attended, the effects are small, certainly compared to the previous results for friendship and residence. The impact of kinship confirms our previous findings about the central role of endogamy in perpetuating communal divisions. While there has been some increase in mixed marriages in Northern

Ireland since the late 1960s, the results of the current analysis suggest that the expansion in integrated education has not contributed to this increase. Similar patterns in relation to the extent of religious exclusivity in social contact between the two communities also emerge when Protestants, Catholics and those claiming no religious affiliation are considered separately.[20]

The results based on our investigation of the relationship between the educational system and inter-community contact are unambiguous. Individuals who had experienced an integrated education are not only more likely to hold opinions that support cross-community contact but they are also more likely to carry those opinions into their daily patterns of social interaction. In other words, regardless of whether attitudes or behaviour are examined, it is individuals who had experienced an integrated education who are the most likely to cross the religious divide.

Evaluating the role of integrated education

The roots of public attitudes towards contact between the two religious communities are complex. The results presented above indicate that school background is a significant factor in shaping these opinions, but we would equally expect that a range of other factors such as age, educational attainment as well as political opinion should also play a role. In order to take account of these various factors, a multivariate analysis was conducted to predict the impact of school background on attitudes towards integration in a school, neighbourhood, or workplace setting. Each model controls for socio-demographic background, political support and the level of contact between the two religious communities.

The results in Table 7.6 demonstrate that even when a range of background factors are taken into account, including levels of contact between the two religious communities, individuals who have experienced an integrated education – either formally or informally – are significantly more likely to endorse a religiously mixed environment than those who had not.

Focusing initially on the school environment, the results suggest individuals who attended a religiously mixed school were significantly more likely than those who attended a religious segregated one to say that they would prefer to send their children to a religiously mixed school. It is those who had experienced an integrated education who stand out as the most inclusive in their views. Religious identification, education, political ideology and particularly cross-community contact are also important in shaping attitudes towards religious integration in a school setting. For example, in all three cases, those with high levels of cross-community

Table 7.6 Type of school, social contact and attitudes towards integration, limited pooled sample

	School		Neighbourhood		Workplace	
	Est	(SE)	Est	(SE)	Est	(SE)
Religion (Protestant)						
Catholic	-0.17**	(0.05)	0.53**	(0.06)	0.36**	(0.09)
No religion	0.68**	(0.08)	0.42**	(0.08)	0.25*	(0.12)
Gender (male)	-0.07	(0.04)	-0.31**	(0.05)	-0.43**	(0.07)
Age (years)	-0.01	(0.01)	0.01**	(0.01)	0.01	(0.01)
Education (tertiary)						
Secondary	-0.08	(0.05)	-0.07	(0.07)	-0.03	(0.09)
No qualification	-0.21**	(0.06)	-0.32**	(0.07)	-0.25**	(0.10)
Party support (DUP)						
UUP	-0.13**	(0.05)	0.03	(0.06)	0.11	(0.08)
Alliance	0.76**	(0.07)	0.80**	(0.09)	0.57**	(0.14)
SDLP	-0.10	(0.05)	0.02	(0.07)	0.23*	(0.09)
Sinn Fein	-0.65**	(0.07)	-0.86**	(0.08)	-0.75**	(0.10)
Cross-community contact						
Relatives (high)	-0.87**	(0.12)	-0.44**	(0.15)	-1.00**	(0.27)
Friends (high)	-1.35**	(0.14)	-2.05**	(0.18)	-2.84**	(0.32)
Neighbours (high)	-0.24*	(0.09)	-2.68**	(0.14)	-1.10**	(0.19)

School type (segregated)					
Integrated	0.67**	(0.17)	−0.16	(0.16)	0.13	(0.29)
Fairly mixed	0.61**	(0.09)	0.40**	(0.11)	0.41*	(0.18)
Constant	3.38**		4.98**		6.00**	
Pseudo R-squared	0.08		0.16		0.12	
(N)	(11,141)		(11,133)		(10,319)	

Significant at ** $p < 0.01$; * $p < 0.05$

Logistic regression results showing parameter estimates and (in parentheses) robust standard errors predicting the probability of support for mixing in schools, neighbourhoods and workplaces scored 0 (segregation/no preference) and 1 (mixing). All models include year dummy variables for unobserved heterogeneity. Protestant is the omitted category for religious affiliation, tertiary education is the omitted category for education, DUP is the omitted category for party support, and segregated school is the omitted category for school type. See Tables 7.4 and 7.5 for question wording

Source: Northern Ireland Surveys, Restricted Pooled Sample, 1998–2010

contact are consistently the most negative in their views. While at first glance this result may seem counter-intuitive, part of the explanation probably rests with the desire among those with limited cross-community contacts to increase the opportunity for such contacts for their children.

Religious identification also has a consistent effect. Compared to Protestants (the omitted category of comparison), those who claim no religious identity are significantly more likely to adopt a positive stance on religious mixing in a school setting, while Catholics are consistently negative in their views. There are less consistent effects for education and political ideology. Education has a negative effect, although only among individuals who lack a formal educational qualification; this group is significantly less likely than those with a tertiary education to say that they would prefer to send their children to an integrated school. As expected from our earlier analysis, political ideology is also important in determining attitudes towards integration. Compared to DUP supporters (the omitted category of comparison), Alliance Party supporters are significantly more likely to say that they would prefer to send their children to a mixed school, while UUP and Sinn Fein supporters are consistently negative in their views.

Similar patterns emerge with respect to more integrated neighbourhoods and workplaces. However, in both cases it is those who had attended an informally integrated, or fairly mixed, school who stand out as being the most inclusive in their views. Individuals who had attended such a school were significantly more likely than those who had attended a religious segregated one to say that they would prefer to live or work in a religiously mixed setting. This relationship is net of the level of contact between the two communities. Religious identification, education, political ideology and particularly cross-community contact also emerge as important in shaping support for residential and workplace integration. Contrary to our previous analysis, however, both gender and age are also significant determinants, with both older individuals and females being the most positive in their views.

These results about the role of the educational system and inter-community contact are unambiguous. Individuals who had experienced an integrated education are not only more likely to hold opinions that support cross-community contact but they are also more likely to demonstrate such contact in their daily lives. In other words, an integrated education makes a difference not just to an individual's opinions, but to one's behaviour as well. Moreover, the positive effect of integrated schooling remains even when a range of potentially confounding factors, including the possible mediating effects of cross-community contact, are taken into account.

Conclusion

The question of how educational systems operate in post-conflict societies has become an increasing area of interest for researchers, policymakers and governments. Education is often viewed as a primary mechanism for facilitating long-term changes in attitudes and behaviour that can have a lasting impact on community relations. Yet, it is also clear from the available studies that the nature of the relationship between education and conflict is under-researched and inconclusive (see Smith, 2005). This finding is particularly apparent with respect to evaluating the impact of the educational system on relations between the two main religious communities in Northern Ireland.

The churches themselves remain unconvinced about the impact of the type of school on attitudes and behaviour. The traditional view of the Catholic Church is that the issue of segregated schooling is largely irrelevant in explaining the conflict since the key cause is the inequitable treatment of the Catholic minority (see Gallagher and Coombs, 2007). While the Protestant churches have been less forthright in their views on integrated education, with various leaders making mildly positive statements, many Protestant religious leaders take the same view as their Catholic counterparts. They argue that integrated education undermines Christian values and that integrated schooling alone will not solve communal antagonism.

The opinion surveys on which the results presented here are based have not been designed to provide a definitive answer to the impact of the educational system on community relations. Nevertheless, they suggest that attendance at an integrated school has positive long-term benefits for community relations. Our evidence in support of this proposition is fourfold. First, regardless of religious background, individuals who had attended an integrated school were more likely to adopt a more inclusive view of community relations. Second, this relationship holds regardless of whether attitudes towards community contact or actual levels of social contact between the communities are considered. Third, the positive effect of integrated schooling remains even when a range of potentially confounding factors, including levels of cross-community contact, are taken into account. Fourth, our study – based on the adult population – suggests that the positive effect of integrated education extends into later life. As the numbers experiencing integrated schooling grows, these individuals have the potential to break down social barriers and become important advocates for change.

As important as integrated education appears to be in fostering social contact across the religious divide, it is not the only solution for prejudice

and ethnic division. Integrated schooling alone cannot tackle the mutually reinforcing problems of segregation, real and perceived disadvantage,
and divergent political aspirations that continue to underpin community
relations (Hughes and Donnelly, 2002, 2004; Hayes and McAllister,
2004). Nevertheless, our results do suggest that an integrated education
system is a fruitful place to start in conflict resolution. Education should
be a key element within a wider strategy for addressing communal relations and community divisions, not just in Northern Ireland but also in
other post-conflict societies.

Notes

1 See, for example, Bush and Saltarelli (2000), Smith and Vaux (2003), Davies
   (2004) and Lange (2012).
2 For a comprehensive review, see McGlynn et al. (2004).
3 Crucial components of the 1930 Education Act were the management
   of voluntary schools, which was broadened to include the clergy and
   their funding, half of which now came from the state. This discrepancy
   in funding was partially removed in 1968, but it was not until 1993 that
   the discrepancy in capital funding was finally abolished (see McGrath,
   2000).
4 Prominent among these was the McIvor initiative in 1974 which attempted
   to establish a third category of 'shared school', available to Catholic and
   Protestant parents alike. The subsequent 1978 Education Act allowed for
   the existing controlled or maintained schools to transform to an integrated
   status if they met certain conditions (see Bardon, 2009).
5 There is an extensive literature on the curriculum; see, for example, Darby
   et al. (1977) and Murray (1985).
6 With the collapse of the power-sharing executive in May 1974 following
   the Ulster Workers' Council strike and the introduction of direct rule from
   Westminster, the McIvor plan was quietly shelved by the British government,
   and the issue of integrated education virtually disappeared from discussion
   until the 1978 Education Act. In the mid-1990s, as a result of falling numbers plus reforms introduced in the 1989 Education Reform (Northern
   Ireland) Order which facilitated integrated education, a significant number
   of Protestant schools began to avail of this facility.
7 An exception was the Alliance Party. The 1978 Education Act, which
   allowed the transformation of existing maintained or controlled schools
   to an integrated status, was initially introduced as a private member's bill
   in the House of Lords by an Alliance peer, Lord Dunleath, in January 1978
   and completed its passage through the Commons in May 1978.
8 See O'Connor (2002) for a detailed historical account of this issue.
9 ACT was originally set up by a group of Catholic parents in response to
   the refusal of the Catholic Church in 1973 to administer the sacrament of

confirmation to their children because they were attending state-controlled schools, but it quickly became an interdenominational movement (see Bardon, 2009).

10 Peter Robinson, whose constituency Lagan College was originally temporarily located in, voiced strong objections to its opening and voted against the proposal. For the first couple of weeks, the children, parents and teachers had to run a gauntlet of hostile DUP supporters as they made their way into the school (Bardon, 2009: 117).

11 See the Northern Ireland Council for Integrated Education (NICIE) website – http://www.nicie.org – for further statistical information and a detailed account of this issue.

12 The first school to take this step did so to avoid closure.

13 Government figures indicate that there were 84,605 unfilled places in Northern Ireland schools in 2011. In September 2011, the Minister for Education, John O'Dowd, announced that he had asked all schools to conduct an 'immediate viability audit' with a view to the closure of nonperforming schools.

14 In a speech at La Mon Hotel in Belfast in October 2010, Peter Robinson characterized the school system as a 'benign form of apartheid which is fundamentally damaging to our society' and called for the abolition of religiously segregated schools in favour of a single school system. Robinson did not object to single-faith schools *per se* but instead argued that they should not be funded by the state. As Robinson put it, 'I don't in any way object to churches providing and funding schools for those who choose them. What I do object to is the state providing and funding church schools'.

15 Sinn Fein's education spokesperson, John O'Dowd, was more vocal in his response when he described Peter Robinson's remarks as nothing more than a thinly disguised sectarian attack on Catholic education. According to O'Dowd, 'The principle of children going to school together no-one can argue against. However, I expect that is not the motivation behind the DUP leader's statement. What we are witnessing is an attack on the Catholic education sector'.

16 The DUP have long pointed to the irrelevance of integrated schools as state schools are available and belong to both traditions. By contrast, Sinn Fein regards the expansion of integrated education as a cynical ploy by the British government to undermine national identity and divert attention away from the disadvantages and inequalities experienced by nationalists.

17 This was a view also previously endorsed by the UUP leader, David Trimble. He regarded the failure of the first minister of education to introduce a compulsorily integrated education system in 1924 as a 'lost opportunity'.

18 Criticizing what he referred to as the 'head-on-collision course' adopted by Peter Robinson, Martin McGuinness stressed the importance of trying to 'achieve and continue to build consensus about the need to develop shared services'.

19 The accuracy of these estimates is also supported by the age distribution of the respondents reporting experiencing formally integrated education: of those aged 18–24 years when they were interviewed, 6 per cent said that they attended a formally integrated school, compared to just 1 per cent of those aged 70 or over.

20 The results should, however, be treated with caution given the small number of cases in some cells.

8

The legacy of political violence

At the heart of all efforts to bring about reconciliation in post-conflict societies is the question of how to deal with the victims of violence. The resolution of this issue is often considered the litmus test of a successful peace endeavour for societies emerging from conflict. Irrespective of whether restorative or retributive forms of justice are applied to a conflict, the recognition of the needs of victims and the ability to deal effectively with their concerns is considered essential to the stability of any post-conflict settlement. The existence of a large group of disaffected and aggrieved victims who feel that their suffering has not been adequately addressed has the potential to undermine what are often delicately balanced peace agreements. Northern Ireland is no exception to this worldwide pattern.

Despite the central role that victims occupy in reconciliation, what constitutes a victim in practice is contested. Much of the literature on post-conflict societies emphasizes how a person can be simultaneously both a victim and a perpetrator. As Borer (2003: 1115), based on her investigation of the South African Truth and Reconciliation Process, puts it, 'not all victims are the same, nor are all perpetrators the same...some victims are also perpetrators'. There is a further complication in that many individuals who qualify for either victim or perpetrator status are unwilling to accept the label. Many perpetrators refer to their status as ex-combatants, or even victims, in order to justify their recourse to armed conflict. Many victims, by contrast, seek to distance themselves from the perceived passivity of the label preferring instead the title 'survivor' (Bouris, 2007; Brewer, 2010).

A similar difficulty arises when we consider the identification of victims in Northern Ireland. More than any other factor, the question of how to deal with victims has emerged as one of the most contentious issues of the past decade. While much research has been devoted to the controversial question of who qualifies as a victim, the question of how society should remember and atone for the suffering inflicted on them remains largely unexplored (Smyth, 2007). The ability to address the needs of victims lies at the heart of post-conflict politics, offering the hope of reconciliation and a shared future but providing a further justification for perpetuating the violence and reproducing the grievances of the past if reconciliation should fail (Nagle and Clancy, 2010).

This chapter focuses on the nature and extent of victimhood in Northern Ireland and public attitudes towards how to deal with the injustices inflicted on them in the past. The first section outlines the nature of the 1998 Belfast Agreement with reference to the rights of victims. The second and third sections, using a range of official government statistics and our extensive collection of public opinion surveys, examine both the nature and extent of victimhood and the main perpetrators of the violence. Finally, building on this examination, we investigate public attitudes towards dealing with the violent legacy of the past, particularly in terms of the rights of victims.

Identifying victims

On 22 May 1998, the Belfast Agreement was ratified by 71 per cent of voters, formally ending almost three decades of civil strife. For the first time, representatives from both religious communities came together to endorse an elite-driven political accommodation designed to respect their differing traditions and to end the political violence. Unlike previous political initiatives, a key aspect of the Agreement was to acknowledge the suffering of the victims of violence and to support groups who were working with them. Such an acknowledgement was considered necessary not only to ensure public support for the Agreement, particularly in light of the release of political prisoners,[1] but also for the success of the process of reconciliation. As the Agreement put it, '... it is essential to acknowledge and address the suffering of the victims of violence as a necessary element of reconciliation' (Northern Ireland Office, 1998: 22). Mechanisms that were put in place to address the needs of victims included the establishment of a Northern Ireland Victims Commission as well as the promise of sufficient resources to meet the needs of victims.[2] In addition, the Agreement acknowledged the right of victims to 'remember' the past, although it did not indicate how this might be achieved (Lundy and McGovern, 2008a).

From the very beginning of the peace process, how to deal with the needs of victims generated much controversy, not least in terms of who could be defined as a victim (see Smyth, 2007; Ferguson et al., 2010; Brewer, 2010). Claims and counterclaims raged about who should be considered a 'legitimate' victim. Early government-sponsored approaches to the problem used an inclusive definition of victimhood, based primarily on the suffering of individuals and their families. More recently, individuals and victims organizations, particularly with unionist links,[3] have sought to introduce a more exclusive definition, or a hierarchy of victimhood, distinguishing 'innocent victims' from those who had been engaged in 'terrorist' activity (see Smyth, 2003).

These distinctions are evident in the government report on victims prepared by Sir Ken Bloomfield, a retired senior public servant. Bloomfield (1998: 14) advanced an inclusive definition of victimhood, although his failure to address the issue of victims of state violence angered many nationalists and republicans.[4] He suggested that at some level every citizen could be considered a victim of the Troubles and included in his classification was not only the 'surviving injured' but those 'who care for them' as well as 'close relatives who mourn their dead'.[5] The Agreement itself offered a more restricted definition, as simply anyone who had been a 'victim of violence'. However, it was the controversy following the publication of the Report of the Consultative Group on the Past (2009) that highlighted the divisions over who should count as a 'true' victim. Proposing that the nearest relative should be awarded a one-off payment of £12,000, many victim groups and politicians were outraged, arguing that such a payment would indicate a moral equivalence between those who committed violence and the 'innocents' who were simply victims of such violence. Such was the public outcry that none of the report's recommendations were implemented.

The political parties have also been divided on the issue of victims and have frequently clashed over how to define them. The main unionist parties have subscribed to exclusive definitions of victimhood, suggesting a fundamental difference between 'innocent' or 'deserving' victims, or those who have suffered at the hands of terrorists, and 'those who deserved it', such as individuals who were involved in the terror campaign. As the DUP (2003: 4) put it, 'We contend that there is a fundamental distinction between those who have suffered at the hands of terrorist groups and former terrorists who contributed to the terrorist campaign and wrought untold suffering through the period of the Troubles'. By contrast, the nationalist/republican parties have a much more inclusive definition of victimhood. The SDLP interpretation includes any individual whose life has been 'altered as a result of the division and bitterness within society', both in Northern Ireland and elsewhere, as well as those 'who might have been perceived by some to have brought the suffering upon themselves' (see SDLP, 1999). Loyalist and republican ex-prisoners are equally divided on the issue with former republican prisoners being much more inclusive than former loyalist prisoners in their views (Shirlow and McEvoy, 2008).

In addition to determining who the real victims are, almost every other aspect of victimhood has been challenged since the 1998 Agreement.

Neil Ferguson and his colleagues (2010) observe that such disputes have ranged from the allocation of funding to even the choice of the victim commissioners. These competing claims over how to address the violence of the past are not just restricted to Northern Ireland but are present in all societies emerging from conflict. In Northern Ireland, however, they are exacerbated by a political culture of victimhood. As Marie Breen-Smyth (2007) concludes, both loyalists and republican paramilitaries used the status of 'victim' to justify their own acts of violence and in so doing have cast the other community in the role of aggressor or perpetrator of their suffering. It has been argued that these competing moral claims to victimhood have formed the major fault line of the Northern Ireland peace process and stymied the introduction of a range of initiatives – such as a truth and reconciliation commission – to deal with the past (Brewer and Hayes, 2011).

Patterns of suffering

The Northern Ireland state was born in violence in the early 1920s. Between 1920 and 1922 alone, an estimated 428 people were killed, two-thirds of them Catholic. Although the level of violence decreased significantly over the following four decades as Northern Ireland entered a period of relative calm, sporadic outbreaks of political violence continued – most notably the IRA campaign of the mid-1950s, which resulted in the deaths of a further 26 people (O'Leary and McGarry, 1993). The post-1968 conflict, however, easily surpasses all other episodes in both scale and intensity. The statistics of violence suggest that, relative to population size, the conflict approached that of a war rather than a local insurgency, with substantial numbers of the population being exposed to many aspects of the violence – from intimidation and physical injury to being caught up in a bomb explosion or riot. While the levels of political violence have declined substantially since the mid-1990s, the cumulative level of deaths, injuries and grievances that constitute the legacy of the past is now considerable.

More people have died in the most recent conflict in Northern Ireland – 3,380 by 2011[6] – than in any similar period in Ireland over the past two centuries, with the possible exception of the Irish Civil War. By international standards, the conflict is 'low intensity', given both the small population (just under 1.8 million) and limited geographical area. However, the relative impact of the violence on the local population has been substantial.[7] In addition, 50,156 people have been injured, representing just under 3 per cent of the population, many of whom feel abandoned by the Northern Ireland government and are increasing reliant on the benefit system to meet their financial needs.[8] If we extrapolate these figures to Britain, some 126,000 people would have died, with 1.8 million injured. This represents just under half of all British deaths (265,000) during the Second World War. The large number of incidents underlies the intensity of the conflict, with 37,718 shooting incidents and 16,704 bomb explosions recorded between 1969 and 2011. Such levels of violence, maintained over a long period of time, have inevitably drawn many people into paramilitary organizations. Estimates of paramilitary membership are difficult to make with any accuracy, but police statistics show that, since 1972, a total of 20,165 people have been charged with terrorist offences.[9] Again, extrapolating these figures to Britain shows that nearly three-quarters of a million people would have been charged with a terrorist offence.

The main casualties in war are invariably civilians, and the Northern Irish conflict is no exception to this pattern. Of the 3,380 deaths that have occurred in Northern Ireland since 1969, the overwhelming majority have been civilian (see Table 8.1). Civilians now account for 7 out of every 10 deaths that have occurred during the course of the present conflict. While the number of civilian deaths has declined dramatically since the 1998 Agreement, they still account for 117 deaths or under just 4 per cent of the total. The security forces, by contrast, have experienced a smaller proportion of deaths. The British Army (the second largest group) emerges as the second major casualty accounting for 454 deaths – or just over 1 in every 10 deaths and only 2 in the post-Agreement period. By any standards, what people in Northern Ireland euphemistically called 'the Troubles' was, in fact, a war that was experienced disproportionally by the civilian population.

The evidence concerning direct and indirect exposure to victimization supports the conclusion that the civilian population has borne the brunt of the violence. The results in the first part of Table 8.2 suggest that the

Table 8.1 The affiliation of those killed, 1969–2011

	Percentages	N
Police	6.0	202
Police Reserve	3.0	102
Army	13.4	454
UDR/RIR	6.0	203
Civilian	71.6	2,419
Total	100.0	3,380

Figures include RIR (Home Services Battalion)
Source: Police Service of Northern Ireland (http://psni.police.uk)

Table 8.2 Nature and extent of victimhood, 1995–2011

	(Percentages)			
	1995	1998	2004	2011
(All respondents)				
Direct victimization				
Victim of violent incident	10	14	16	21
Indirect victimization				
Family member/relative killed or injured	18	21	26	36
Know someone killed or injured	69	56	62	60
Self-assessed victimization				
Consider oneself a victim of the Troubles	—	—	22	26
(N)	(982)	(948)	(1,800)	(1,500)
(Protestants only)				
Direct victimization				
Victim of violent incident	8	13	15	20
Indirect victimization				
Family member/relative killed or injured	17	21	25	36
Know someone killed or injured	69	54	61	62
Self-assessed victimization				
Consider oneself a victim of the Troubles	—	—	20	25
(N)	(509)	(479)	(917)	(669)
(Catholics only)				
Direct victimization				
Victim of violent incident	11	16	18	21
Indirect victimization				
Family member/relative killed or injured	22	22	28	34
Know someone killed or injured	59	59	65	59
Self-assessed victimization				
Consider oneself a victim of the Troubles	—	—	24	27
(N)	(335)	(343)	(663)	(611)

The questions were 'Were you a victim of any conflict-related violent incidents? Were any of your family or close relatives killed or injured because of the violence? Do you know anyone (not family or relatives) who were killed or injured in the violence? Overall, do you consider yourself to be a victim of the troubles?'

Sources: Northern Ireland Social Identity Survey, 1995; Northern Ireland Referendum and Election Survey, 1998; Northern Ireland Life and Times, 2004; Northern Ireland Social and Political Attitudes Survey, 2011

conflict has affected the lives of a significant section of the adult popula-tion. The cumulative effects are particularly evident when indirect measures of victimization, such as the death or injury of family members, are considered. For example, in 1995, following the paramilitary ceasefires of 1994, just under one-fifth of all adults in Northern Ireland reported having a family member or close relative injured or killed during the violence; by 2011, this figure had doubled to 36 per cent. As expected, a much larger proportion of the population report knowing someone who was killed or injured – 60 per cent in 2011 – a pattern which has remained reasonably constant over time. Just over one-quarter of the population now consider themselves a victim of the violence, and around one in five claim to have directly experienced it.

The patterns suggest that exposure to victimization is not shared equally between the two main religious communities, as previous research has found (see Hayes and McAllister, 2001b; Smyth, 2003). The second and third parts of Table 8.3 show that while Catholics have uniformly reported higher levels of victimization than Protestants in the past, this is no longer the case. This may be a consequence of the greater willingness of Protestants to express their experience of the conflict now than in the past (see Simpson, 2009). For example, between 1995 and 2004, while a greater proportion of Catholics than Protestants reported having a family member or close relative injured or killed during the violence, by 2011 this difference had been reversed, with Protestants reporting marginally higher levels of victimization than Catholics. An identical pattern emerges with regard to knowledge of a non-family member being killed or injured. Once again, by 2011 Protestants were reporting slightly higher rates of victimization than Catholics – 62 per cent versus 59 per cent. In confirmation of previous research (see Brewer and Hayes, 2011), however, Catholics were consistently more likely to consider themselves a victim of the conflict than Protestants.

Just as levels of victimization and self-perceptions of victimhood are unevenly spread across the two religious communities, perceptions of who should be seen as a victim also varies by religion. The 2004 Northern Ireland Life and Times Survey demonstrates that nearly a quarter of Catholics strongly agreed that all those killed or injured in the conflict, regardless of whether they were members of paramilitary organizations or the security forces, should be seen as victims (see Table 8.3). By contrast, the same figure for Protestants was only 7 per cent. Among Protestants, 29 per cent disagreed strongly with this position compared to just 6 per cent of Catholics. Overall, whereas 7 out of every 10 Catholics agreed that all people who had been killed or injured should be seen as legiti-mate victims of the conflict, only a third of Protestants shared this view.

Table 8.3 Public perceptions concerning the legitimacy of victimhood, 2004

	Protestant	*Catholic*	*All*
All killed or injured are victims			
Strongly agree	7	24	15
Agree	26	46	34
Neither agree or disagree	7	8	8
Disagree	31	16	25
Strongly disagree	29	6	18
Total	100	100	100
(*N*)	(898)	(656)	(1,770)
All those bereaved are victims			
Strongly agree	9	27	16
Agree	46	56	50
Neither agree or disagree	13	8	12
Disagree	21	7	15
Strongly disagree	11	2	7
Total	100	100	100
(*N*)	(901)	(655)	(1,772)

The question was 'When people talk about victims of the troubles there is
sometimes disagreement about who should count as a victim. How much do
you agree or disagree with each of the following statements about victims
of the troubles? All those people who were killed or injured should be seen
as victims equally no matter whether they were paramilitaries or members
of the security forces. All those people who were bereaved as a result of the
conflict should be treated equally no matter whether their loved ones were
paramilitaries or members of the security forces'
Source: Northern Ireland Life and Times, 2004

Protestants clearly have a very different view of victimhood when compared to Catholics.

There is a similar pattern with respect to attitudes towards the
bereaved, with Catholics again emerging as the most inclusive in their
views. The second part of Table 8.3 shows that around one-quarter of
Catholics strongly agreed that all people who are bereaved as a result of
the conflict, regardless of whether or not their loved ones were paramilitaries or members of the security forces, should be treated equally. Only
9 per cent of Protestants shared this view. Moreover, although Protestants
are more likely to recognize the bereaved as legitimate victims of the
conflict than those who had been killed or injured during the Troubles,
Catholics still remain the most inclusive in their views. Among Catholics,
8 out of every 10 endorsed the position that all people who are bereaved

as a result of the conflict should be treated equally as compared to just slightly over half of Protestants.

This relationship between victim status and perceptions of who should count as a victim underscores the complexity of the term victimhood in Northern Ireland. There is no consensus on who constitutes a victim, and, not least, the understanding of the term varies significantly between the two communities. Catholics tend to adopt an inclusive view of victimhood, with all of those who have been killed or injured being regarded as victims. By contrast, Protestants are more exclusive in their approach to victimhood. Indeed, a key factor in determining Protestant attitudes towards who should count as a 'true' victim, which did not emerge for Catholics, is their own feelings of victimization.[10] As we explain below, this is a key difference and one which has profound implications for the process of reconciliation.

The perpetrators of violence

In common with other conflicts, both victims and protagonists to the Northern Ireland conflict do not agree on who is to be held responsible for the violence. While republicans and nationalists have long pointed to the role of the British government and its security forces, often in collusion with loyalist paramilitaries, unionists place the fault firmly at the feet of republican paramilitary organizations like the IRA. However, despite public perceptions and much disagreement about the issue, the objective data in Table 8.4 suggests that only two agencies have been responsible, in various ways, for the majority of the deaths that have occurred during the course of the conflict.

Republican paramilitaries have been responsible for by far the largest number of deaths – 2,152 by mid-November 2006, or 58 per cent of the

Table 8.4 Agencies responsible for those killed, 1969–2006

	Percentages	N
Police/Police Reserve	1.4	51
Army	8.1	302
UDR/RIR	0.2	8
Republicans	57.8	2,152
Loyalists	29.9	1,112
Other	2.6	95
Total	100.0	3,720

Source: McKittrick et al. (2008: 1560)

total. Among the latter, the IRA has been the most active republican group, accounting for 1,768 deaths. The second main agency, the various loyalist organizations, has been responsible for 1,112 deaths, or 30 per cent of the total. The most active group with this category is the Ulster Volunteer Force which has been responsible for 550 deaths. Combining these two paramilitary groups results in a total of 3,264 deaths or 88 per cent of the total. The third agency, the security forces – combining the British Army, the Ulster Defence Regiment/Royal Irish Regiment (UDR/RIR) and the police – has caused the fewest number of deaths, or 10 per cent of the total. The British Army has been responsible for 302 deaths, or 8 per cent of the overall total, and the police and UDR/RIR have been responsible for 59 deaths.

Although the paramilitary organizations have been responsible for nearly 9 out of every 10 deaths during the course of the conflict, this number does not adequately capture the scale of the suffering inflicted on the population. As self-designated 'protectors' of their community, paramilitary groups have also engaged in a range of other violent activities, including racketeering, bank robberies and so-called punishment beatings. The brutality of punishment beatings should not be underestimated (see Knox, 2001). The beatings are usually inflicted with baseball bats (often spiked with nails), hammers or ever power tools; when shots are fired, they are intended to permanently maim the victim. Within the nationalist community, such attacks are predominantly directed at young working-class males, for offences such as joyriding and other types of antisocial behaviour such as petty crime. Punishment attacks in the loyalist community, by contrast, involve older males and are often related to internal disciplinary matters, as well as to feuds involving criminal activity such as drugs and the control of territory (Hamill, 2011).

Such attacks numbered almost 5,000 in the period since 1982, almost equally divided between shootings and assaults (see Table 8.5). Over the period, republicans were involved in 2,216 such attacks and loyalists in 2,730. Overall, loyalist paramilitaries were more likely than republican

Table 8.5 Casualties as a result of paramilitary violence, 1982–2011

	Republican	Loyalist	All
Shootings	47	48	47
Assaults	53	52	53
Total	100	100	100
(N)	(2,216)	(2,730)	(4,946)

Source: Police Service of Northern Ireland (http://psni.police.uk)

paramilitaries to engage in these activities, although their greater propensity to use such attacks is a relatively recent phenomenon, in part deriving from a series of internal loyalist feuds which date from the mid-1990s.

Although the number of paramilitary-style shootings has fluctuated considerably since the early 1970s, as the data in Figure 8.1 demonstrates, republican paramilitaries have traditionally been more likely to engage in these activities than loyalist paramilitaries up until the early 1990s. For example, throughout the 1970s and early 1980s, the number of republicans who engaged in paramilitary-style shootings outnumbered loyalists by more than two to one. By contrast, throughout the 1990s loyalists had increasingly replaced republicans as the primary perpetrators of this activity. Between 1998 and 2002 alone, in the immediate aftermath of the Agreement, loyalists were responsible for 63 per cent of all shooting incidents (405 in total) compared to 235 which were attributed to republicans.[11]

A similar pattern emerges with respect to paramilitary assaults. Throughout the 1980s, the main perpetrators of this activity were again republican paramilitaries; since then, loyalists have significantly outstripped republicans. In fact, as the data in Figure 8.2 demonstrates,

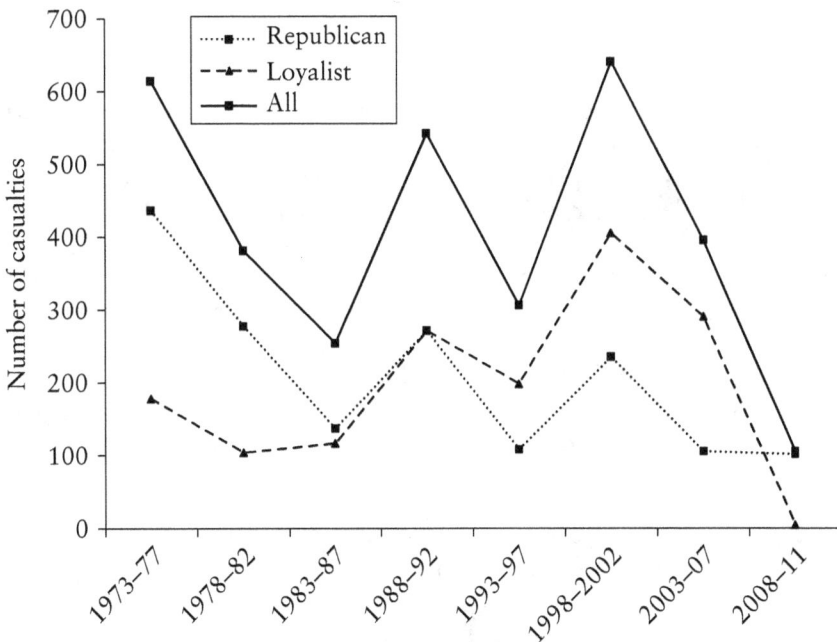

Figure 8.1 Casualties as a result of paramilitary-style shootings, 1973–2011
Source: Police Service of Northern Ireland (http://psni.police.uk)

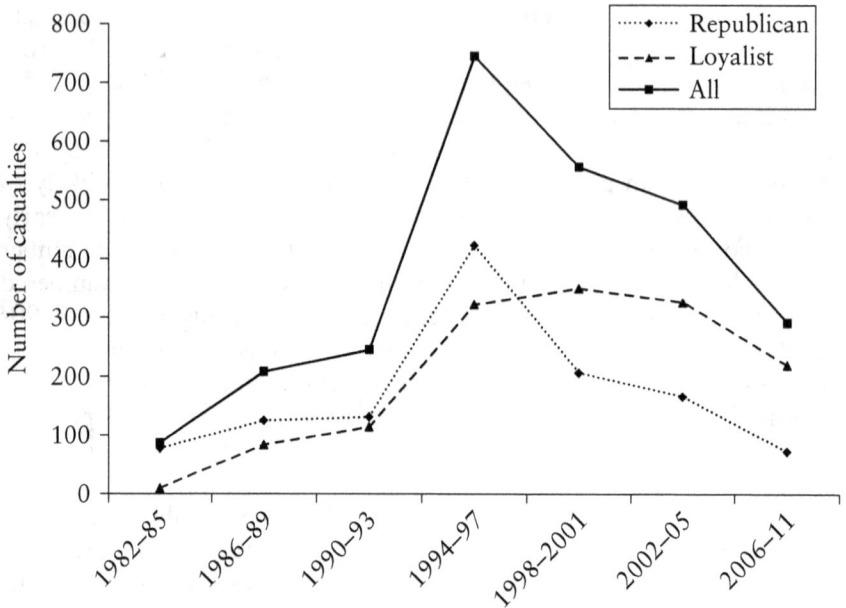

Figure 8.2 Casualties caused by paramilitary assaults, 1982–2011
Source: Police Service of Northern Ireland (http://psni.police.uk)

assaults have now become an almost exclusively loyalist paramilitary activity. Some of the decline in paramilitary assaults, particularly among Catholics, may be explained by the increasing condemnation of such practices by leading republican figures, such as Martin McGuinness. Other contributory factors include increasing communal support for non-violent alternatives to punishment beating through community-based restorative justice programs, in which former prisoners are heavily involved (see Shirlow and McEvoy, 2008; Shirlow *et al.*, 2010).

Despite the prominence of paramilitary groups as the main perpetrators of the violence in terms of deaths and injuries, there is much dispute among the public as to who they hold primarily responsible for the conflict. The 2004 Life and Times Survey asked the respondents who they considered to be responsible for the conflict. Table 8.6 shows the first five mentions for Protestants, Catholics and those who explicitly claimed no religious affiliation. The results show that there is no clear consensus on who is primarily responsible for the conflict. Among Protestants, culpability is shared between Irish/nationalist paramilitaries, mainly the IRA, and civilians from both communities. Among Catholics, culpability is mainly directed at the British government and its security

Table 8.6 Public perceptions about responsibility for the conflict, 2004

Protestants	Per cent	Catholics	Per cent	Others	Per cent
1. Irish/nationalist paramilitaries	24	1. British/unionist government/security forces	37	1. Civilians from both sides	25
2. Civilians from both communities	21	2. Civilians from both communities	21	2. British/unionist government/security forces	17
3. Multiple Irish/nationalist agencies	14	3. Multiple British/unionist agencies	6	3. Paramilitaries from both sides	10
4. British/unionist government/security forces	7	4. Multiple Irish/nationalist agencies	6	4. Irish/nationalist paramilitaries	8
5. Paramilitaries from both sides	6	5. Paramilitaries from both sides	4	5. Government/security forces from both sides	6
(N)	(906)		(656)		(206)

The question was 'Looking back at "the Troubles" now, who do you think was primarily responsible for the conflict?' Only the first five mentions are shown

Source: Northern Ireland Life and Times Survey, 2004

forces: 37 per cent see them as being responsible for the conflict, compared to just 7 per cent of Protestants. Among those who state that they have no religion, the first ranked agency is civilians from both sides.

There are, then, marked differences between the two religious communities in terms of whom they hold primarily responsible for the conflict. No single agency is identified as the main cause by a majority of the respondents, and for the most part blame is assigned to a variety of government, paramilitary and civilian agencies spanning the two communities. This willingness to attribute culpability to such a wide range of agencies, including that of the civilian population, underlines the difficulties in addressing the legacy of the past through a process of reconciliation. It is to the disputed topic of reconciliation that we now turn.

Dealing with the past

Over the last decade, the emergence of numerous 'peace processes' to resolve long-standing conflicts has generated much debate. The ability to deal with the violent legacy of the past has now moved to centre stage as a key mechanism in conflict resolution and national reconciliation (see, e.g., Bell, 2003a; Hamber, 2009; Brewer, 2010; Hayner, 2011). Government-sponsored initiatives to deal with the past include a range of disparate and sometimes overlapping activities, such as the establishment of truth commissions, amnesty dispensations, public inquiries, criminal investigations and prosecutions. Of these initiatives, truth commissions, established under many names, have become one of the most common options for societies emerging from conflict. As Priscilla Hayner (2011: xiv) notes, between 1974 and 1999, some 40 truth commissions have been undertaken, 21 of which were created in the last decade alone. It is now accepted that some form of truth recovery process is central for societies trying to come to terms with the violent legacy of their past (see Hamber, 2009; Hayner, 2011).

Despite the growing international literature as to the importance of dealing with the past, to date efforts to address the legacy of the conflict in Northern Ireland have been both piecemeal and divisive (see Bell, 2003b; Lundy and McGovern, 2008a, 2008b). In comparison to other post-conflict societies – such as South Africa, Uganda, Argentina and Chile, all of whom opted for a truth and reconciliation process – there has been no similar state-led initiative in Northern Ireland. There have, however, been a number of government-sponsored 'truth recovery' initiatives, such as the establishment of the Serious Crime Review Team (now the Historical Enquiries Team),[12] the Independent Commission for the Location of Victims' Remains[13] as well as a series of judicial inquiries – Stevens (2003), Cory (2004) and Saville (2010) – into the role of the security forces (see Brewer, 2010: 175–80). Of the judicial inquiries, the Saville Inquiry was by far the most profligate and extensive, running for 12 years and costing £195 million.[14]

A number of unofficial 'truth' recovery processes have also been established (see Lundy and McGovern, 2008a; Brewer, 2010). Unlike official truth recovery mechanisms which are state-sanctioned, unofficial truth recovery mechanisms are operated by civil society organizations and include memorialization, documentation and storytelling. These range from highly localized storytelling initiatives[15] to more extensive cross-community initiatives, such as the Healing Through Remembering project. Formally launched in October 2001, this project includes individuals drawn from a wide range of political, social and community backgrounds whose primary aim is to consider how best to deal with the past. After extensive consultations, the Healing Through Remembering project identified 14 key approaches to dealing with the past. Along with storytelling and oral history, memorials, museums, public and collective commemorations, and a financial response for victims, it also recommended that a formal truth recovery process should be considered, though only as one part of dealing with the past (see Hamber, 2008).

A similar list of options was discussed in November 2004 when the Northern Ireland Affairs Committee (NIAC) examined submissions on the issue of how to deal with the past. Although all stressed the value of unofficial mechanisms of truth recovery, there were deep divisions in relation to establishing an official truth recovery process (see Smyth, 2007: 108–42). Views ranged from those who favoured such an initiative (led by nationalist human rights and victims organizations) to those who favoured it in the future (led by the Northern Ireland Human Rights Commission and the Community Relations Council) and those who opposed it (led by loyalist ex-prisoners, Protestant victims groups and groups associated with the security forces). Given the divergence in opinion, the NIAC concluded that the establishment of an official process was 'virtually impossible'. Instead, it recommended that unofficial processes, such as local story or truth telling – sometimes cynically referred to as the 'talk about yourselves' option – should be actively pursued, a view that was subsequently endorsed by the British government. Later calls for the establishment of a legacy commission (a truth commission by another name), such as that advocated by the Consultative Group on the Past (2009), have not been acted upon (see Lundy, 2010).

Like the interested groups, public opinion is also sharply divided on a truth commission. For many unionists, any official truth recovery mechanism is viewed as a 'republican agenda' and as a comprehensive attempt

Table 8.7 Public support for a truth commission, 2011

	Protestant	Catholic	Other	All
Strongly agree	5	19	16	12
Agree	31	52	31	40
Neither agree nor disagree	23	16	23	20
Disagree	31	10	17	21
Strongly disagree	10	3	12	7
	100	100	100	100
(N)	(602)	(555)	(190)	(1,347)

The question was 'Here are some ways that people have suggested the legacy of the troubles should be dealt with. Please say how much you agree or disagree with the following: A Truth Commission'
Source: Northern Ireland Social and Political Attitudes Survey, 2011

to 're-write the past' (Lundy and McGovern, 2008a, 2008b). Ethnographic research on the Protestant community suggests, however, that many individuals who were previously reticent to talk about their experiences of the conflict now feel the need to do so, particularly in light of the perceived republican agenda that casts them in the role of perpetrator (see Simpson, 2009). Nationalists, in contrast, have been much more supportive of such an initiative. Even republican ex-prisoners, who as one of the main perpetrators of the conflict have potentially much to lose in such a process, are overwhelmingly in support. Indeed Marie Breen-Smyth (2007:158–9) has concluded that the level of republican support for truth recovery is 'remarkable' and may be explained by their desire to draw a line under their paramilitary activity in the past and thereby gain democratic acceptability.[16]

Recent public opinion data with respect to a truth commission as a mechanism to deal with the past lends further support to this diversity in views. As the results in Table 8.7 show, the population is now about equally divided – 52 per cent versus 48 per cent – between those who support such a commission and those who do not or are undecided in their views. Moreover, this support for a truth recovery mechanism is lukewarm at best; just 12 per cent strongly endorse the proposal. As we would expect, there are marked differences between the two religious communities, with Catholics the most supportive in their opinions. Around 1 in every 7 Catholics favour the proposal, compared to almost half that proportion among Protestants. In addition, almost 1 in 4 Protestants have no view on the issue.

Table 8.8 Public support for dealing with the legacy of the Troubles, 2011

	Protestant	Catholic	Other	All
	(Per cent strongly agree or agree)			
	(All respondents)			
More public inquiries	23	52	31	36
Public apologies from those who did wrong	67	79	70	73
More police investigations/ prosecutions	58	65	59	61
Memorials/centres of remembrance	42	54	49	48
Support for victims	84	92	88	88
More compensation	30	50	34	39
Community initiatives	81	92	86	86
(N)	(669)	(611)	(208)	(1,488)
	(Victims only)			
Truth commission	30	72	53	51
More public inquiries	20	53	28	35
Public apologies from those who did wrong	67	76	62	70
More police investigations/ prosecutions	59	61	61	60
Memorials/centres of remembrance	44	60	50	52
Support for victims	82	96	85	89
More compensation	39	55	38	46
Community initiatives	77	94	81	86
(N)	(153)	(151)	(49)	(353)

The question was 'Here are some ways that people have suggested the legacy of the troubles should be dealt with. Please say how much you agree or disagree with the following: More public inquiries; public apologies from those who did wrong; more police investigations and prosecutions; memorials or centres of remembrance; support for victims; more compensation; initiatives within communities to help people come to terms with the past.' Ns vary for individual items
Source: Northern Ireland Social and Political Attitudes Survey, 2011

Truth commissions are not the only way in which a society emerging from conflict can come to terms with its past; as noted earlier, there are also other official and unofficial options. The first part of Table 8.8 examines levels of public support for some of these alternatives. The most popular mechanisms are support for victims, followed by community initiatives and public apologies; public inquiries and memorials are least popular. In general, all of the measures find more support among Catholics than Protestants, but several differences stand out. In particular, more than twice as many Catholics as Protestants favour more public inquiries, and Catholics are also more favourable to compensation. This greater antipathy among Protestants towards inquiries and compensation is probably a response to the enormous expense of the Saville inquiry as well as the past record of inquiries in concentrating almost exclusively on the deaths of Catholic civilians at the hands of security forces. Higher levels of support for public apologies among Catholics can be explained by the disproportionate use of such apologies by the British government for past injustices towards the nationalist community.

The results also suggest limited support within both communities for memorials and centres of remembrance. Just over half of Catholics support such a practice compared to 42 per cent of Protestants. This lack of widespread public endorsement within both communities for such forms of commemoration reflects the contested and sectarian uses to which such memorials have been subjected to in the past. Indeed, Brian Graham and Yvonne Whelan (2007: 494) argue that the proliferation of such memorials and monuments by paramilitary associations has been used as one way 'of continuing the war by other means'. As a consequence, memorials are discredited by a substantial proportion of the population.

The second part of Table 8.8 shows the views of the victims towards how to deal with the past. The patterns largely replicate those found among the general population with several exceptions. First, there is more support among victims for memorials, particularly among Catholics. Second, there is also more support among victims in both communities for more compensation. Perhaps surprisingly, victims are very similar to the general population in their views of truth commissions; Catholics who report being a victim of the violence are more than twice as likely to support such a commission as Protestants. Overall, however, it is perhaps surprising that the differences between victims within the two communities are not larger.

Not only is there a lack of consensus on who is a victim of the conflict, there is no agreement on how to engineer a reconciliation and to deal with the legacy of the past. Other post-conflict societies, most notably South Africa, adopted a truth commission; in many cases, these mechanisms have been viewed as generally succeeding in their goals. Public opinion in Northern Ireland about how to achieve lasting reconciliation underscores the deep divisions that exist. While a majority of Catholics would accept a truth commission, Protestants will not, even among those who have been victims of the conflict. Moreover, the use of memorials, often regarded as the least divisive means of recognizing a conflict, produces a negative response from Protestants and a lukewarm one from Catholics. In short, it would appear that there is no clear way forward to progress the process of reconciliation.

Conclusion

Following 30 years of widespread violence, which approached the level of a war rather than a low-intensity conflict, the people of Northern Ireland now face the painful process of achieving a post-conflict reconciliation. The experience of violence has permeated the whole society. The survey evidence presented in this chapter has shown that around 1 in 5 of the population have had direct experience of violence, while more than 1 in 3 have had a family member or relative killed or injured. Perhaps the most telling indicator is the 1 in 4 of the population who consider themselves a victim of the conflict.

The key to the success of the process of reconciliation is how to address the needs of victims. As this chapter has made clear, this process will be no easy task. Protestants and Catholics disagree profoundly on who should be counted as a victim as well as who they regard as responsible for the conflict. Similar divisions emerge over the most appropriate mechanisms to deal with the past. With such lack of agreement, it is perhaps not surprising that government-sponsored attempts to initiate a process of reconciliation, such as the Report of the Consultative Group on the Past, have resulted in failure. Moreover, public inquiries, such as the Saville Inquiry into the deaths caused by the security forces on 'Bloody Sunday' in 1972, have produced even more division, with Protestants regarding the exercise as a profligate attempt to pursue a republican agenda. In the light of these findings, it is perhaps not surprising that the process of post-conflict reconciliation has almost been as difficult as the process of finding a basis for halting the violence.

Yet, despite these deep-seated divisions, there are also some grounds for optimism. First, unlike the deafening silence in the past, debates about how to deal with the violent legacy of the past have gained increasing political and public momentum in recent years. There is now a tentative acceptance among the public as well as the political elite that Northern Ireland must address the issue of its turbulent and violent past. Moreover, even members of the Protestant population, who have traditionally been the most reticent in their views, have increasingly voiced their desire for Northern Ireland to confront and deal with its violent past. The importance of this growing acceptance of the necessity to deal with the past cannot be overestimated. As evidence from other post-conflict societies demonstrates, it is only by confronting and facing up to one's violent past that societal reconciliation and healing between previously warring groups can genuinely take place (Hamber 2009; Hayner 2011).

Second, there is a growing international recognition that any such initiatives in dealing with the past must be broadly inclusive and driven by consensus. Moreover, victims need to be central to the process (Brewer, 2010). Again, the evidence from Northern Ireland is somewhat encouraging in this regard. As our survey evidence attests, there is now a growing awareness of the needs of victims within both religious communities, with 1 in 7 adults pointing towards support for victims as a vital mechanism for dealing with the legacy of the past. Nevertheless, deep divisions over who counts as a 'true' victim remain and point to the fact that the needs of victims – whoever 'they' may be – are now both officially and unofficially recognized as a key mechanism in dealing with the past.

Third, there is a growing recognition among scholars that no single model for dealing with the past – such as a formal truth commission – should be considered exclusively. Instead, a variety of mechanisms, particularly those locally based and reflective of the needs of victims, need to be also considered (Hamber, 2008). Again, the evidence is encouraging. The survey data shows that there is already a high level of public support for such community-based initiatives within both communities. However, these locally based mechanisms, such as unofficial storytelling, will not be sufficient in themselves to address the legacy of Northern Ireland's violent and traumatic past. As lessons from the international community attest, not only must victims be allowed to tell their stories, but these stories need to be officially heard and acknowledged (Hayner, 2011).

Finally, leadership, primarily by political representatives, will be crucial. The vital role of Archbishop Desmond Tutu in contributing to the overall success of the South African Truth Commission is often mentioned. However, the evidence from Northern Ireland is less encouraging, and although all the political parties now acknowledge the need to confront the past, deep divisions remain in terms of the mechanisms by which this should be achieved. Furthermore, these deep divisions are replicated among the general public at large. While there have been some recent political initiatives, such as an emerging consensus on the need to convene all-party talks to address the issue, progress remains slow. As the lessons from the international community on truth recovery teach us, addressing the needs of victims and dealing with the legacy of a violent past is a complex and time-consuming process, fraught with difficulty and open to much dispute (Hamber, 2009).

Notes

1 In what has been described as 'one of the most controversial aspects of the peace process', 447 prisoners were released – 194 loyalists, 241 republicans and 12 non-aligned – under the provisions of the Northern Ireland Agreement (see McEvoy *et al.*, 2004).

2 By international standards, the amount of money paid out to victims groups in Northern Ireland has been considerable. John Brewer (2010: 173) estimates that between 1998 and 2008, the Northern Ireland Office channelled £36.4 million to victims compared to just over £400,000 to ex-prisoner groups. This does not include the £400 million of public money spent over the same period on the official inquiry into Bloody Sunday, the £33 million to finance the work of the Victims Commission and the £8.4 million given to the Police Service of Northern Ireland (PSNI) to conduct enquiries into unsolved murders from the past.

3 Since the inception of the first paramilitary ceasefires in 1994 and particularly since the 1998 Belfast Agreement, there has been a significant growth in the number of victims' groups. These groups hold a wide diversity of political positions and have different understandings of what constitutes a victim. Government estimates suggest that at least 60 are currently in receipt of public monies (see Brewer, 2010: 174–5).

4 As Connolly (2006: 421–2) notes, not only did the Bloomfield Report devote only two paragraphs to victims killed by state actors, but it made no recommendations as to how the gap in accountability for state-sponsored violence should be addressed. By contrast, it explicitly affirmed the 'innocence' of policemen, soldiers, employees of the prison service and other state agents who died in the conflict.

5 In a parallel commission established in the Republic of Ireland to review whether services within its jurisdiction met the needs of those who suffered from the conflict in Northern Ireland, a much narrower approach was adopted. Here, victims were defined as 'those directly affected by acts of violence, rather than indirectly affected by the troubles in general' (see Wilson, 1999: 5).

6 Estimates of deaths due to political violence vary. The most reliable statistics concerning deaths in Northern Ireland come for the PSNI. All figures presented here have been calculated using official PSNI estimates (see http://psni.police.uk). However, they do not provide details of the agencies responsible for those killed. McKittrick *et al.* (2008) provide this additional information, the details of which are presented in Table 8.4.

7 There is a large literature on the effects of the violence on the population. See, for example, Fay *et al.* (1999), Morrissey and Smyth (2002), Cairns *et al.* (2003) and Muldoon *et al.* (2005). For personalized accounts of the human costs of the conflict, see Smyth and Fay (2000), McKittrick *et al.* (2008), McKay (2008) and Simpson (2009).

8 See Breen-Smyth (2012) for the most recent and comprehensive account of this issue.

9 Figures for persons charged with terrorist offences date from 31 August 1972. They include those charged with terrorist and serious public disorder offences (1972–2002) and those charged under Section 41 of the Terrorist Act (2003–11).

10 Even when a range of background variables are taken into account using multivariate analysis, self-assessed victimhood remains a significant net predictor of who should be considered a 'true victim'. Protestants who perceived themselves as victims of the Troubles were significantly less likely to count either the bereaved or those who were killed or injured as legitimate victims of the conflict. Neither exposure to victimization or feelings of victimization was a significant net predictor of views about who should be seen as a victim among Catholics.

11 Part of the sharp rise in loyalist activity can be accounted for by a series of internal feuds within the loyalist community that occurred in 2002–03 involving the Ulster Defence Association (UDA).

12 Launched in January 2006 as a separate unit of the PSNI, the purpose of the Historical Enquiries Team is to re-examine all deaths attributable to the violence during the period 1968–99, currently estimated at 3,268 cases (see Lundy, 2011). However, a recent evaluation of the unit was highly critical of its operation and suggested that former British soldiers were being treated much more favourably as compared to non-state or paramilitary suspects (see Lundy, 2012).

13 The Independent Commission for the Location of Victims' Remains was established in 1999 in order to locate the remains of 16 people, referred to colloquially as 'the disappeared'. All had gone missing as a result of their believed abduction and murder by the IRA. To date, nine bodies have been recovered.

14 The Saville Inquiry investigated the killing of 14 people in Londonderry in 1972 by the British army, while both the Stevens and Cory inquiries focused primarily on alleged collusion between the security forces and loyalist paramilitaries in the deaths of Catholic civilians. The Stevens and Cory reports supported claims of collusion, and the Saville inquiry laid the responsibility for the deaths of the civilians firmly with the British Army. However, no prosecutions have taken place of police or army personnel. In 2010, David Cameron publicly apologized for Bloody Sunday describing the actions of the soldiers as 'unjustified and unjustifiable' and saying that 'what happened should never have happened'. In September 2011, the Ministry of Defence announced that it would pay compensation to the families of those killed or injured, some of whom have rejected the government's offer.

15 Examples include the Ardoyne Commemoration Project as well as other collective memory work undertaken by groups such as An Crann/The Tree, the Ballymurphy Women's Group and the Duchas project in west Belfast (see Brewer, 2010: 179–80).

16 Sinn Fein had originally requested legislation to be introduced to allow its members who were fugitives from Northern Ireland to return home. However, they withdrew their support for the ill-fated 2005 Northern Ireland Offences Bill when it became clear that the proposed law would amount to an amnesty for all unsolved conflict-related acts, including those committed by the security forces, prior to the signing of the 1998 Agreement.

9

Conclusion

The post-cold war era has witnessed a proliferation of intrastate conflicts based on ethnic differences. Intrastate conflicts, or civil wars, have now replaced interstate conflicts, or international wars, as the most prevalent and deadliest form of violence in the international system today (Wallensteen, 2012). Currently, 95 per cent of wars are civil wars, and the large majority are ethnic conflicts. Moreover, as Collier *et al.* (2009) note, once they break out, civil wars are particularly difficult to stop: about half of the countries emerging from civil war slip back into violence within five years, and this pattern is particularly marked when the antagonists are mobilized along ethnic lines (Kreutz, 2010).

As intrastate conflicts have proliferated, so too have international efforts to resolve them via peace agreements. Although traditionally the majority of intrastate conflicts have ended when one of the warring parties achieves victory over the other, an increasing number of these confrontations have been brought to an end through negotiated settlements (Hartzell, 1999). Indeed, since 1990 negotiated settlements have become more common than victories. As Christine Bell (2006: 373) notes, 'Some 50 percent of civil wars have terminated in peace agreements since 1990...numerically, these settlements amount to over 300 peace agreements in some 40 jurisdictions'. The vast majority of these political settlements are based on power-sharing solutions in which the key actors are guaranteed a place in government. In effect, the underlying rational of international mediation in such conflicts is to 'encourage parties to adopt power-sharing in exchange for war' (Sisk, 2008: 196).

Two approaches have dominated efforts at resolving intercommunal division in ethnically divided post-conflict societies: consociationalism and integration. While both approaches advocate inclusive solutions to ethnic conflict, or solutions that are based on interethnic accommodation, bargaining and reciprocity, they differ fundamentally on whether the institutional structures should be built on the ethnic groups or transcend them (see Sisk, 2002).

A key assumption underlying the consociational approach is that because ethnic identities are robust and historically resilient, the best way of dealing with them is to acknowledge their importance and build them into the new political structures of government. Thus, the key elements of a consociational approach include a grand coalition representing the main segments of society; proportionality in representation; community (segmental) autonomy, particularly in terms of cultural issues; and mutual vetoes on key decisions (see Nagle and Clancy, 2010). While advocates of the consociational model of governance concede that this may result in some short-term problems in terms of political and communal division, they suggest that over time it can create the conditions for a permanently peaceful and inclusive society. As Arend Lijphart (1977: 42), the original architect of consociationalism, put it, 'Its approach is not to abolish or weaken segmental cleavage but to recognise them explicitly and to turn the segments into constructive elements of stable democracy'.

By contrast, the integrationist approach has a less benign view of ethnicity and seeks to eschew ethnic groups as the building blocks of society. Viewing the existence of such divisions as inherently destructive to democratic politics, it purposively seeks to integrate society along these communal lines of division. Thus, the primary goal of the integrationist approach is to facilitate the development of multiethnic political coalitions by providing incentives to decouple politics from identity and ethnicity. Political conflict should therefore coalesce around other cleavages, or cross-cutting forms of division, such as social class. To facilitate this change, proponents of this approach suggest that the electoral system should encourage pre-election pacts across ethnic lines, while the constitution should be based on nonethnic federalism in order to disperse political power (see Sisk, 2008: 203). It is this desire to foster ethnic accommodation among the political elite by promoting and rewarding 'ethnically blind' cross-cutting allegiances which lies at the heart of an integrative approach to conflict resolution. As David Horowitz (2003: 15), a leading proponent of the integrationist approach, puts it, 'My own preferred course involves the use of political incentives to encourage interethnic moderation'.

The balance sheet

The 1998 Belfast Agreement was a consociational model of power-sharing, albeit with a federal and confederal component (McGarry and O'Leary, 2009). Based on the principle of 'parity in esteem', a key assumption of the Agreement was that entrenched communal divisions could be accommodated and eventually ameliorated through institutionalized power-sharing arrangements. McGarry and O'Leary (2006b: 264) argue that the implementation of this model has been the key to sustainable peace in Northern Ireland: 'there is hard evidence that the peace process has brought greater security and stability because it was attached to an inclusive consociational settlement'. Moreover, even critics of consociationalism, such as Rupert Taylor (2009b: 7), concede that this form of democratic governance has become the system of choice for deeply divided societies, and, given its successful application to Northern Ireland, it now 'shines as the brightest star in the new consociational universe.' As Mac Ginty (2009) points out, it is now common to read that the Northern Ireland peace process and the power-sharing forms which underpin it provide a successful model for violently divided societies to follow and imitate.

As we noted in Chapter 1, not all analysts of Northern Ireland politics remain convinced as to the suitability of consociationalism in resolving deep-seated ethnic divisions. While the criticisms of consociationalism are numerous, two related objections have been put forward, particularly in how it has been applied to the 1998 Belfast Agreement. First, it is argued that such arrangements privilege certain divisive identities (such as ethnicity) over other integrating or cross-cutting identities (such as class or gender). Second, instead of resolving conflict, elite-driven consociational power-sharing arrangements often entrench existing identities and promote sectarianism. One of the most vocal critics has been Rupert Taylor (2009a: 320), who argues that 'the Belfast Agreement reinforces and perpetuates sectarian division'.

How do we evaluate these competing arguments? Has the ratification of the Belfast Agreement and the consociational power-sharing arrangements that underpin it led to an amelioration of communal division in Northern Ireland? Or, as many of its opponents suggest, has its implementation actually further entrenched sectarian divisions? To address this question, we examine the key academic debates surrounding the main sources of contention since the ratification of the Agreement in 1998: disputes over continuing manifestations of the conflict and efforts to deal with its past, support for the new political arrangements, and the current state of community relations.

There is no doubt that the most obvious physical manifestation of the conflict – political violence – has been radically reduced, if not completely eradicated, since the ratification of the Agreement in 1998. As our evidence in Chapter 8 shows, the human costs of political violence in terms of deaths and paramilitary attacks have all but ceased since 1998. Of the 3,380 deaths since the start of the Troubles in 1969,

97 per cent have occurred in the pre-Agreement period. Nevertheless, while the number of civilians killed since 1998 has dramatically decreased, they still make up 177 deaths. An overview of the number of casualties as a result of paramilitary-style attacks, or so-called punishment beatings, also shows a considerable reduction. Although there was an upsurge in such activity between 1998 and 2002, most notably within the loyalist community, paramilitary attacks now stand at their lowest level since records began.

Supporters of consociationalism, such as John McGarry and Brendan O'Leary (2009: 51), link the end of political violence in Northern Ireland with the introduction of power-sharing. Even sceptics of the Agreement now accept that, despite the continuing activity of so-called 'dissident' republican groups as well as the recent upsurge in paramilitary-style attacks by ex-Provisional IRA members seeking to rid their communities of drugs, there remains little prospect of any widespread return to violence (see Tonge, 2012). Thus, at least as far as the eradication of widespread political violence is concerned, both the Agreement and the consociational power-sharing arrangements that underpin it must be considered a resounding success.

Nevertheless, unresolved issues stemming from nearly 30 years of conflict remain, notably how to deal with the victims of violence and how to come to terms with the violent legacy of the past. As our analysis in Chapter 8 showed, although the conflict in Northern Ireland may be considered low intensity by international standards, the direct and indirect impact of the violence on the civilian population has been substantial. Currently, just over one-quarter of the population now consider themselves to be a victim of violence, and around 1 in 5 claim to have directly experienced it. Yet, in common with other societies emerging from conflict, opinions differ sharply in terms of who counts as a 'true' victim as well as who is considered primarily responsible for the conflict. Despite a formal acknowledgement in the Agreement as to the need to both address and recognize the rights of victims, these issues remain unresolved.

Given the contested nature of victimhood, it is not surprising that Northern Ireland has so far been unable to deal with the violent legacy of its past. Despite its importance, efforts to address the past have been both piecemeal and divisive. Unlike other post-conflict societies such as South Africa, there have been no state-led initiatives or even public support for a mechanism such as a truth commission, one of the most common methods of coming to terms with a violent past. Moreover, public support for such an initiative remains sharply differentiated on religious grounds. While Protestants remain strongly opposed and see it as little more than a republican instrument to 're-write their violent past', Catholics are more supportive. The inability of Northern Ireland to deal with the contested issue of victimhood and how to come to terms with its violent past poses the greatest threat to the current peace settlement.

In terms of the second criteria on which we can evaluate the success of the 1998 Agreement – support for the new political arrangements – despite an unstable beginning, the institutions established by the Agreement are now operating effectively and without interruption. When the third assembly was dissolved in March 2011, it marked the first time in Northern Ireland's history that a devolved government had completed its full term in office. Moreover, once sworn political enemies, such as Peter Robinson and Martin McGuinness, are now sharing power in their joint decision-making capacity as first and deputy first minister, respectively. Since the reestablishment of the assembly in May 2007, not only have relations between ministers become more cooperative but the assembly itself has become a much more effective legislative body.

This increasing stability in devolved government via a power-sharing assembly has been accompanied by a significant movement away from traditional zero-sum constitutional issues. As we demonstrated in Chapter 4, Catholic support for maintaining the link with Britain has increased considerably during the post-Agreement period. At 51 per cent of the population, it now stands evenly balanced between those who wish to remain in the UK versus those who seek the reunification of Ireland. Moreover, election campaigns traditionally based on divisions over the constitutional position are being replaced by a greater emphasis on socioeconomic issues, albeit with electoral preferences being still rigidly divided along traditional communal lines. For example, the recent 2011 assembly election, which focused almost exclusively on the economy, health and education, has been characterized as one of the most 'bread and butter' elections in modern Northern Ireland history.

The struggle to achieve stability in governance has not been without political cost. We found in Chapter 4 that in addition to increasing polit- ical disengagement and electoral apathy, political pillarization remains widespread. The old centre ground of Northern Ireland politics, occu- pied by the Alliance Party and, more recently, the Northern Ireland Women's Coalition, as well as by the traditionally more moderate UUP and SDLP, has weakened considerably. Not least, cross-community bridg- ing of the electoral divide between the two dominant ethnic blocks – the DUP and Sinn Fein – remains almost non-existent. Despite their domi- nance and electoral security, these two parties continue to engage in 'ethnic outbidding' within their respective blocks. Even public support for the principles of the Agreement and the new political arrangements embodied within it has declined steadily. This is particularly the case among Protestants, who believe that the Agreement has disproportionately benefited Catholics at their expense.

Political stability is also compromised by the sharp polarization in political identity. Even the rise of a Northern Irish identity, a phenomenon particularly marked among the young, will do little to alleviate this communal division. The traditional reinforcement of these overlapping albeit bipolar identities – Protestant/British/unionist versus Catholic/Irish/nationalist – and their zero-sum influence on political outlooks continues to derail efforts to bring about a genuine political transformation. Moreover, this uncertainty will remain given the 'interim' nature of the settlement (see Weller, 2009) and the lack of consensus on the constitutional future of Northern Ireland. Repeated calls from within both communities for a referendum on the constitutional question – the most recent being in March 2012 – point to its re-emergence as an increasingly destabilizing force in future years. Although the armed conflict in Northern Ireland has ceased, consensus politics based on an overarching accommodation between the two political traditions remains as illusionary as ever.

The third criteria on which to evaluate the effectiveness of the Belfast Agreement is community relations. Despite improvements on both the political and security front, there remains considerable tension at the community level. As our analyses throughout this book have consistently demonstrated, Northern Ireland remains deeply divided and segregated along religious lines. While religious observance has declined, religious belonging remains high by international standards and is structured around the Protestant/Catholic cleavage. And, while the conflict is not inherently religious in nature, religious identity continues to act as the focal point for demarcating and entrenching communal division. Although opportunities for social contact exist, the two communities continue to go to separate schools, live in separate areas and lead separate lives. This pattern is particularly marked among the less educated and the young for whom increasing segregation, not integration, is the norm. Moreover, as the results in Chapter 7 confirm, a key factor in perpetuating this division is the religiously segregated educational system. The old adage that 'high fences make good neighbours' continues to inform and reflect contemporary community relations in Northern Ireland.

While community relations have not improved, there are some grounds for optimism. After a difficult start, the number of integrated schools has grown considerably and the vast majority of the population now support integrated education. Even the political elite, traditionally

the least supportive of integrated education, now recognizes the importance of religiously integrated schooling in breaking down communal
division. The increasing public acceptance of some form of integrated
education cannot be overestimated. Our analyses show that attendance
at either an informally or formally integrated school has significant
positive long-term benefits for community relations. Individuals who
report attending an integrated school are more likely to interact with
others across the religious divide. Despite these benefits, the widespread
introduction of integrated education will not be an easy task; the Catholic
Church remains vehemently opposed to such a move and, for the most
part, support within the Protestant churches remains economically
driven and tepid at best.

There can be no doubt that Northern Ireland has been radically
transformed since the ratification of the Agreement in 1998. There have
been many notable achievements, the most important being the
eradication of physical force but also the increasing stability of the
political institutions. Whatever the many twists and turns in relation to
the decommissioning of paramilitary weapons, the guns are now 'silent'
and the stop-start nature of the political institutions has finally been
overcome. Many issues are still unresolved, particularly in the area of
community relations. These include the deep hostility between the two
main religious communities and their increasingly segregated living
arrangements, the failure of the newly established institutions and their
political representatives to break down communal division and the
inability to confront effectively the legacy of Northern Ireland's violent
past. Moreover, many of the structures that contributed to the rise of the
violence in the first place, such as the religiously segregated school
system, remain in place. The post-1998 period has been marked by
conflict regulation rather than conflict transformation; a lasting
transformation of social and political relations has yet to emerge.

Lessons for post-conflict societies

Our investigation has a number of important implications for post-
conflict peace-building agendas based on consociational models of
governance. At the most basic level, the Northern Ireland experience
shows that consociational power-sharing agreements can regulate, if not
completely resolve, conflict. The application of the model to a range of
post-conflict societies, such as Bosnia-Herzegovina, shows that political
systems operating on a consociational basis can and do lead to peaceful
settlements. Even in Northern Ireland, long considered one of the most
violent and intractable of conflicts, bitter protagonists can eventually be

brought to the negotiating table to reach an agreed solution to the conflict. The lesson from Northern Ireland is that even prolonged conflicts can sooner or later be resolved and that consociational power-sharing can achieve this objective.

The process of conflict resolution via the establishment of a negotiated political settlement is, however, slow and tortuous. As noted in Chapter 1, since the start of the present conflict in 1969, there had been at least six failed attempts before the Belfast Agreement was finally reached in 1998. Even by Northern Ireland standards, the implementation of the 1998 settlement was a slow and fractious affair. As in other post-conflict societies, at the heart of problem were competing claims in interpretation, a complete lack of trust between the negotiators and doubts that the parties to the agreement could deliver on their side of the bargain. These difficulties were exemplified by the problems in achieving the decommissioning of paramilitary weapons. The bitter and protracted disputes about decommissioning seriously undermined public support for the Agreement and undermined the stability of its political institutions for almost a decade. The Northern Ireland experience confirms that implementing a peace settlement can often be harder than negotiating the original settlement.

The Northern Ireland experience also shows that the role of political leaders and their ability to mobilize the support of their followers is cru-cial to any settlement. The primary function of leaders during peace negotiations is not so much to help their opponents reach a settlement as to 'deliver their own people' (Darby and Mac Ginty, 2008: 365). However, the simple delivery of one's community is not enough; dealing with other leaders, many of whom have been previously directly involved in the conflict, is also a key dimension of political leadership in post-conflict societies. As Gormley-Heenan (2001: 11) notes, this need to secure the peace while maintaining the support of one's party and con-stituents means that leadership skills are needed as much within parties as between them. The lessons from Northern Ireland, particularly in relation to unionist politicians, point to the difficulty in accommodating these competing goals. As Peter Robinson (2012) commented, 'reaching agreement with historic enemies is hard. Persuading your own people that it is the right thing to do is harder still'.

Another lesson of Northern Ireland is that an exclusive concentration on the political components of the conflict is not enough. For genuine conflict transformation to take place, the economic dimensions of the conflict as experienced by ordinary citizens must also be addressed. As Senator George Mitchell (2012), who chaired the Northern Ireland peace talks, put it, 'The importance of economic opportunity ... in conflict resolution cannot be overstated. It is critical'. However, despite economic improvements during the mid-1990s, Northern Ireland remains a divided and unequal society, with rising levels of inequality within, rather than between, the two religious communities. Moreover, within both communities, it is individuals living in the poorest areas – many of whom bore the brunt of the conflict – who continue to experience the highest levels of unemployment and deprivation, a phenomenon that is particularly marked among the less educated and the young. It is this marginalized group who are the primary producers of low-level-intensity conflict, such as rioting and confrontation at interface areas, and most sectarian in their views. As the Northern Ireland experience and lessons from other societies emerging from conflict warn us, it is often young people in the communities who have suffered the most from the conflict who are most likely to undermine the peace process and provide the catalyst for a return to violence (see Borer *et al.* 2006).

A precondition for a successful settlement is the inclusion of militants, or their representatives, in the peace negotiations. Darby and Mac Ginty (2008: 361) are correct when they suggest that 'a lasting agreement is impossible unless it actively involves those with the power to bring it down'. What distinguishes the Belfast Agreement from previous attempts at a settlement is the participation of armed organizations in the negotiations. Their inclusion, however, must be accompanied by efforts to reintegrate them into mainstream society. As the lessons from Northern Ireland demonstrate, ex-paramilitaries can act as a source of continuing communal division, capable of derailing the peace process, but if they are given a place at the negotiating table, they can also be an important source of reconciliation.

A successful peace settlement must recognize the needs of victims and deal with the injustices inflicted on them in the past. The Northern Ireland experience brings the difficulties in achieving this objective into sharp relief. To date, there remains no consensus between the two communities or their respective politicians in terms of who counts as a victim, let alone how to meet their needs. Many of the provisions of the Agreement, such as the early release of political prisoners, were deeply offensive to victims, particularly among Protestants, who saw themselves as pawns in the inexorable pursuit of peace. While the reintegration of ex-militants may be necessary to initiate a peace process, they must also be genuine efforts to accommodate the victims, many of whom see themselves as unwanted reminders of the past. As Darby and Mac Ginty (2008) note and the Northern Ireland experience also reminds us, efforts to deal with the concerns of victims must be confronted at a much earlier stage in the peace process.

While the peace process in Northern Ireland has gone farther than anyone could have imagined prior to 1998, it remains an 'interim' settlement and a return to violence cannot be ruled out. The aspirations that each community and their political leaders hold in terms of what they consider a just and ultimate solution to the conflict – Northern Ireland remaining part of the United Kingdom versus its reunification with the Republic of Ireland – remain incompatible. As Wolff (2007: 64) correctly states, 'the same stretch of territory cannot, at the same time, be part of the UK and part of the Republic of Ireland'. Thus, the lessons from Northern Ireland suggest that while the parking of the territorial claim for the sake of political progress can in the short-term manage the conflict, the roots of the conflict remain intact and may re-emerge. A second stage of any peace process is therefore to address these fundamental divisions and move from an interim settlement to a permanent one.

Appendix

Data sources

Northern Ireland Loyalty Survey (1968). Conducted between March and August 1968, the Loyalty Survey is based on a multistage stratified random sample, representative of the adult population. Funded by the Economic and Social Research Council and using a questionnaire design, it is based on personal interviews involving 1,291 respondents aged 20 years or more, with a response rate of 87 per cent. The study was designed to provide the first systematic examination of religious and political issues in Northern Ireland, including attitudes towards discrimination and intermarriage, the constitutional position, support for the government and attitudes towards the main political parties. The principal investigator of the survey was Richard Rose, and the data are available from the UK Data Archive at the University of Essex (see http://www.data-archive.ac.uk/).

Northern Ireland Social Mobility Survey (1973). Conducted between January and June 1973, the Northern Ireland Social Mobility Survey is based on a multistage stratified random sample, representative of the male adult population. Funded by the Economic and the Social Research Council and using a questionnaire design, it is based on personal interviews involving 2,416 respondents aged 18–64 years old, with a response rate of 75 per cent. The study was designed to investigate trends, correlates and determinants of social mobility in Northern Ireland. The principal investigator of the study was John A. Jackson. The data are available from the UK Data Archive at the University of Essex (see http://www.data-archive.ac.uk/).

Northern Ireland Attitude Survey (1978). Conducted between July and October 1978, the Northern Ireland Attitude Survey is based on a one-stage stratified random sample, representative of the adult population. Funded by the Nuffield Foundation, the Ford Foundation, the Committee for Social Science Research in Ireland and the Economic and Social Research Institute and using a questionnaire design, it is based on personal interviews involving 1,277 respondents aged 18 years or more, with a response rate of 64 per cent. The study was designed to probe Northern Ireland attitudes, including national identity, religious attitudes, law and order, attitudes towards the European Community and views on the constitutional position of Northern Ireland. The principal investigators of the survey were Edward Moxon-Browne in Northern Ireland and Earl E. David and Richard Sinnott in the Republic of Ireland. The data are available from the UK Data Archive at the University of Essex (see http://www.data-archive.ac.uk/).

Northern Ireland Social Attitudes Surveys (1989–96). Initiated in 1989 and usually conducted between February and April each year, the Northern Ireland Social Attitudes Surveys are based on a multistage stratified random sample, representative of the adult population. The surveys have been conducted annually between 1989 and 1996 except in the years when a general election was held, such as in 1992. Funded originally by the Nuffield Foundation and Central Community Relations Unit (1989–91) and later by a range of government departments in Northern Ireland (1993–96) and using a questionnaire design, it is based on personal interviews with respondents aged 18 years or more and also involves a small self-completion section. The sample size has fluctuated over the years, ranging from its highest level of 1,519 in 1994 to 786 in 1996. The response rate has also varied – from its highest level of 71 per cent in 1991 to 62 per cent in 1996 – cumulating in an average response rate of 68 per cent over the seven survey periods of study.

Like its companion survey in Britain – the British Social Attitudes Survey – the main purpose of the surveys is to examine continuity and change in attitudes in respect to a range of social, economic, political and moral issues. The Northern Ireland Social Attitudes Survey was also a member of the International Social Survey Programme and thus contained a module of questions which are replicated cross-nationally. The principal investigator was Social and Community Planning and Research, who run the British Social Attitudes series and which became the National Centre for Social Research in 1999. The data are available from the UK Data Archive at the University of Essex (see http://www. data-archive.ac.uk/).

Northern Ireland Election Survey (1992). Conducted immediately after the UK general election in April 1992 and based on a one-stage stratified random sample, the survey is representative of the adult population. Funded by the Economic and Social Research Council and the Northern Ireland Office and using a questionnaire design, it is based on personal interviews involving 1,947 respondents aged 17 years or more, with a response rate of 78 per cent. The principal investigators of the survey were Sydney Elliott, John Ditch and Edward Moxon-Browne. The study was designed to investigate social and political attitudes in Northern Ireland, including the social basis of political allegiances, perceptions of national identity and voting and party preference. The data are available from the UK Data Archive at the University of Essex (see http://www.data-archive.ac.uk/).

Northern Ireland Social Identity Survey (1995). Conducted between April and June 1995 and based on a proportionate stratified random sample, the Northern Ireland Social Identity Survey is representative of the adult population. Funded by the Central Community Relations Unit in Northern Ireland and using a questionnaire design, it is based on personal interviews involving 982 respondents aged 18 years or more, with a response rate of 63 per cent. The study was designed to examine perceptions of and attitudes towards national identity in Northern Ireland. The principal investigators of the survey were Karen Trew and Denny Benson. The data are not publicly available.

Northern Ireland Referendum and Election Survey (1998). Conducted immediately after the Northern Ireland Assembly elections in June 1998 and based on a one-stage stratified random sample, the survey is representative of the adult population. Funded by the Economic and Social Research Council and using a questionnaire design, it is based on personal interviews involving 950 respondents aged 18 years or more plus a small self-completion component, with an overall response rate of 71 per cent. The study was designed to examine voting behaviour in the May 1998 referendum and the subsequent Northern Ireland Assembly election, attitudes to politics, the political system and constitutional affairs in Northern Ireland. The principal investigators of the survey were John Curtice, Bernadette C. Hayes, Geoff Evans and Lizanne Dowds. The data are available from the UK Data Archive at the University of Essex (see http://www.data-archive.ac.uk/).

Northern Ireland Life and Times Surveys (1998–2010). The Northern Ireland Life and Times Surveys evolved from the 1989–96 Northern Ireland Social Attitudes Surveys. Officially launched in October 1998 and conducted annually since then, usually in the late autumn period (October–February), the surveys have been based on either a stratified or systematic random sample and are representative of the adult population. Funded from a variety of sources, including the Economic and Social Research Council, the Nuffield Foundation, Atlantic Philanthropies as well as a range of government departments in Northern Ireland, and using a questionnaire design, it is based on personal interviews with respondents aged 18 years or more and also involves a small self-completion element. The sample size has fluctuated over the years, ranging from its highest level of 2,200 in 1999 to 1,179 in 2007. The response rate has also varied – ranging from its highest level of 70 per cent in 1999 to 58 per cent in 2010 – resulting in an average response rate of 63 per cent over the 13 surveys.

Like the earlier Northern Ireland Social Attitudes Surveys, the main purpose of the surveys is to record the attitudes, values and beliefs of the people in Northern Ireland, particularly in terms of a range of social policy issues. Like its predecessor, the survey is a member of the International Social Survey Programme and thus also contains a module of questions that are replicated cross-nationally across 30 nations. The data are publicly available from the Northern Ireland Access Research Knowledge website (see http://www.ark.ac.uk/).

Northern Ireland Young Life and Times Surveys (1998–2010). The Northern Ireland Young Life and Times Survey was also launched in October 1998 with the intention that it would run alongside its adult version. In the first three years of the survey, the Young Life and Times Surveys were directly linked to the adult survey in two ways. First, around 400–450 young people aged 12–17 who were living in the household of an adult Northern Ireland Life and Times respondent were chosen to participate in the study, which took the form of a paper questionnaire. Second, the questions mainly consisted of a subset of the questions of the adult questionnaire, with additional questions which were viewed as of relevance to young people. In 2001, this methodology was reviewed as the level of use of the young person's survey was markedly lower than that of the adult survey.

When the Young Life and Times restarted in 2003, the link with the adult survey was dropped, and a different methodology was developed, whereby all 16-year-olds were invited to take part in the study via the use of the Child Benefit Register. Since its relaunch in 2003, the sample size of the Young Life and Times has grown considerably, ranging from its highest level of 941 respondents in 2007 to 627 in 2006. The response rate has consistently fallen since 2003, from its highest level of 46 per cent in 2003 to just 21 per cent in 2010, resulting in an average response rate of 33 per cent over the eight surveys. As with the adult survey, the Young Life and Times Survey has been funded from a variety of sources including the Economic and Social Research Council as well as a range of government departments in Northern Ireland. The data are publicly available from the Northern Ireland Access Research Knowledge website (see http://www.ark.ac.uk/).

Northern Ireland Election Survey (2003). Conducted between November 2003 and January 2004, immediately after the 2003 Northern Ireland Assembly elections, and based on a multistage stratified sample, the Northern Ireland Election Survey is representative of the adult population. Funded by the Economic and Social Research Council and using a questionnaire design, it is based on personal interviews involving 1,000 respondents aged 18 years or more plus a small self-completion element, with an overall response rate of 62 per cent. The study was designed to examine changing voting behaviour between the 1998 and 2003 elections and the potential effect this would have on the Assembly and related institutions. The principal investigators of the survey were Bernadette C. Hayes, Lizanne Dowds, Geoff Evans and Paul Mitchell. The data are available from the UK Data Archive at the University of Essex (see http://www.data-archive.ac.uk/).

Northern Ireland Election Survey (2010). Conducted between May and June 2010, immediately after the 2010 Westminster general election, and based on a one-stage stratified sample, the Northern Ireland Election Survey is representative of the adult population. Funded by the Economic and Social Research Council and using a questionnaire design, it is based on personal interviews involving 1,000 respondents aged 18 years or more, with an overall response rate of 63 per cent. The study was designed to examine the demographics of party support, perceptions of the parties and opinions on the performance of the Northern Assembly and Executive as well the Northern Ireland electorate's view of the 2010 election. The principal investigators of the survey were Jonathan Tonge, Bernadette C. Hayes and Paul Mitchell. The data are available from the UK Data Archive at the University of Essex (see http://www.data-archive.ac.uk/).

Northern Ireland Social and Political Attitudes Survey (2011). Conducted between April and August 2011, the survey is based on a multistage stratified random sample and is representative of the adult population. Funded by the Leverhulme Trust and using a questionnaire design, it is based on personal interviews involving 1,500 respondents aged 18 years or more, with a response rate of 59 per cent. The study was designed to examine perceptions of victimhood and its consequences for a range of sociopolitical attitudes. The principal investigators of the survey were John D. Brewer and Bernadette C. Hayes. The data are not publicly available.

Northern Ireland Pooled Surveys (1989–2010). The pooled Northern Ireland Surveys are a combined data set which includes the representative samples of the adult population conducted between 1989 and 2010. It is based on personal interviews involving 31,417 respondents aged

Table A.1 Northern Ireland data sources

Name	Year of survey	Sample size/ range	Response/average response rate (per cent)
Northern Ireland Loyalty Survey	1968	1,291	87
Northern Ireland Social Mobility Survey	1973	2,416	75
Northern Ireland Attitude Survey	1978	1,277	64
Northern Ireland Social Attitude Surveys	1989–91; 1993–96	786–1,519	68
Northern Ireland Election Survey	1992	1,947	78
Northern Ireland Social Identity Survey	1995	982	63
Northern Ireland Referendum and Election Survey	1998	950	71
Northern Ireland Life and Times Surveys	1998–2010	1,179–2,200	63
Northern Ireland Young Life and Times Surveys	1998–2000	400–450	n/a
Northern Ireland Young Life and Times Surveys	2003–10	627–941	33
Northern Ireland Election Survey	2003	1,000	62
Northern Ireland Election Survey	2010	1,000	63
Northern Ireland Social and Political Attitudes Survey	2011	1,500	59
Northern Ireland Pooled Surveys	1989–2010	31,417	n/a

18 years or more. The pooled surveys included in the combined data set are Northern Ireland Social Attitudes Surveys (1989–96), Northern Ireland Election Survey (1992), Northern Ireland Referendum and Election Survey (1998), Northern Ireland Life and Times Surveys (1998–2010) and the Northern Ireland Election Survey (2003).

The main purpose of the pooled surveys is to overcome the small sample size that has hindered many investigations on a range of issues in the past, namely, those dealing with divisions within the two main religious communities rather than between them. Two versions of the pooled data set are used in this book. A complete version which incorporates all the surveys conducted between 1989 and 2010 is used for the bulk of the analysis. In addition, to investigate those who experienced a formally integrated education, we use a more limited version. This version is based on 22,041 respondents and includes the Northern Ireland Referendum and Election Survey (1998), Northern Ireland Life and Times Surveys (1998–2010) and the Northern Ireland Election Survey (2003). A version of the 1989–2010 pooled data set is available from Surveys Online on the Northern Ireland Access Research Knowledge website (see http://www.ark.ac.uk/sol/).

References

Adshead, Maura and Jonathan Tonge. 2009. *Politics in Ireland: Convergence and Divergence in a Two-Polity Island*. Basingstoke: Palgrave Macmillan.

Allport, Gordon W. 1954. *The Nature of Prejudice*. Cambridge, MA: Addison-Wesley.

Andeweg, Rudi B. 2000. 'Consociational Democracy.' In Nelson W., Polsby (ed), *Annual Review of Political Science*, vol. 3. Palo Alto, CA: Annual Reviews.

Annan, Kofi A. 2002. *Prevention of Armed Conflict: Report of the Secretary General*. New York: United Nations.

Appleby, R. Scott. 2000. *The Ambivalence of the Sacred: Religion, Violence, and Reconciliation*. Oxford: Rowman and Littlefield.

Arthur, Paul. 1999. 'Anglo-Irish Relations and Constitutional Policy.' In Paul Mitchell and Rick Wilford (eds), *Politics in Northern Ireland*. Boulder, CO: Westview Press.

Arthur, Paul. 2000. *Special Relationships: Britain, Ireland, and the Northern Ireland Problem*. Belfast: Blackstaff Press.

Arthur, Paul and Keith Jeffery. 1988, second edition 1996. *Northern Ireland Since 1968*. Oxford: Blackwell.

Aughey, Arthur. 1989. *Under Siege: Ulster Unionism and the Anglo-Irish Agreement*. Belfast: Blackstaff Press.

Aughey, Arthur. 2000. 'The 1998 Agreement: Unionist Responses.' In Michael Cox, Adrian Guelke and Fiona Stephen (eds), *A Farewell to Arms?: From 'Long War' to Long Peace in Northern Ireland*. Manchester: Manchester University Press.

Bardon, Jonathan. 2009. *The Struggle for Shared Schools in Northern Ireland*. Belfast: Ulster Historical Foundation.

Bean, Kevin. 2007. *The New Politics of Sinn Fein*. Liverpool: Liverpool University Press.

Bell, Christine. 2003a. *Peace Agreements and Human Rights*. Oxford: Oxford University Press.

Bell, Christine. 2003b. 'Dealing With the Past in Northern Ireland.' *Fordham International Law Journal* 26: 1095–118.

Bell, Christine. 2006. 'Peace Agreements: Their Nature and Legal Status.' *American Journal of International Law* 100: 373–412.

Bloomfield, David. 1997. *Peacemaking Strategies in Northern Ireland: Building Complementarity in Conflict Management Theory*. Basingstoke: Palgrave Macmillan.

Bloomfield, Kenneth. 1998. *We Will Remember Them: Report of the Northern Ireland Victims Commission*. Belfast: Northern Ireland Office.

Boal, Fred W. 1995. *Shaping a City: Belfast in the Late Twentieth Century*. Belfast: Institute of Irish Studies, Queen's University of Belfast.

Borer, Tristan Anne. 2003. 'A Taxonomy of Victims and Perpetrators: Human Rights and Reconciliation in South Africa.' *Human Rights Quarterly* 25: 1088–116.

Borer, Tristan Anne, John Darby and Siobhan McEvoy-Levy. 2006. *Peacebuilding After Peace Accords: The Challenges of Violence, Truth, and Youth*. Notre Dame: University of Notre Dame Press.

Bouris, Erica. 2007. *Complex Political Victims*. Sterling, VA: Kumarian Press.

Brass, Paul R. 1991. *Ethnicity and Nationalism: Theory and Comparison*. London: Sage.

Breen, Richard. 1996. 'Who Wants a United Ireland? Constitutional Preferences Among Catholics and Protestants.' In Richard Breen, Paula Devine and Lizanne Dowds (eds), *Social Attitudes in Northern Ireland: The Fifth Report*. Belfast: Appletree Press.

Breen-Smyth, Marie. 2012. *Injured in the Troubles: The Needs of Individuals and Their Families*. Northern Ireland: Wave Trauma Centre.

Brewer, John D. 2003a. 'Northern Ireland: Peacemaking among Protestants and Catholics.' In Mary Ann Cejka and Thomas Bamat (eds), *Artisans of Peace: Grassroots Peacemaking among Christian Communities*. New York: Orbis.

Brewer, John. 2003b. 'Are There Any Christians in Northern Ireland?' In Ann Marie Grey, Katrina Lloyd, Paula Devine, Gillian Robinson and Deirdre Heenan (eds), *Social Attitudes in Northern Ireland: The Eight Report*. London: Pluto Press.

Brewer, John D. 2010. *Peace Processes: A Sociological Approach*. Cambridge: Polity Press.

Brewer, John D. and Bernadette C. Hayes. 2011. 'Victims as Moral Beacons: Victims and Perpetrators in Northern Ireland.' *Contemporary Social Science* 6: 73–88.

Brewer, John D. and Gareth I. Higgins. 1998. *Anti-Catholicism in Northern Ireland, 1600–1998*. London: Macmillan.

Brewer, John D., Gareth I. Higgins and Francis Teeney. 2011. *Religion, Civil Society, and Peace in Northern Ireland*. Oxford: Oxford University Press.

Brown, Kris and Roger Mac Ginty. 2003. 'Public Attitudes Towards Partisan and Neutral Symbols in Post-Agreement Northern Ireland.' *Identities: Global Studies in Culture and Power* 10: 83–108.

Bruce, Steve. 1986. *God Save Ulster! The Religion and Politics of Paisleyism*. Oxford: Clarendon Press.

Bruce, Steve. 1994. *At the Edge of the Union*. Oxford: Oxford University Press.

Bruce, Steve. 1999. *Choice and Religion: A Critique of Rational Choice*. Oxford: Oxford University Press.

Bruce, Steve. 2002. *God is Dead: Secularization in the West*. Oxford: Blackwell.

Bush, Kenneth D. and Diana Saltarelli. 2000. *The Two Faces of Education in Ethnic Conflict*. Florence: Innocenti Research Centre, UNICEF.

Byrne, Sean. 2001. 'Consociational and Civil Society Approaches to Peacebuilding in Northern Ireland.' *Journal of Peace Research* 38: 327–52.

Cairns, Ed, John Mallett, Christopher Lewis and Ronnie Wilson. 2003. *Who Are the Victims? Self-Assessed Victimhood and the Northern Irish Conflict*. Belfast: Northern Ireland Statistics and Research Agency.

Cassidy, Clare and Karen Trew. 1998. 'Identities in Northern Ireland: A Multidimensional Approach.' *Journal of Social Issues* 54: 725–40.

Catholic Bishops of Northern Ireland. 2001. *Building Peace, Shaping the Future*. Armagh: Ara Coeli.

Clark, Alistair and Rick Wilford. 2012. 'Political Institutions, Engagement and Outreach: The Case of the Northern Ireland Assembly.' *Parliamentary Affairs* 65: 380–403.

Coakley, John. 2008. 'Ethnic Competition and the Logic of Party System Transformation.' *European Journal of Political Research* 47: 766–93.

Coakley, John. 2009. 'Implementing Consociation in Northern Ireland.' In Rupert Taylor (ed), *Consociational Theory: McGarry and O'Leary and the Northern Ireland Conflict*. London: Routledge.

Coakley, John. 2010. *Adapting Consociation to Northern Ireland*. Dublin: Institute of British-Irish Studies Discussion Paper No. 8.

Collier, Paul, Hoeffler, Anke and Dominic Rohner. 2009. 'Beyond Greed and Grievance: Feasibility and Civil War'. *Oxford Economic Papers* 61: 1–27.

Compton, Paul A. 1985. 'An Evaluation of the Changing Religious Composition of the Population in Northern Ireland.' *Economic and Social Review* 16: 201–24.

Compton, Paul A. and John Coward. 1989. *Fertility and Family Planning in Northern Ireland*. Aldershot: Avebury.

Connolly, Christopher K. 2006. 'Living on the Past: The Role of Truth Commissions in Post-Conflict Societies and the Case Study of Northern Ireland.' *Cornell International Law Journal* 39: 401–33.

Connor, Walker. 1973. 'The Politics of Ethnonationalism.' *Journal of International Affairs* 27: 1–21.

Consultative Group on the Past. 2009. *Report of the Consultative Group on the Past*. Belfast: OFMDFM.

Cory, Peter. 2004. *Cory Collusion Inquiry Report*. London: HMSO.

Coulter, Colin. 1999. *Contemporary Northern Ireland: An Introduction*. London: Pluto Press.

Curtice, John. 2006. 'A Stronger or Weaker Union? Public Reactions to Asymmetric Devolution in the United Kingdom.' *Publius: The Journal of Federalism* 36: 95–113.

Dalton, Russell J., David Farrell and Ian McAllister. 2011. *Political Parties and Democratic Linkage: How Parties Organize Democracy*. Oxford: Oxford University Press.

Darby, John. 1976. *Conflict in Northern Ireland: The Development of a Polarised Community*. Dublin: Gill and Macmillan.

Darby, John, Dominic Murray, D. Batts, Seamus Dunn, Sean Farren and J. Harris. 1977. *Education and Community in Northern Ireland: Schools Apart?* Coleraine: New University of Ulster.

Darby, John and Roger Mac Ginty. 2008. 'Conclusion: Peace Processes, Present, and Future.' In John Darby and Roger Mac Ginty (eds), *Contemporary Peacemaking: Conflict, Peace Processes and Post-War Reconstruction.* London: Macmillan.

Davies, Lynn. 2004. *Education and Conflict: Complexity and Chaos.* London: Routledge.

de Breadun, Deaglan. 2001. *The Far Side of Revenge: Making Peace in Northern Ireland.* Cork: Collins Press.

Democratic Unionist Party. 2003. *A Voice for Innocent Victims: The Democratic Unionist Party's Policy on Innocent Victims of Terrorism.* Belfast: Democratic Unionist Party.

Department of Education of Northern Ireland. 2011. *Religion of Pupils by School Type and Management Type, 2010/11.* Available at http:/www.deni. gov.uk/pupil religion series updated 1011-3. Accessed 10 January 2012.

Deutsch, Karl W. 1966 [1953]. *Nationalism and Social Communication: An Inquiry into the Foundations of Nationality.* Cambridge, MA: Technology Press.

Devine, Paula and Dirk Schubotz. 2004. *Us and Them?* Belfast: Access Research Knowledge Research Update, Number 28.

Dixon, Jeffrey C. and Michael S. Rosenbaum. 2004. 'Nice to Know You? Testing Contact, Cultural and Group Threat Theories of Anti-Black and Anti-Hispanic Stereotypes.' *Social Science Quarterly* 85: 257–80.

Dixon, Paul. 2001. *Northern Ireland: The Politics of War and Peace.* Basingstoke: Palgrave Macmillan.

Dixon, Paul. 2002. 'Political Skills or Lying and Manipulation? The Choreography of the Northern Ireland Peace Process.' *Political Studies* 50: 725–41.

Donais, Timothy. 2005. *The Political Economy of Peacebuilding in Post-Dayton Bosnia.* London: Routledge.

Donnelly, Caitlin. 2004. 'What Price Harmony? Teachers' Methods of Delivering an Ethos of Tolerance and Respect for Diversity in an Integrated School in Northern Ireland.' *Educational Research* 46: 3–16.

Donnelly, Caitlin and Joanne Hughes. 2006. 'Contact, Culture and Context: Evidence from Mixed Faith Schools in Northern Ireland and Israel.' *Comparative Education* 42: 493–516.

Ellingsen, Tanja. 2005. 'Towards a Revival of Religion and Religious Clashes?' *Terrorism and Political Violence* 17: 305–32.

Elliott, Sydney. 1973. *Northern Ireland Parliamentary Election Results, 1921–1972.* Chichester: Political Reference Publications.

Elliott, Sydney. 1999. 'The Referendum and Assembly Elections in Northern Ireland.' *Irish Political Studies.* 14: 138–49.

Elliott, Sydney and W. D. Flackes. 1999. *Northern Ireland: A Political Dictionary, 1968–1999.* Belfast: Blackstaff.

English, Richard. 2003. *Armed Struggle: A History of the IRA*. London: Macmillan.

Evans, Geoffrey and Mary Duffy. 1996. 'Building Bridges? The Political Implications of Electoral Integration for Northern Ireland.' *British Journal of Political Science* 26: 123–40.

Evans, Jocelyn and Jonathan Tonge. 2001. 'Northern Ireland's Third Tradition(s): The Alliance Party Surveyed.' *Journal of Elections, Public Opinion and Parties* 11: 104–18.

Evans, Jocelyn and Jonathan Tonge. 2003. 'The Future of the "Radical Centre." Northern Ireland after the Good Friday Agreement.' *Political Studies* 51: 26–50.

Evans, Jocelyn and Jonathan Tonge. 2009. 'Social Class and Party Choice in Northern Ireland's Ethnic Blocs.' *West European Politics* 32: 1012–30.

Fahey, Tony, Bernadette C. Hayes and Richard Sinnott. 2006. *Conflict and Consensus: A Study of Values and Attitudes in the Republic of Ireland and Northern Ireland*. Leiden: Brill.

Farren, Sean. 1976. 'Culture and Education in Ireland.' *Compass, The Journal of the Irish Association for Curriculum Development* 5: 25–35.

Fay, Marie-Therese, Mike Morrissey and Marie Smyth. 1999. *Northern Ireland's Troubles: The Human Costs*. London: Pluto Press.

Ferguson, Neil, Mark Burgess and Ian Hollywood. 2010. 'Who Are the Victims?: Victimhood Experiences in Post-Agreement Northern Ireland.' *Political Psychology* 31: 857–86.

Finke, Roger and Rodney Stark. 2005. *The Churching of America, 1776–2005: Winners and Losers in Our Religious Economy*. New Brunswick, NJ: Rutgers University Press.

Fox, Jonathan. 2004. *Religion, Civilization, and Civil War: 1945 Through the New Millennium*. Lanham, MD: Lexington.

Fulton, John. 2002. 'Religion and Enmity in Ireland: Institutions and Relational Beliefs.' *Social Compass* 49: 189–202.

Gallagher, Tony. 1995. *Majority Minority Review 1. Education in a Divided Society: A Review of Research and Policy*. Coleraine: University of Ulster.

Gallagher, Tony. 2003. 'Education and Equality in Northern Ireland.' In Owen Hargie and David Dickson (eds), *Researching the Troubles: Social Science Perspectives on the Northern Ireland Conflict*. London: Mainstream.

Gallagher, Tony. 2004. *Education in Divided Societies*. Basingstoke: Palgrave Macmillan.

Gallagher, Tony and Alyson Coombs. 2007. 'The Impact of Integrated Education on Religious Beliefs.' In Fiona Leach and Mairead Dunne (eds), *Education, Conflict and Reconciliation: International Perspectives*. Oxford: Peter Lang.

Galtung, Johan. 1996. *Peace By Peaceful Means*. London: Sage.

Ganiel, Gladys. 2008. *Evangelicalism and Conflict in Northern Ireland*. Basingstoke: Palgrave Macmillan.

Ganiel, Gladys and Paul Dixon. 2008. 'Religion, Pragmatic Fundamentalism and the Transformation of the Northern Ireland Conflict.' *Journal of Peace Research* 45: 419–36.

Gillis, John R. (ed). 1994. *Commemorations: The Politics of National Identity*. Princeton, NJ: Princeton University Press.

Gormley-Heenan, Cathy. 2001. *From Protagonist to Pragmatist: Political Leadership in Societies in Transition*. University of Ulster: INCORE.

Graham, Brian and Peter Shirlow. 1998. 'An Elusive Agenda: The Development of a Middle Ground in Northern Ireland.' *Area* 30: 245–54.

Graham, Brian and Yvonne Whelan. 2007. 'The Legacies of the Dead: Commemorating the Troubles in Northern Ireland.' *Environment and Planning D: Society and Space* 25: 476–95.

Hadden, Tom, Colin Irwin and Frederick W. Boal. 1996. *Separation or Sharing: The Peoples Choice*. Belfast: Fortnight Educational Trust.

Hadfield, Brigid. 1992. 'The Northern Ireland Constitution.' In Brigid Hadfield (ed), *Northern Ireland: Politics and the Constitution*. Buckingham: Open University Press.

Hamber, Brandon. 2008. 'Putting the Past in Perspective.' Paper Presented at the 'Putting the Past in Perspective' Seminar, Queen's University Belfast, 17 May.

Hamber, Brandon. 2009. *Transforming Societies After Political Violence: Truth, Reconciliation and Mental Health*. London: Springer.

Hamill, Heather. 2011. *The Hoods: Crime and Punishment in Belfast*. Princeton, NJ: Princeton University Press.

Harris, Rosemary. 1972. *Prejudice and Tolerance in Ulster: A Study of Neighbours and 'Strangers' in a Border Community*. Manchester: Manchester University Press.

Hartzell, Caroline A. 1999. 'Explaining the Stability of Negotiated Settlements to Intrastate Wars.' *Journal of Conflict Resolution* 43: 3–22.

Hayes, Bernadette C. 2000. 'Religious Independents within Western Industrialized Nations: A Socio-Demographic Profile.' *Sociology of Religion* 61: 191–207.

Hayes, Bernadette C. and Ian McAllister. 1995. 'Religious Independents in Northern Ireland: Origins, Attitudes and Significance.' *Review of Religious Research* 37: 65–83.

Hayes, Bernadette C. and Ian McAllister. 2001a. 'Who Voted for Peace? Public Support for the 1998 Northern Ireland Peace Agreement.' *Irish Political Studies* 16: 73–94.

Hayes, Bernadette C. and Ian McAllister. 2001b. 'Sowing Dragon's Teeth: Public Support for Political Violence and Paramilitarism in Northern Ireland.' *Political Studies* 49: 901–22.

Hayes, Bernadette C. and Ian McAllister. 2004. *The Political Impact of Secularisation in Northern Ireland*. Dublin: Institute for British-Irish Studies Working Paper No. 36.

Hayes, Bernadette C. and Ian McAllister. 2009a. 'Religion, Identity and Community Relations Among Adults and Young Adults in Northern Ireland.' *Journal of Youth Studies* 12: 385–403.

Hayes, Bernadette C. and Ian McAllister. 2009b. 'Education as a Mechanism for Conflict Resolution in Northern Ireland.' *Oxford Review of Education* 35: 437–50.

Hayes, Bernadette C., Ian McAllister and Lizanne Dowds. 2005. 'The Erosion of Consent: Protestant Disillusionment with the 1998 Northern Ireland Agreement' *Journal of Elections, Public Opinion and Parties* 15: 147–67.

Hayes, Bernadette C., Ian McAllister and Lizanne Dowds. 2007. 'Integrated Education, Intergroup Relations, and Political Identities in Northern Ireland.' *Social Problems* 54: 454–82.

Haymes, Thomas. 1997. 'What is Nationalism Really? Understanding the Limitations of Rigid Theories in Dealing with the Problems of Nationalism and Ethnonationalism.' *Nations and Nationalism* 3: 541–57.

Hayner, Priscilla B. 2011. *Unspeakable Truths: Transitional Justice and the Challenge of Truth Commissions*. New York: Routledge.

Healey, John, Mark Gill and Declan McHugh. 2005. *MPs and Politics in Our Time*. London: Dod's Parliamentary Communications.

Heaney, Seamus. 1975. *North*. London: Faber & Faber.

Herz, Dietmar. 1986. 'The Northern Ireland Policy of the Irish Republic.' In Brian Girvin and Roland Sturm (eds), *Politics and Society in Contemporary Ireland*. Aldershot: Gower.

Hewstone, Miles, Jared B. Kenworthy, Ed Cairns, Nicole Tausch, Joanne Hughes, Tania Tam, Alberto Voci, Ulrich von Hecker and Catherine Pinder. 2008. 'Stepping Stones to Reconciliation in Northern Ireland: Intergroup Contact, Forgiveness and Trust.' In Arie Nadler, Thomas E. Malloy and Jeffrey D. Fisher (eds), *The Social Psychology of Intergroup Reconciliation*. Oxford: Oxford University Press.

Hillyard, Paddy, Grace Kelly, Eithne McLaughlin, Demi Patsios and Mike Tomlinson. 2003. *Bare Necessities: Poverty and Social Exclusion in Northern Ireland*. Belfast: Democratic Dialogue.

Holme, Jennifer Jellison, Amy Stuart Wells and Anita Tijerina Revilla. 2005. 'Learning Through Experience: What Graduates Gained by Attending Desegregated High Schools.' *Equity & Excellence in Education* 38: 14–24.

Horgan, Goretti and Marina Monteith. 2009. *What Can We Do To Tackle Child Poverty in Northern Ireland?* York: Joseph Rowntree Foundation.

Horowitz, Donald L. 1985. *Ethnic Groups in Conflict*. Berkeley: University of California Press.

Horowitz, Donald L. 1990. 'Making Moderation Pay: The Comparative Politics of Ethnic Conflict Management.' In Joseph V. Montville (ed), *Conflict and Peacemaking in Multiethnic Societies*. Lexington, MA: Lexington Books.

Horowitz, Donald L. 1991. *Democratic South Africa? Constitutional Engineering in a Divided Society*. Berkeley: University of California Press.

Horowitz, Donald L. 2000 [1985]. *Ethnic Groups in Conflict*. Berkeley: University of California Press.

Horowitz, Donald L. 2002. 'Explaining the Northern Ireland Agreement: The Sources of an Unlikely Constitutional Consensus.' *British Journal of Political Science* 32: 193–220.

Horowitz, Donald L. 2003. 'The Cracked Foundations of the Right To Secede.' *Journal of Democracy* 14: 5–17.

Hout, Michael and Claude S. Fischer. 2002. 'Why More Americans Have No Religious Preference: Politics and Generations.' *American Sociological Review* 67: 165–90.

Hughes, Joanne. 2007. 'Peace, Reconciliation and a Shared Future: A Policy Shift or More of the Same?' *Community Development Journal* 44: 22–37.

Hughes, Joanne and Caitlin Donnelly. 2002. 'Ten Years of Social Attitudes to Community Relations in Northern Ireland.' In Ann Marie Gray, Katrina Lloyd, Paula Devine, Gillian Robinson and Deirdre Heenan (eds), *Social Attitudes in Northern Ireland: The Eight Report*. London: Pluto Press.

Hughes, Joanne and Caitlin Donnelly. 2004. 'Attitudes Towards Community Relations in Northern Ireland: Signs of Optimism in the Post Cease-Fire Period?' *Terrorism and Political Violence* 16: 567–92.

Hughes, Joanne, Andrea Campbell, Miles Hewstone and Ed Cairns. 2007. 'Segregation in Northern Ireland: Implications for Community Relations Policy.' *Policy Studies* 28: 35–53.

Hume, John. 1996. *Personal Views: Politics, Peace and Reconciliation in Ireland*. Boulder, CO: Roberts Rinehart.

Huntington, Samuel P. 1996. *The Clash of Civilizations and the Remaking of the World Order*. New York: Simon and Schuster.

Iannaccone, Laurence R. 1994. 'Why Strict Churches are Strong.' *American Journal of Sociology* 99: 1180–211.

Independent Commission on the Future for Housing in Northern Ireland. 2010. *Report of the Independent Commission on the Future for Housing in Northern Ireland*. Northern Ireland: Chartered Institute of Housing.

Inglehart, Ronald and Christian Welzel. 2005. *Modernization, Cultural Change, and Democracy: The Human Development Sequence*. Cambridge: Cambridge University Press.

Ipsos MORI. 2011. *Attitudinal Survey on Integrated Education*. Belfast: Integrated Education Fund. Available at http://www.ief.org.uk/resources/publications/. Accessed 12 January 2012.

Irvin, Cynthia and Sean Byrne. 2004. 'The Perception of Economic Aid in Northern Ireland and Its Role in the Peace Process.' In Jorg Neuheiser and Stefan Wolff (eds), *Peace at Last? The Impact of the Good Friday Agreement on Northern Ireland*. New York: Berghahn.

Irwin, Colin. 2002. *The People's Peace Process in Northern Ireland*. Basingstoke: Palgrave Macmillan.

Jardine, Edgar F. 1994. 'Demographic Structure in Northern Ireland and its Implications for Constitutional Preference.' *Journal of the Statistical and Social Inquiry Society of Ireland* 27: 193–220.

Jarman, Neil and Chris O'Halloran. 2001. 'Recreational Rioting: Young People, Interface Areas and Violence.' *Childcare in Practice* 7: 2–16.

Kahler, Miles. 2006. 'Territoriality and Conflict in an Age of Globalization.' In Miles Kahler and Barbara F. Walter (eds), *Territoriality and Conflict in an Era of Globalization*. Cambridge: Cambridge University Press.

Kenway, Peter, Tom MacInnes, Aveen Kelly and Guy Palmer. 2006. *Monitoring Poverty and Social Exclusion in Northern Ireland 2006*. York: Joseph Rowntree Foundation.

Knox, Colin. 2001. 'The "Deserving" Victims of Political Violence: "Punishment" Attacks in Northern Ireland.' *Criminal Justice* 11: 181–99.

Knox, Colin. 2011. 'Cohesion, Sharing and Integration in Northern Ireland.' *Environment and Planning C: Government and Policy* 29: 548–66.

Knox, Colin and Joanne Hughes. 1996. 'Crossing the Divide: Community Relations in Northern Ireland.' *Journal of Peace Research* 33: 83–98.

Kreutz, Joakim. 2010. 'How and When Armed Conflicts End: Introducing the UCDP Conflict Termination Dataset.' *Journal of Peace Research* 47: 243–50.

Lange, Matthew. 2012. *Educations in Ethnic Violence: Identity, Educational Bubbles, and Resource Mobilization.* Cambridge: Cambridge University Press.

Lederach, John Paul. 1997. *Building Peace: Sustainable Reconciliation in Divided Societies.* Washington, DC: United States Institute of Peace.

Liechty, Joseph and Cecelia Clegg. 2001. *Moving Beyond Sectarianism: Religion, Conflict and Reconciliation in Northern Ireland.* Dublin: Columbia Press.

Lijphart, Arend. 1968a. *The Politics of Accommodation: Pluralism and Democracy in the Netherlands.* Berkeley: University of California Press.

Lijphart, Arend. 1968b. 'Typologies of Democratic Regimes.' *Comparative Political Studies* 1: 3–24.

Lijphart, Arend. 1969. 'Consociational Democracy.' *World Politics* 21: 207–25.

Lijphart, Arend. 1977. *Democracy in Plural Societies: A Comparative Exploration.* New Haven, CT: Yale University Press.

Lijphart, Arend. 1999. *Patterns of Democracy: Government Forms and Performance in Thirty-Six Countries.* New Haven, CT: Yale University Press.

Lipset, Seymour Martin, and Stein Rokkan. 1967. 'Introduction'. In Seymour Martin Lipset and Stein Rokkan (eds), *Party Systems and Voter Alignments.* New York: Free Press.

Lundy, Patricia. 2010. 'Commissioning the Past in Northern Ireland.' *Review of International Affairs* 60: 101–33.

Lundy, Patricia. 2011. 'Paradoxes and Challenges of Transitional Justice at the "Local" Level: Historical Inquiries in Northern Ireland.' *Contemporary Social Science* 6: 89–106.

Lundy, Patricia. 2012. *Assessment of the Historical Inquiries Team (HET) Review Processes and Procedures in Royal Military Police (RMP) Investigation Cases.* Jordanstown: University of Ulster.

Lundy, Patricia and Mark McGovern. 2008a. 'Truth, Justice and Dealing with the Legacy of the Past in Northern Ireland, 1998–2008.' *Ethnopolitics* 7: 177–93.

Lundy, Patricia and Mark McGovern. 2008b. 'A Trojan Horse? Unionism, Trust and Truth-Telling in Northern Ireland.' *International Journal of Transitional Justice* 2: 42–62.

Lynn, Brendan. 1997. *Holding the Ground: The Nationalist Party in Northern Ireland, 1945–72.* Aldershot: Ashgate.

McAllister, Ian. 1977. *The Northern Ireland Social Democratic and Labour Party: Political Opposition in a Divided Society.* London: Macmillan.

McAllister, Ian. 1982. 'The Devil, Miracles and the Afterlife: The Political Sociology of Religion in Northern Ireland.' *British Journal of Sociology* 33: 330–47.

McAllister, Ian. 2004. 'The Armalite and the Ballot Box': Sinn Fein's Electoral Strategy in Northern Ireland.' *Electoral Studies* 23: 123–42.

McAllister, Ian and Stephen White. 2007. 'Political Parties and Democratic Consolidation in Postcommunist Societies.' *Party Politics* 13: 197–216.

McAllister, Ronald J. 2000. 'Religious Identity and the Future of Northern Ireland.' *Policy Studies Journal* 28: 843–57.

McAuley, James W. 2004. '"Just Fighting to Survive": Loyalist Paramilitary Politics and the Progressive Unionist Party.' *Terrorism and Political Violence* 16: 522–43.

McAuley, James W., Jonathan Tonge and Andrew Mycock. 2011. *Loyal to the Core? Orangeism and Britishness in Northern Ireland.* Dublin: Irish Academic Press.

McCartney, Clem. 2003. *International Review of Public Policies Towards Improving Inter-Community Relations.* Londonderry: International Conflict Research Institute, University of Ulster.

McEvoy, Kieran, Peter Shirlow and Karen McElrath. 2004. 'Resistance, Transition and Exclusion: Politically Motivated Ex-Prisoners and Conflict Transformation in Northern Ireland.' *Terrorism and Political Violence* 16: 646–70.

McGarry, John and Brendan O'Leary. 1995. *Explaining Northern Ireland.* Oxford: Blackwell.

McGarry, John and Brendan O'Leary. 2006a. 'Consociational Theory, Northern Ireland's Conflict, and Its Agreement. Part 1: What Consociationlists can Learn from Northern Ireland.' *Government and Opposition* 41: 43–64.

McGarry, John and Brendan O'Leary. 2006b. 'Consociational Theory, Northern Ireland's Conflict, and Its Agreement 2. What Consociationlists can Learn from Northern Ireland.' *Government and Opposition* 41: 249–77.

McGarry, John and Brendan O'Leary. 2009. 'Power Shared After the Deaths of Thousands.' In Rupert Taylor (ed), *Consociational Theory: McGarry and O'Leary and the Northern Ireland Conflict.* London: Routledge.

McGarry, John, Brendan O'Leary and Richard Simeon. 2008. 'Integration or Accommodation? The Enduring Debate in Conflict Resolution.' In Sujit Choudry (ed), *Constitutional Design for Divided Societies.* Oxford: Oxford University Press.

McGlynn, Claire. 2003. 'Integrated Education in Northern Ireland in the Context of Critical Multiculturalism.' *Irish Educational Studies* 22: 1–28.

McGlynn, Claire, Ulrike Niens, Ed Cairns and Miles Hewstone. 2004. 'Moving Out of Conflict: The Contribution of Integrated Schools in Northern Ireland to Identity, Attitudes, Forgiveness and Reconciliation.' *Journal of Peace Education* 1: 147–63.

McGovern, Mark. 2004. '"The Old Days are Over": Irish Republicanism, the Peace Process and the Discourse of Equality.' *Terrorism and Political Violence* 16: 622–45.

McGrath, Michael. 2000. *The Catholic Church and Catholic Schools in Northern Ireland.* Dublin: Irish Academic Press.

McGuinness, Martin. 2012. 'The Northern Ireland Case Study.' Speech at the Organization for Security and Co-operation in Europe Conference, 'Shared Future: Building and Sustaining Peace, the Northern Ireland Case Study.' Dublin: Royal Hospital Kilmainham, 27 April.

McIntyre, Anthony. 1995. 'Modern Irish Republicanism: The Product of British State Strategies.' *Irish Political Studies* 10: 97–121.

McKay, Susan. 2008. *Bear in Mind These Dead*. London: Faber and Faber.

McKeown, Ciaran. 1984. *The Passion of Peace*. Chester Springs, PA: Dufour.

McKittrick, David, Seamus Kelters, Brian Feeney, Chris Thornton and David McVea. 2008. *Lost Lives: The Stories of the Men, Women and Children Who Died as a Result of the Northern Ireland Troubles*. Edinburgh: Mainstream.

McLaughlin, Eithne and Neil Faris. 2004a. *The Section 75 Equality Duty: An Operational Review*, vol. 1. Belfast: OFMDFM.

McLaughlin, Eithne and Neil Faris. 2004b. *The Section 75 Equality Duty: An Operational Review*, vol. 2. Belfast: OFMDFM.

McMichael, Gary. 1999. *Ulster Voice: In Search of a Common Ground in Northern Ireland*. Boulder, CO: Roberts Rinehart.

McQuaid, Ronald and Emma Hollywood. 2008. *Educational Migration and Non-Return in Northern Ireland*. Belfast: Northern Ireland Equality Commission.

Mac Ginty, Roger. 2009. 'The Liberal Peace at Home and Abroad: Northern Ireland and Liberal Internationalism.' *British Journal of Politics and International Relations* 11: 690–708.

Mac Ginty, Roger, Orla T. Muldoon and Neil Ferguson. 2007. 'No War, No Peace: Northern Ireland after the Agreement.' *Political Psychology* 28: 1–11.

Macrory Report. 1970. *Review Body on Local Government in Northern Ireland*, Cmnd 540 (NI). Belfast: HMSO.

Mair, Peter. 1987. 'Breaking the Nationalist Mould: The Irish Republic and the Anglo-Irish Agreement.' In Paul Teague (ed), *Beyond the Rhetoric: Politics, the Economy, and Social Policy in Northern Ireland*. London: Lawrence and Wishart.

Mair, Peter. 1997. *Party System Change: Approaches and Interpretations*. Oxford: Clarendon Press.

Mallie, Eamonn and McKittrick, David. 1997. *The Fight for Peace: The Secret Story of the Irish Peace Process*. London: Mandarin.

Mitchell, Claire. 2006. *Religion, Identity and Politics in Northern Ireland: Boundaries of Belonging and Belief*. Aldershot: Ashgate.

Mitchell, Claire. 2008a. 'Religious Change and Persistence.' In Colin Coulter and Michael Murray (eds), *Northern Ireland After the Troubles: A Society in Transition*. Manchester: Manchester University Press.

Mitchell, Claire. 2008b. 'For God and ... Conflict Transformation? The Churches' Dis/engagement with Contemporary Loyalism.' In Aaron Edwards and Stephen Bloomer (eds), *Transforming the Peace Process in Northern Ireland: From Terrorism to Democratic Politics*. Dublin: Irish Academic Press.

Mitchell, Claire and James Tilley. 2004. 'The Moral Minority: Evangelical Protestants in Northern Ireland and Their Political Behaviour.' *Political Studies* 52: 585–602.

Mitchell, George J. 2012. 'The Northern Ireland Case Study.' Speech at the Organization for Security and Co-operation in Europe Conference, 'Shared Future: Building and Sustaining Peace, the Northern Ireland Case Study.' Dublin: Royal Hospital Kilmainham, 27 April.

Mitchell, Paul and Geoffrey Evans. 2009. 'Ethnic Party Competition and the Dynamics of Power Sharing in Northern Ireland.' In Rupert Tayor (ed), *Consociational Theory: McGarry and O'Leary and the Northern Ireland Conflict*. London: Routledge.

Mitchell, Paul, Geoffrey Evans and Brendan O'Leary. 2009. 'Extremist Outbidding in Ethnic Party Systems is Not Inevitable: Tribune Parties in Northern Ireland.' *Political Studies* 57: 397–421.

Moffat, Chris (ed). 1993. *Education Together for a Change: Integrated Education and Community Relations in Northern Ireland*. Belfast: Fortnight Educational Trust.

Montgomery, Alison, Grace Fraser, Claire McGlynn, Alan Smith and Tony Gallagher. 2003. *Integrated Education in Northern Ireland: Integration in Practice*. Report 2. Coleraine: UNESCO Centre, University of Ulster.

Morgan, Valerie, Seamus Dunn, Ed Cairns and Grace Fraser. 1992. *Breaking the Mould: The Roles of Parents and Teachers in the Integrated Schools in Northern Ireland*. Coleraine: Centre for the Study of Conflict, University of Ulster.

Morgan, Valerie and Grace Fraser. 1999. 'When Does 'Good News' Become 'Bad News'? Relationships Between Government and the Integrated Schools in Northern Ireland.' *British Journal of Educational Studies* 47: 364–79.

Morrissey, Mike and Marie Smyth. 2002. *Northern Ireland After the Good Friday Agreement: Victims, Grievance and Blame*. London: Pluto Press.

Morrow, Duncan, Birrell, Derek, Greer John and Terry O'Keeffe. 1991. *The Churches and Inter-Community Relations*. Coleraine: Centre for the Study of Conflict, University of Ulster.

Moxon-Browne, Edward. 1991. 'National Identity in Northern Ireland.' In Peter Stringer and Gillian Robinson (eds), *Social Attitudes in Northern Ireland*. Belfast: Appletree Press.

Muldoon, Orla T., Katharina Schmid, Ciara Downes, John Kremer and Karen Trew. 2005. *The Legacy of the Troubles*. Belfast: School of Psychology, Queen's University Belfast.

Muldoon, Orla T., Karen Trew, Jennifer Todd, Nathalie Rougier and Katrina McLaughlin. 2007. 'Religious and National Identity after the Belfast Good Friday Agreement.' *Political Psychology* 28: 89–103.

Murray, Dominic. 1985. *Worlds Apart: Segregated Schools in Northern Ireland*. Belfast: Appletree Press.

Murray, Gerard. 1998. *John Hume and the SDLP*. Dublin: Irish Academic Press.

Murray, Gerard and Jonathan Tonge. 2005. *Sinn Féin and the SDLP: From Alienation to Participation*. London: Hurst.

Murtagh, Brendan. 2003. 'Territoriality, Research and Policy Making in Northern Ireland.' In Owen Hargie and David Dickson (eds), *Researching the Troubles: Social Science Perspectives on the Northern Ireland Conflict*. London: Mainstream.

Nagle, John and Mary-Alice C. Clancy. 2010. *Shared Society or Benign Apartheid: Understanding Peace-Building in Divided Societies*. Hampshire: Palgrave Macmillan.

Norris, Pippa and Ronald Inglehart. 2004. *Sacred and Secular: Religion and Politics Worldwide*. Cambridge: Cambridge University Press.

Northern Ireland Assembly. 2011. Written Answers to Questions. Official Report (Hansard) Friday 16th Volume 66, No WA2. Available at http://archive.niassembly.gov.uk/qanda/2007mandate/writtenans/2009/pdf/100312.pdf. Accessed 10 March 2102.

Northern Ireland Council for Integrated Education. 2004a. *IE Movement: Taking the Fear out of Difference*. Available at http://www.nicie.org. Accessed 20 December 2011.

Northern Ireland Council for Integrated Education. 2004b. *What is Integrated Education?* Available at http://www.nicie.org. Accessed 20 December 2011.

Northern Ireland Executive. 2008. *Programme for Government 2008–2011*. Belfast: OFMDFM.

Northern Ireland Office. 1998. *Good Friday Agreement*. Belfast: Northern Ireland Office.

Northern Ireland Statistics and Research Agency. 2001. *Northern Ireland Census, 2001*. Key Statistics, Table KS07c. Available at http://www.nisranew.nisra.gov.uk/Census/Census2001Output/KeyStatistics/keystats.html. Accessed 10 January 2010.

Oberschall, Anthony. 2007. *Conflict and Peacebuilding in Divided Societies: Responses to Ethnic Violence*. London: Routledge.

Oberschall, Anthony and L. Kendall Palmer. 2005. 'The Failure of Moderate Politics: The Case of Northern Ireland.' In Ian O'Flynn and David Russell (eds), *Power Sharing: New Challenges for Divided Societies*. London: Pluto Press.

O'Brien, Brendan. 1999. *The Long War: The IRA and Sinn Fein*. New York: Syracuse University Press.

O'Connor, Fionnuala. 1993. *In Search of a State: Catholics in Northern Ireland*. Belfast: Blackstaff Press.

O'Connor, Fionnuala. 2002. *A Shared Childhood: The Story of Integrated Education in Northern Ireland*. Belfast: Blackstaff Press.

Office of the First Minister and Deputy First Minister. 2002. *Review of Community Relations Policy: Report of the Review Team*. Belfast: Stormont.

Office of the First Minister and Deputy First Minister. 2005. *A Shared Future*. Belfast: Stormont.

Office of the First Minister and Deputy First Minister. 2010. *Programme for Cohesion, Sharing and Integration*. Belfast: Stormont.

O'Leary, Brendan. 1989. 'Coercive Consociationalism in Northern Ireland.' *Political Studies* 37: 562–88.

O'Leary, Brendan. 1999. 'The Nature of the Agreement.' *Fordham Journal of International Law* 22: 1628–67.

O'Leary, Brendan and Paul Arthur. 1990. 'Northern Ireland as the Site of State- and Nation-Building Failures.' In John McGarry and Brendan O'Leary (eds), *The Future of Northern Ireland*. Oxford: Clarendon Press.

O'Leary, Brendan and John McGarry. 1993. *The Politics of Antagonism: Understanding Northern Ireland*. London: Athlone Press.

Osborne, Robert D. 2004. 'Education and the Labour Market.' In Bob Osborne and Ian Shuttleworth (eds), *Fair Employment in Northern Ireland: A Generation On*. Belfast: Blackstaff Press.

Osborne, Robert D. 2006. 'Equality in Higher and Further Education in Northern Ireland.' In Caitlin Donnelly, Penny McKeown and Bob Osborne (eds), *Devolution and Pluralism in Education in Northern Ireland*. Manchester: Manchester University Press.

Osborne, Robert D. and Ian Shuttleworth (eds). 2004. *Fair Employment in Northern Ireland: A Generation On*. Belfast: Blackstaff Press.

Petersen, Roger D. 2002. *Understanding Ethnic Violence: Fear, Hatred, and Resentment in Twentieth-Century Eastern Europe*. Cambridge: Cambridge University Press.

Pettigrew, Thomas F. 1997. 'Generalized Intergroup Effects on Prejudice.' *Personality and Social Psychology Bulletin* 23: 173–85.

Pettigrew, Thomas F. 1998. 'Intergroup Contact Theory.' *Annual Review of Psychology*. 4: 65–85.

Pettigrew, Thomas F. and Linda R. Tropp. 2006. 'A Meta-Analytic Test of Intergroup Contact Theory.' *Journal of Personality and Social Psychology* 90: 751–83.

Price, Simon and David Saunders. 1995. 'Economic Expectations and Voting Intentions in the UK, 1979–87: A Pooled Cross-Section Approach.' *Political Studies* 43: 451–71.

Purdie, Bob. 1990. *Politics in the Streets: The Origins of the Civil Rights Movement in Northern Ireland*. Belfast: Blackstaff Press.

Purvis, Dawn. 2010. *Educational Underachievement and the Protestant Working Class: A Summary of Research for Consultation*. Belfast: OFMDFM.

Roberts, Hugh. 1990. 'Sound Stupidity: The British Party System and the Northern Ireland Question.' In John McGarry and Brendan O'Leary (eds), *The Future of Northern Ireland*. Oxford: Clarendon Press.

Robinson, Peter. 2012. 'The Northern Ireland Case Study.' Speech at the Organization for Security and Co-operation in Europe Conference, 'Shared Future: Building and Sustaining Peace, the Northern Ireland Case Study.' Dublin: Royal Hospital Kilmainham, 27 April.

Rokeach, Milton. 1979. *Understanding Human Values: Individual and Societal*. New York: Free Press.

Roof, Wade Clark. 1993. *A Generation of Seekers: The Spiritual Journeys of the Baby Boom Generation*. San Francisco, CA: Harper Collins.

Rose, Richard. 1971. *Governing Without Consensus*. London: Faber and Faber.

Rose, Richard. 1976. *Northern Ireland: Time of Choice*. London: Macmillan.

Rose, Richard and Ian McAllister. 1983. 'Can Violent Conflict be Resolved By Social Change? Northern Ireland as a Test Case'. *Journal of Conflict Resolution* 27: 533–57.

Rose, Richard and Derek Urwin. 1969. 'Social Cohesion, Political Parties, and Strains in Regimes.' *Comparative Political Studies* 2: 7–67.

Rothchild, Donald and Philip G. Roeder. 2005. 'Dilemmas of State-Building in Divided Societies,' In Philip G. Roeder and Donald Rothchild (eds), *Sustainable Peace: Power and Democracy After Civil Wars.* London: Cornell University Press.

Rowan, Brian. 2003. *Armed Peace: Life and Death After the Ceasefires.* Edinburgh: Mainstream.

Ruane, Joseph and Jennifer Todd. 1992. 'Diversity, Division and the Middle Ground in Northern Ireland.' *Irish Political Studies* 7: 73–98.

Ruane, Joseph and Jennifer Todd. 1996. *The Dynamics of Conflict in Northern Ireland.* Cambridge: Cambridge University Press.

Saville, Mark, Lord. 2010. *Report of the Bloody Sunday Inquiry.* London: HMSO.

Sayrs, Lois W. 1989. *Pooled Time Series Analysis.* London: Sage, Quantitative Applications in the Social Sciences, No. 70.

Schubotz, Dirk and Gillian Robinson. 2006. 'Cross-Community Integration and Mixing: Does it Make a Difference?' *Research Update* 43: 1–4.

Shapiro, Ian. 1996. *Democracy's Place.* New York: Cornell University Press.

Sherkat, Darren E. and John Wilson. 1995. 'Preferences, Constraints and Choices in Religious Markets: An Examination of Religious Switching and Apostasy.' *Social Forces* 73: 993–1026.

Shirlow, Peter and Kieran McEvoy. 2008. *Beyond the Wire: Former Prisoners and Conflict Transformation in Northern Ireland.* London: Pluto Press.

Shirlow, Peter and Brendan Murtagh. 2006. *Belfast: Segregation, Violence and the City.* London: Pluto Press.

Shirlow, Peter, Jonathan Tonge, James McAuley and Catherine McGlynn. 2010. *Abandoning Historical Conflict? Former Political Prisoners and Reconciliation in Northern Ireland.* Manchester: Manchester University Press.

Shuttleworth, Ian G. and Christopher D. Lloyd. 2009. 'Are Northern Ireland's Communities Dividing? Evidence from Geographically Consistent Census of Population Data, 1971–2001.' *Environment and Planning A* 41: 213–29.

Simpson, Kirk. 2009. *Unionist Voices and the Politics of Remembering the Past in Northern Ireland.* Basingstoke: Palgrave Macmillan.

Sisk, Timothy D. 2002. *Power Sharing and International Mediation in Ethnic Conflicts.* Washington, DC: United States Institute of Peace.

Sisk, Timothy D. 2008. 'Power-Sharing After Civil Wars: Matching Problems To Solutions.' In John Darby and Roger Mac Ginty (eds), *Contemporary Peacemaking: Conflict, Violence and Peace Processes.* Hampshire: Palgrave Macmillan.

Smith, Alan. 2001. 'Religious Segregation and the Emergence of Integrated Schools in Northern Ireland.' *Oxford Review of Education* 27: 559–75.

Smith, Alan. 2005. 'Education in the Twenty-First Century: Conflict, Reconstruction and Reconciliation.' *Compare* 35: 373–91.

Smith, Alan and Tony Vaux. 2003. *Education, Conflict and International Development*. London: Department for International Development.

Smyth, Jim and Andreas Cebulla. 2008. 'The Glacier Moves? Economic Change and Class Structure.' In Colin Coulter and Michael Murray (eds), *Northern Ireland After the Troubles: A Society in Transition*. Manchester: Manchester University Press.

Smyth, Marie Breen. 2003. 'Putting the Past in Its Place: Issues of Victimhood and Reconciliation in Northern Ireland's Peace Process.' In Nigel Biggar (ed), *Burying The Past: Making Peace and Doing Justice After Civil Conflict*. Washington, DC: Georgetown University Press.

Smyth, Marie Breen. 2007. *Truth Recovery and Justice After Conflict: Managing Violent Pasts*. London: Routledge.

Smyth, Marie and Marie-Therese Fay (eds). 2000. *Personal Accounts from Northern Ireland's Troubles: Public Conflict, Private Loss*. London: Pluto Press.

Social Democratic and Labour Party. 1999. *Victims, We Will Remember Them*. Belfast: SDLP.

Stevens, Sir John. 2003. *Stevens Inquiry: Overview and Recommendations*. Available from http://www.madden-finucane.com/english/index.aspx. Accessed 15 December 2010.

Tajfel, Henri (ed). 1978. *Differentiation Between Social Groups*. London: Academic Press.

Taylor, Rupert. 2001. 'Consociation or Social Transformation?' In John McGarry (ed), *Northern Ireland and the Divided World*. Oxford: Oxford University Press.

Taylor, Rupert. 2009a. 'The Injustice of a Consociational Solution to the Northern Ireland Problem.' In Rupert Taylor (ed), *Consociational Theory: McGarry and O'Leary and the Northern Ireland Conflict*. London: Routledge.

Taylor, Rupert. 2009b. 'Introduction: The Promise of Consociationary Theory.' In Rupert Taylor (ed), *Consociational Theory: McGarry and O'Leary and the Northern Ireland Conflict*. London: Routledge.

Todd, Jennifer and Joseph Ruane. 2010. *From 'A Shared Future' to 'Cohesion, Sharing and Integration': An Analysis of Northern Ireland's Policy Framework Documents*. Dublin: Institute for British Irish Studies.

Tonge, Jonathan. 2003. 'Victims of Their Own Success? Post-Agreement Dilemmas of Political Moderates in Northern Ireland.' *Global Review of Ethnopolitics* 3: 39–59.

Tonge, Jonathan. 2004. '"They Haven't Gone Away, You Know": Irish Republican Dissidents and Armed Struggle'. *Terrorism and Political Violence* 16: 671–93.

Tonge, Jonathan. 2012. '"No-one Likes Us, We Don't Care:" Dissident Irish Republicans and Mandates.' *Political Quarterly* 83: 219–26.

Trew, Karen. 1994. 'What it Means to be Irish Seem from A Northern Perspective.' *Irish Journal of Psychology* 6: 28–36.

Trew, Karen. 1996. 'National Identity.' In Richard Breen, Paula Devine and Lizanne Dowds (eds), *Social Attitudes in Northern Ireland: The Fifth Report*. Belfast: Appletree Press.

Trew, Karen. 1998. 'The Northern Irish Identity.' In Anne J. Kershen (ed), *A Question of Identity*. Aldershot: Ashgate.

Voas, David and Alasdair Crockett. 2005. 'Religion in Britain: Neither Believing nor Belonging.' *Sociology* 39: 11–28.

Voas, David and Rodney Ling. 2010. 'Religion in Britain and the United States.' In Alison Park, John Curtice, Katarina Thomson, Miranda Phillips, Elizabeth Clery and Sarah Butt (eds), *British Social Attitudes: The 26th Report*. London: Sage.

Walker, Graham. 2004. *A History of the Ulster Unionist Party: Protest, Pragmatism and Pessimism*. Manchester: Manchester University Press.

Wallensteen, Peter. 2012. *Understanding Conflict Resolution*. London: Sage, 3rd Edition.

Weller, Marc. 2009. 'Settling Self-Determination Conflicts: Recent Developments.' *European Journal of International Law* 20: 111–65.

Wells, Amy Stuart, Jennifer Jellison Holme, Anita Tijerina Revilla and Awo Korantemaa Atanda. 2009. *Both Sides Now: The Story of School Desegregation's Graduates*. Berkeley: University of California Press.

Whyte, John. 1990. *Interpreting Northern Ireland*. Oxford: Clarendon Press.

Wilford, Rick. 2000. 'Designing the Northern Ireland Assembly.' *Parliamentary Affairs* 53: 577–90.

Wilford, Rick (ed). 2001. *Aspects of the Belfast Agreement*. Oxford: Oxford University Press.

Wilford, Rick. 2007. 'Inside Stormont: The Assembly and the Executive.' In Paul Carmichael, Colin Knox and Robert D. Osborne (eds), *Devolution and Constitutional Change in Northern Ireland*. Manchester: Manchester University Press.

Wilford, Rick and Robin Wilson. 2000. 'A "Bare Knuckle Ride": Northern Ireland.' In Robert Hazell (ed), *The State and the Nations: The First Year of Devolution in the United Kingdom*. Thorverton, UK: Imprint Academic.

Wilford, Rick and Robin Wilson. 2001. 'Northern Ireland: Endgame.' In Alan Trench (ed), *The State of the Nations 2001: The Second Year of Devolution in the United Kingdom*. Thorverton, UK: Imprint Academic.

Wilford, Rick and Robin Wilson. 2008. 'Northern Ireland: Devolution Once Again.' In Alan Trench (ed), *The State of the Nations 2008*. Exeter, UK: Imprint Academic.

Wilson, John P. 1999. *A Place and a Name: Report of the Victims Commission*. Dublin: Stationary Office.

Wilson, Robin. 2007. 'Rhetoric Meets Reality: Northern Ireland's Equality Agenda.' *Benefits*. 15: 151–62.

Wolff, Stefan. 2007. *Ethnic Conflict: A Global Perspective*. Oxford: Oxford University Press.

World Bank. 2005. *Reshaping the Future: Education and Postconflict Reconstruction*. Washington, DC: World Bank.

Index

EU authorised representative for GPSR:
Easy Access System Europe, Mustamäe tee 50,
10621 Tallinn, Estonia
gpsr.requests@easproject.com

www.ingramcontent.com/pod-product-compliance
Lightning Source LLC
Chambersburg PA
CBHW071734270326
41928CB00013B/2676